SERMON STUDIES ON THE EPISTLES

SERMON STUDIES ON THE EPISTLES

(ILCW Series B)

Richard D. Balge
General Editor

Curtis A. Jahn
Manuscript Editor

NORTHWESTERN PUBLISHING HOUSE
Milwaukee, Wisconsin

Library of Congress Card 93-83035
Northwestern Publishing House
1250 N. 113th St., Milwaukee, WI 53226-3284
© 1993 by Northwestern Publishing House.
Published 1993
Printed in the United States of America
ISBN 0-8100-0486-0

CONTENTS

Preface   11

FIRST SUNDAY IN ADVENT   13
1 Corinthians 1:3-9

SECOND SUNDAY IN ADVENT   17
2 Peter 3:8-14

THIRD SUNDAY IN ADVENT   21
1 Thessalonians 5:16-24

FOURTH SUNDAY IN ADVENT   25
Romans 16:25-27

CHRISTMAS DAY — NATIVITY OF OUR LORD   29
Hebrews 1:1-9

FIRST SUNDAY AFTER CHRISTMAS   36
Colossians 3:12-17

NEW YEAR'S DAY   42
Romans 1:1-7

SECOND SUNDAY AFTER CHRISTMAS   47
Ephesians 1:3-6,15-18

EPIPHANY OF OUR LORD   53
Ephesians 3:2-12

FIRST SUNDAY AFTER EPIPHANY—
THE BAPTISM OF OUR LORD   57
Acts 10:34-38

SECOND SUNDAY AFTER EPIPHANY   62
1 Corinthians 6:12-20

THIRD SUNDAY AFTER EPIPHANY   66
1 Corinthians 7:29-31

FOURTH SUNDAY AFTER EPIPHANY   70
1 Corinthians 8:1-13

FIFTH SUNDAY AFTER EPIPHANY   75
1 Corinthians 9:16-23

SIXTH SUNDAY AFTER EPIPHANY   80
1 Corinthians 9:24-27

SEVENTH SUNDAY AFTER EPIPHANY   83
2 Corinthians 1:18-22

EIGHTH SUNDAY AFTER EPIPHANY   87
2 Corinthians 3:1b-6

TRANSFIGURATION — LAST SUNDAY AFTER EPIPHANY   92
2 Corinthians 3:12—4:2

ASH WEDNESDAY   97
2 Corinthians 5:20b—6:2

FIRST SUNDAY IN LENT   101
Romans 8:31-39

SECOND SUNDAY IN LENT   105
Romans 5:1-11

THIRD SUNDAY IN LENT   110
1 Corinthians 1:22-25

FOURTH SUNDAY IN LENT   114
Ephesians 2:4-10

FIFTH SUNDAY IN LENT   118
Hebrews 5:7-9

SIXTH SUNDAY IN LENT — PALM SUNDAY   122
Philippians 2:5-11

MAUNDY THURSDAY   124
1 Corinthians 10:16-17

GOOD FRIDAY   128
Hebrews 4:14—5:10

EASTER SUNDAY — RESURRECTION OF OUR LORD   134
1 Corinthians 15:19-26

SECOND SUNDAY OF EASTER   140
1 John 5:1-6

THIRD SUNDAY OF EASTER   145
1 John 1:1—2:2

FOURTH SUNDAY OF EASTER   150
1 John 3:1,2

FIFTH SUNDAY OF EASTER   154
1 John 3:16-24

SIXTH SUNDAY OF EASTER   160
1 John 4:1-11

ASCENSION OF OUR LORD   164
Ephesians 1:16-23

SEVENTH SUNDAY OF EASTER   170
1 John 4:13-21

PENTECOST   175
Acts 2:22-36

HOLY TRINITY — FIRST SUNDAY AFTER PENTECOST   180
Romans 8:14-17

SECOND SUNDAY AFTER PENTECOST   184
2 Corinthians 4:5-12

THIRD SUNDAY AFTER PENTECOST   190
2 Corinthians 4:13-18

FOURTH SUNDAY AFTER PENTECOST   194
2 Corinthians 5:1-10

FIFTH SUNDAY AFTER PENTECOST   199
2 Corinthians 5:14-21

SIXTH SUNDAY AFTER PENTECOST   204
2 Corinthians 8:1-9,13,14,21-24a

SEVENTH SUNDAY AFTER PENTECOST   209
2 Corinthians 12:7-10

EIGHTH SUNDAY AFTER PENTECOST   212
Ephesians 1:3-14

NINTH SUNDAY AFTER PENTECOST   219
Ephesians 2:13-22

TENTH SUNDAY AFTER PENTECOST   224
Ephesians 4:1-7,11-16

ELEVENTH SUNDAY AFTER PENTECOST   228
Ephesians 4:17-24

TWELFTH SUNDAY AFTER PENTECOST   235
Ephesians 4:30—5:2

THIRTEENTH SUNDAY AFTER PENTECOST   239
Ephesians 5:15-20

FOURTEENTH SUNDAY AFTER PENTECOST   243
Ephesians 5:21-31

FIFTEENTH SUNDAY AFTER PENTECOST   248
Ephesians 6:10-20

SIXTEENTH SUNDAY AFTER PENTECOST   253
James 1:17-22,26,27

SEVENTEENTH SUNDAY AFTER PENTECOST   257
James 2:1-5,8-10,14-18

EIGHTEENTH SUNDAY AFTER PENTECOST   261
James 3:16—4:6

NINETEENTH SUNDAY AFTER PENTECOST   265
James 4:7-12

TWENTIETH SUNDAY AFTER PENTECOST   272
Hebrews 2:9-11

TWENTY-FIRST SUNDAY AFTER PENTECOST   275
Hebrews 3:1-6

TWENTY-SECOND SUNDAY AFTER PENTECOST   279
Hebrews 4:9-16

TWENTY-THIRD SUNDAY AFTER PENTECOST   284
Hebrews 5:1-10

TWENTY-FOURTH SUNDAY AFTER PENTECOST   290
Hebrews 7:23-28

TWENTY-FIFTH SUNDAY AFTER PENTECOST   294
Hebrews 9:24-28

TWENTY-SIXTH SUNDAY AFTER PENTECOST   298
Hebrews 12:25-29

TWENTY-SEVENTH SUNDAY AFTER PENTECOST   302
Hebrews 12:1,2

LAST SUNDAY AFTER PENTECOST   307
Revelation 1:4b-8

REFORMATION DAY   312
Romans 3:19-28

FESTIVAL OF HARVEST   316
2 Corinthians 9:6-15

MISSION FESTIVAL   322
Romans 10:11-17

THANKSGIVING DAY   326
Philippians 4:6-20

PREFACE

Northwestern Publishing House has published six earlier volumes of sermon studies on ILCW text series. In 1982 Professor Ernst H. Wendland edited the Series C Gospels for publication in the United States, after they had been published for use in WELS sister churches around the world.

Favorable response and the widespread use of the ILCW series encouraged the publication of studies on Series B Old Testament in 1984, Series A Epistles in 1986, and Series B Gospels in 1987. All of them were edited by Professor Wendland.

Because of his involvement in other important work, Professor Wendland declined to edit a fifth volume. Pastor Mentor E. Kujath, Northwestern's editor-in-chief at the time, asked the homiletics department of Wisconsin Lutheran Seminary to participate in the publication of a volume on the Series A Gospels.

Partly because the earlier volumes were being used by pastors in Lutheran churches not of our fellowship, the department honored Pastor Kujath's request. A time-honored reluctance to offer "canned" materials for use by pastors was offset by a desire to share our evangelical conservative approach to Scripture and to sermonizing with other preachers in other church bodies. Series A Gospels was published in 1989 and Series C Epistles followed in 1991.

Preaching on epistle texts, especially longer texts, presents a number of special challenges. They are not "story" texts, although there is always a story behind them. They frequently contain more than one abstract doctrinal concept, and sermonic efforts easily become doctrinal treatises. A preacher trained to do thorough exegesis feels conscience-bound to expound a text thoroughly, and this may result in a product that is more exegetical essay than practical sermon. A frequent solution is to shorten the text, and this may be done after the preacher has done thorough work on the entire text in its context.

For the most part, however, the outlines suggested in this book show how a preacher can utilize the text in its entirety. The preacher who emphasizes what the outlines emphasize, not giving equal weight to each and every thought of the text, will find most of them usable.

The contributors to this volume are for the most part parish pastors; a few teach in Lutheran high schools or synodical academies.

Their work was a labor of love, done with a high degree of cooperation and without remuneration.

Listed alphabetically, these were the contributors: Frederick S. Adrian, Paul W. Alliet, Kenneth R. Arndt, Richard D. Balge, James A. Bare, David J. Beckmann, Jon R. Bitter, William R. Carter, Frederick W. Casmer, Mark A. Cordes, Charles L. Cortright, Randall L. Cutter, Leroy P. Dux, William H. Favorite, Lester G. Fritz, Beck H. Goldbeck, Tim H. Gumm, Richard L. Gurgel, David E. Haag, Keith R. Haag, Thomas W. Haar, Gerald C. Hintz, Stephen C. Hintz, David L. Huebner, James R. Huebner, David C. Hussmann, Bruce A. Janisch, Robert D. Johannes, Daniel W. Kelm, Mark T. Kipfmiller, David P. Kolander, Thomas C. Kutz, James L. Langebartels, Gregory P. Lenz, Allen L. Lindke, Joel W. Lintner, Joel T. Luetke, Ronald W. Mehlberg, James W. Naumann, Joel I. Nitz, David A. Nottling, James H. Oldfield, Lawrence O. Olson, Leon E. Piepenbrink, Donald J. Pieper, Kelly D. Pochop, James F. Pope, Robert F. Raasch, Bradley E. Ragner, Terry W. Reich, Jonathan E. Rimmert, Jonathan J. Rockhoff, William J. Schaefer II, Jeffrey L. Schallert, Douglas R. Scherschel, John C. Schneidervin, Daniel L. Schoeffel, Thomas A. Schulz, Raymond W. Schumacher, Jeffrey L. Schone, David D. Sellnow, John F. Unnasch, Paul W. Vander Galien, Roger D. Wahl, Jeffrey A. Weber, Paul O. Wendland, Lynn E. Wiedmann, James G. Witt III, Paul M. Workentine, Joel M. Zank.

Eleven epistles, plus Acts and Revelation, are represented in Series B. A brief introductory sketch is offered at the first appearance of a text from each of the books. Where it seemed helpful, additional isagogical material was provided with one or more later appearances of the same book.

Not all of the studies in this volume include references to the other Scripture readings for the day. Some of them make reference to the readings in "Homiletical Suggestions." Sometimes there is mention in the discussion of the text.

With this book this editor has completed his assignment in the nine-volume project. May the Lord of the Church bless the use of this book and the entire series by those who preach and for those who hear.

Richard D. Balge

FIRST SUNDAY IN ADVENT

The Scriptures

Old Testament — *Isaiah 63:16b,17; 64:1-8*
Epistle — *1 Corinthians 1:3-9*
Gospel — *Mark 13:32-37*

The Text — 1 Corinthians 1:3-9

Paul's first letter to the Christians at Corinth, not preserved, was intended to resolve problems in that congregation. The congregation replied with a letter which asked several questions, but which also challenged the apostle's authority. Then Paul wrote the epistle which we know as First Corinthians. Written from Ephesus around the year 55, it reveals what the problems, questions, and challenges of the Corinthian believers were. It answers these, and in doing so provides inspiration and instruction for Christians everywhere, in every age.

The letter addresses the problem of party spirit in the congregation (1:10—4:21). It treats practical questions of moral delinquency, of the misuse of freedom, and of false doctrine (5:1—11:34). It instructs on the nature and use of spiritual gifts (12:1—14:40), with special focus on the greatest gift, love (12:31—13:13). Then follows the great resurrection chapter, 1 Corinthians 15. Chapter 16 deals with personal and business matters.

The sermon text includes Paul's greeting and a prayer of thanksgiving for God's goodness to the congregation.

v. 3 — *Grace and peace to you from God our Father and the Lord Jesus Christ.*

These are the most familiar words of the text because they are so often used as a pulpit greeting. Here is an opportunity for the preacher to help himself and his hearers understand them as a concise gospel message, more than a conventional way in which to start a sermon.

Grace is the unmerited favor of God which prompted him to elect us in eternity, redeem us in time, call us by the gospel, and preserve us in faith. Objectively, peace is what God has declared and established in Christ for all people. Subjectively, it is that quiet assurance of God's favor which is ours since we are justified by faith.

There are two implicit confessions of Christ's divine nature here. One is that the ἀπὸ is not repeated before "the Lord Jesus Christ."

This expresses his unity with God our Father. The other is κύριος, the Septuagint's consistent rendering of Jahweh.

"Jesus" reminds us that the Lord became man to save us. "Christ" signifies that he is the Lord's Anointed, God's Man sent to do God's work in God's good time.

Where is the Holy Spirit in this? He is doing what he always does, pointing to the Father and the Son, imparting their grace and peace.

v. 4 — *I always thank God for you because of his grace given you in Christ Jesus.*

Constant in prayer, Paul is grateful for grace. The first and essential gift, to which many gifts have been added, is God's favorable disposition in connection with his Son toward sinners. Christ Jesus lived the perfect life of love which the law demands. He offered himself as the unblemished sacrifice for sin. God raised him from the dead because that life and death satisfied his justice.

This grace was preached to the Corinthians. By grace they believed the message. By grace they have been kept in faith and equipped for the life of faith. For this grace Paul thanks God.

vv. 5,6 — *For in him you have been enriched in every way—in all your speaking and in all your knowledge—because our testimony about Christ was confirmed in you.*

Not by themselves or in their own right, but in Christ Jesus ("him"), they have been enriched. Note the passive. They have not made themselves rich in speaking and knowledge.

There is another passive, "was confirmed." The imagery underlying ἐβεβαιώθη is that of a strong root or a secure anchor. What Paul and his co-workers testified concerning Christ has taken firm hold in his readers. He is confidently thankful that it will remain. Their enrichment in all speaking and all knowledge is in accord with (καθώς) the gospel's strong root and secure hold on them.

There are people who speak, even eloquently, without knowledge and there is no rich blessing in that. There are also people who know and do not speak, for lack of ability or lack of caring. When knowing and speaking are combined to share the "testimony about Christ," that is reason for thanksgiving. The thanks belongs to God.

v. 7 — *Therefore you do not lack any spiritual gift as you eagerly wait for our Lord Jesus Christ to be revealed.*

The basic χάρις of verse 4 has been generously augmented and supplemented with χαρίσματα. Listed in detail at 1 Corinthians 12:8-

11 and discussed in chapters 12 to 14, these gifts from the Spirit equip them with what they need for their spiritual life and mission. These gifts are community property, "given for the common good" (1 Cor 12:7). Not every believer has every gift, but no believer lacks some gift (1 Pe 4:10).

In his exalted state the Lord is hidden from our eyes, known only to the eyes of faith. Faith eagerly awaits his revelation on his "day" (v. 8). Spiritual gifts equip the believer for the wait and are part of the Spirit's assurance that "our Lord Jesus Christ (will) be revealed."

v. 8 — *He will keep you strong to the end, so that you will be blameless on the day of our Lord Jesus Christ.*

"He will keep you strong" renders βεβαίωσει, future of promise. He will root you firmly and anchor you securely. He will give you the gift of perseverance, preserve you in faith "to the end." It is not wrong to think here of the end of earthly life, temporal death. More likely, however, the end of time is meant, "the day of our Lord Jesus Christ." The variant reading παρουσία is an interpretation of what "the day" (ἡμέρα) is.

"Blameless" has the sense of not chargeable, not liable to accusation. There can be no thought that this is an achievement on our part. The entire Scripture, this text and βεβαίωσει in this verse make clear that it is God's doing and that it is by grace.

v. 9 — *God, who has called you into fellowship with his Son Jesus Christ our Lord, is faithful.*

The keeping of the promise of verse 8 is guaranteed by the faithfulness of God. He who called us will not forget us or forsake us. Indeed, the grace and peace of verse 3 are undergirded by his faithfulness.

Four times in these verses Paul gives the Savior his full title, Lord Jesus Christ. Twice more he names Christ and twice he uses pronouns (αὐτῷ in verse 5 and ὅς in verse 8). This is a Christ-centered beginning for a Christ-centered letter to Christians who are too confident in their "spiritual superiority." They are in grave spiritual danger on both the doctrinal and moral fronts. Paul is calling their attention back to him who is the cause and guarantee of salvation. Through Paul, the Spirit who gave them so many gifts is redirecting their attention to him who is God's fundamental Gift.

By the gospel God has called us to share with his Son in all that he has merited and won. That includes all the blessings mentioned in these verses, and more besides.

16

Homiletical Suggestions

Advent is a season of recollection, recalling the promises of the Old Testament and interpreting them in the light of their New Testament fulfillment. Isaiah's acknowledgment of Israel's sin, and his plea to the Lord to deal with his people as a Father, are an example of such recollection. They help elucidate the emphasis on grace in the sermon text.

Advent anticipates the Feast of the Nativity, the celebration of Christ's first coming with grace and peace. It reminds us that the joy of God's salvation and the Spirit's other gifts are mediated to us by the "testimony about Christ" (1 Co 1:6) in Word and Sacrament.

The Gospel reading reminds us that Advent is also a season of preparation for our Lord's second coming. Indeed, it reminds us that every day is a season for such preparation. The new year of grace will be the last for some people, and may be the final one for all people. And so every day is a day to heed the Savior's words in Mark 13:33-37. "Be on guard! Be alert! . . . Watch!"

The season and the readings suggest this treatment of the text:

God Gives Us a New Year of Grace

1. Let us joyfully hear his gospel (vv. 3,4,6)
2. Let us faithfully use his gifts (vv. 5-7)
3. Let us eagerly wait for his coming (vv. 8,9)

One can divide the text along similar lines and adapt the words of verse 4 as a theme:

Always Thank God for His Grace

1. He gives us peace in Christ (vv. 3,4,6)
2. He has enriched us with spiritual gifts (vv. 5-7)
3. He will keep us in Christ's fellowship (vv. 7b-9)

The preacher who is more comfortable with two-part outlines might try:

Thank God!

1. For the way he has blessed us (vv. 3-7)
2. For the way he will keep us (vv. 8,9)

SECOND SUNDAY IN ADVENT

The Scriptures

> Old Testament — *Isaiah 40:1-11*
> Epistle — *2 Peter 3:8-14*
> Gospel — *Mark 1:1-8*

The Text — 2 Peter 3:8-14

In this epistle Peter is concerned about the souls of his readers. He urges them to make their calling and election sure so that they are ready for God's eternal kingdom (1:10,11). He assures them that they had heard the very words of God, not fables (1:16ff). He alerts them to the presence of false teachers and their faith-destroying ways (chapter 2). In this final chapter the apostle writes about scoffers who live willfully sinful lives because they don't believe Jesus will return (3:3,4). The sermon text continues the thought of being ready for Jesus' return.

v. 8 — *But do not forget this one thing, dear friends: With the Lord a day is like a thousand years, and a thousand years are like a day.*

Jesus will come a second time. By human standards it has been a long time. But God is eternal. This passage in no way indicates that the days of creation were longer than a normal day. The verses preceding and following show that the point is God's eternity, not an interpretation of the creation account.

v. 9 — *The Lord is not slow in keeping his promise, as some understand slowness. He is patient with you, not wanting anyone to perish, but everyone to come to repentance.*

Is the Lord slow or negligent or impotent in not returning as promised? No, he is patient and full of grace. His will is to reach every sinner. He wants no one lost to the flames of hell. He gives time for repentance (1 Ti 2:4). People ought not abuse this patience, but use it to be and remain Christians (2 Co 6:1,2).

v. 10 — *But the day of the Lord will come like a thief. The heavens will disappear with a roar; the elements will be destroyed by fire, and the earth and everything in it will be laid bare.* burned up

Who knows exactly when a thief will come (Lk 12:39,40)? Therefore people live in readiness, with locked doors, alarms, etc. Be ready

18

always for Jesus. Do not procrastinate. People often claim they will get to God's Word and church after they clear up some situation or business. For many the day never comes, as they find other excuses.

When Jesus arrives all creation will be destroyed.

Στοιχεῖα here are the basic elements of creation. All that will remain are God, his Word, and worship. Pay attention to them now. An alternate reading to "will be laid bare" is "will be burned up." Either makes sense here. As to the meaning of "laid bare," consider Romans 2:16. God will judge men's secrets.

> vv. 11,12 — *Since everything will be destroyed in this way, what kind of people ought you to be? You ought to live holy and godly lives as you look forward to the day of God and speed its coming. That day will bring about the destruction of the heavens by fire, and the elements will melt in the heat.*

The end will come suddenly and unexpectedly. Created things will cease to be. In view of this we will want to strive constantly, under God's grace and with the guidance of his Word, to live holy and godly lives.

In verse 12 σπεύδω can be translated either as "to hasten" or as "to be eager for." From our human perspective Christians speed up the day of Jesus' return in two ways. Believers are tools for fulfilling one of the signs of the end in preaching the gospel to all nations (Mt 24:14). Also, again from human perspective, God will shorten the days of the world for the sake of the elect (Mt 24:22).

If we translate "to be eager for," the sermon will express the confidence we have in Jesus for the end. It will also display our desire to be removed from this sin-cursed world (cp. Lk 21:28).

Will the earth be annihilated or will it be purged and then restored? Will God make the new heavens and earth from nothing or from the melted-down remains? Both views are possible and both are held by orthodox Bible scholars. Dr. Siegbert Becker writes of this in his Revelation commentary on page 326-7: "When God says through Isaiah that he would 'make' a new heaven and a new earth he does not use the Hebrew word that was used to describe the creating of the world in the beginning. That would seem to indicate that the second world will not be made out of nothing. . . . Speculation about the exact form of the new heaven and earth should be avoided."

Rather than preach over the heads of the people on this subject, aim at their hearts. Heaven will be an eternally perfect and blissful place. Urge them by the gospel to live in such a way as not to destroy the faith in Jesus' blood, which will get them there.

vv. 13,14 — *But in keeping with his promise we are looking forward to a new heaven and a new earth, the home of righteousness. So then, dear friends, since you are looking forward to this, make every effort to be found spotless, blameless and at peace with him.*

Who is spotless and blameless? Who is righteous? Only those who trust in the holy life and atoning death of Christ are fit for the new heaven and earth. This verse shows what proper waiting for Jesus is. Hearing the gospel, taking the Sacrament, remembering the Savior will keep one ready for his coming. Yes, it is difficult for some to come to hear the Word. In our busy world it's not easy to have time for individual or, especially, family devotions. But it is vital for readiness.

Homiletical Suggestions

The preacher's great challenge in November and December is to offer a fresh sermon each week. So many texts speak about the second coming. The best solution is to stick to the text at hand!

The law can be preached in connection with the destruction of the world and things in it we hold so dear. The idea of judgment, the exhortation to holy lives, and the admonition to set proper priorities also point out sin. The gospel shines in God's patience and in the spotlessness which is ours in Jesus. Peter addresses his readers twice as "dear friends." He speaks to Christians about whom he cares. We do, too.

Sometimes a question serves well as a theme. The text contains a question. The first part of the sermon outlined below tells how we try God's patience with our sins. The second part offers the forgiveness of Jesus and an evangelical admonition to faithfulness in using the means of grace.

What Kind of People Ought We to Be?

1. People who do not abuse God's patience (vv. 8-11)
2. People who look forward to a new world (vv. 12-14)

People have begun to see countdowns to Christmas. They have started or thought about the external celebrations they will have. The big day is approaching. The first part of this sermon urges hearers not to get so tangled with temporal matters that the eternal is neglected. The second part turns the listener to faith in Christ and to the kind of life he desires from us.

The Day Is Coming
1. Don't procrastinate (vv. 8-10)
2. Be prepared (vv. 11-14)

THIRD SUNDAY IN ADVENT

The Scriptures

> Old Testament — *Isaiah 61:1-3,10,11*
> Epistle — *1 Thessalonians 5:16-24*
> Gospel — *John 1:6-8, 19-28*

The Text — 1 Thessalonians 5:16-24

Paul, Silas, Timothy, and Luke had first visited Thessalonica around 51, on Paul's second missionary journey. They had responded to the "Macedonian call" (Ac 16:9,10), which led them to cross over from Troas in Asia Minor to Macedonia.

But their work in Macedonia met fierce persecution. Paul and Silas were forced to leave Thessalonica for Berea (Ac 17). Later, Paul moved on to Athens. There Timothy and Silas rejoined him, but Timothy was sent back to Thessalonica to encourage those new Christians who were facing stiff pressure from Jewish agitators. Timothy's subsequent report gave Paul immense joy, for the Thessalonians were not only faithfully enduring the persecution; they were also faithfully spreading the gospel throughout the whole region.

Then Paul wrote this letter, expressing a strong desire to revisit the Christians of Thessalonica and regretting that he could not do so (2:18). He expresses his deep love for them (2:6-8,11,12), his concern about the persecution they are forced to endure (1:6; 2:14,15) and his desire to return to them again (2:17,18; 3:1-3,10). Certain questions about Christians who had died led Paul to focus on the hope of everlasting life (4:13—5:11). He also gives encouragement for Christian living (4:1-12).

The sermon text is a portion of Paul's final encouragement. It expresses his confidence that God will preserve the Thessalonian Christians in a strong faith, honed and refined by tribulation, matured, magnetic, powerfully transcending—a force that would strengthen the weak among them and enlighten the world.

v. 16 — *Be joyful always;*

One might think that if anyone had reason to despair, these Christians did, on account of the unfair treatment they were receiving. But they knew the example of Jesus, who carried his cross in joyful determination, bent on the world's salvation. They knew they were immensely blessed with the gospel. Persecution only further convinced them that Christ was what mattered most in their lives. They were joyful and Paul encouraged them to continue in that joy.

v. 17 — *Pray continually;*

The KJV translation of ἀδιαλείπτως is literal, "without ceasing." Christians are not alone. They have the privilege of direct communication with their Ally and Friend. Whether danger to body and soul appears imminent or not, Satan is lurking and waiting. Intense prayer struggle with our Advocate will strengthen our position in daily combat with our already defeated foe. Sanctified and trial tested, Christians continually pray that in everything God's will be done and his kingdom come.

v. 18 — *Give thanks in all circumstances, for this is God's will for you in Christ Jesus.*

The Spirit so disciplines Christians that their prayers breathe a spirit of thankfulness. While the worldly are discontented even when living like kings, Christians know their spiritual blessings far surpass the material. They are thankful, even in troubles. They know hardship only strengthens faith.

The second half of the verse offers a reason for the three imperatives (vv. 16-18a). Collectively, they are the antecedent of τοῦτο. God surely desires that his children develop a character of continued joy, thankfulness, and prayer. Such is the nature of one who is "in Christ Jesus."

v. 19 — *Do not put out the Spirit's fire;*

The Spirit will not leave a person he has brought to faith, but such a person can snuff out the Spirit's fire through unbelief. Satan will powerfully tempt persecuted Christians to deny the faith in order to escape bodily pain and anguish. But the Spirit's fire refines us just as fire refines metal by burning off impurities.

v. 20 — *Do not treat prophecies with contempt.*

Ἐξουθενεῖτε, "despise" or "look down upon," can also mean "empty of all authority." By "prophecies" is meant the entire revealed Word of God. Many people give equal or higher authority to human philosophy and wisdom. Certain methods of Bible interpretation do not recognize the inerrancy of Scripture. Some urge tolerance of viewpoints which oppose Scripture. Turning a deaf ear to Scripture is the best way to put out the Spirit's fire. Swapping the diligent study of the Word for the easy life only leads to a soul emptied of meaning, purpose, and life.

vv. 21,22 — *Test everything. Hold on to the good. Avoid every kind of evil.*

Δοκιμάζετε, means "examine, interpret, discern, discover, prove, test." Mindful of Jesus' warning against false prophets, wolves in sheep's clothing, Christians will put all things to the test. The standard is not what seems to make sense or to work best. The standard or rule by which Christians test and discern is God's inspired Word.

Once this test is applied, we are to reject what does not fall into line with God's Word and hold to that which does. Even if the conflict seems small, God still wants us to avoid it. One false teaching leads to another. "A little yeast works through the whole batch of dough" (Ga 5:9).

Εἶδος means "outward form" or "visible appearance." Every manifestation of evil is meant. Christians will strive not only to avoid sin, but even to avoid giving the appearance or impression of it. They know that, too, could shipwreck the faith of others.

v. 23 — *May God himself, the God of peace, sanctify you through and through. May your whole spirit, soul and body be kept blameless at the coming of our Lord Jesus Christ.*

As Christians grow in faith, the Holy Spirit gets involved in every area of their lives. They learn to trust their Savior more each day. Lukewarm faith will eventually die. It will fall prey to temptation and tribulation.

But when faith is put to the test, the Spirit also uses that critical time of testing to confirm and solidify faith, so that it pervades one's "whole spirit, soul and body." Christians then are "blameless" at the second coming of Jesus on Judgment Day. The merits of Christ's perfect life replace their sins in God's eyes. He declares them righteous and just by faith in Jesus.

v. 24 — *The one who calls you is faithful and he will do it.*

One who is faithful is one who keeps his promises. God never broke a single one. This promise is no different. He who calls us to daily repentance and faith will sanctify us and keep us blameless till the coming of Jesus (v. 23).

Homiletical Suggestions

The beautiful prophecy of Isaiah in the Old Testament reading powerfully demonstrates the world's desperate yearning for Israel's Messiah and the rich joy of those who receive the long-awaited freedom in him. No other circumstances in life, mundane, or significant, can rob the Christian of this joy. The reading's focus is joy in the gospel.

The Gospel reading speaks of the ministry of John the Baptist, forerunner of the Savior, who attracted great attention but diverted the attention to the one who would come after him—the Christ. His message: Prepare for his coming by repentance and faith.

The text speaks of joy, prayer, thanksgiving, and perseverance in the gospel, even in the face of persecution. It holds out the promise that God will preserve our faith until Christ's second coming. The preacher thus will likely focus on themes of trust in God's promises, perseverance in good times and bad, God's reliable Word that gives us clear direction, and the Christian's positive outlook on life—a fruit of his faith.

There is a natural three-part division of the text which suggests basic outlines along these lines:

God Will Keep Us Forever True

1. Always living our faith (vv. 16-18)
2. Always in the Word (vv. 19-22)
3. Always trusting him (vv. 23,24)

Keep Focused on Christ

1. He will change your life (vv. 16-18)
2. He will free you from evil (vv. 19-22)
3. He will preserve your faith (vv. 23,24)

One might also construct a two-part outline like the following:

God's Word Prepares Us for Jesus' Coming

1. It changes our lives (vv. 16-18)
2. It preserves our faith (vv. 19-24)

FOURTH SUNDAY IN ADVENT

The Scriptures

> Old Testament — *2 Samuel 7:8-16*
> Epistle — *Romans 16:25-27*
> Gospel — *Luke 1:26-38*

The Text — Romans 16:25-27

The Apostle Paul wrote to the Christians in Rome while he was at Corinth during his third missionary journey (Ac 20:2,3), in A.D. 57 or 58. Although he greatly desired to visit the Roman church (1:11,12), at this time he could not go, since he felt compelled to personally take the offering collected among the Gentile churches in Greece and Asia Minor to the needy saints in Jerusalem (15:25,26). Therefore, he sent this letter to prepare the way for his coming to Rome prior to his projected mission to Spain (1:10-15; 15:23-29). This congregation had not yet benefited from Paul's personal apostolic ministry. Therefore, he also sets forth the basic truths of salvation in this most systematic of all his letters.

Our text is the doxology at the conclusion of the letter. Paul customarily concludes his letters with a doxology or benediction. This one is longer than we find in his other epistles and sums up some of the leading ideas of the letter. In Greek it is a single sentence, which begins (v. 25) and ends (v. 27) by addressing God, with a parenthetical clause between (v. 26).

> vv. 25,26 — *Now to him who is able to establish you by my gospel and the proclamation of Jesus Christ, according to the revelation of the mystery hidden for long ages past, but now revealed and made known through the prophetic writings by the command of the eternal God, so that all nations might believe and obey him—*

Paul commended the Romans to the power of God who brought them to faith and who alone can sustain and preserve his believers in faith. It is quite fitting for him to begin his doxology in this way, since he has just warned his readers to watch out for and keep away from "those who cause divisions and put obstacles in your way that are contrary to the teaching you have learned" (16:17). Whether we are surrounded by false doctrine, temptations to sin, sufferings, or persecution, we can count on God to preserve us in our faith. He always protects those whom he has called to be his own, and he finishes what he has started.

Paul was confident God would strengthen these believers "by my gospel and the proclamation of Jesus Christ." He calls it "my" gospel, not because his gospel was a gospel different from that preached by the other apostles or because it was his own personal possession, but because he received it by direct revelation from Christ himself (Gal 1:12).

Next follows a phrase which defines the gospel. It is "the proclamation of Jesus Christ" (epexegetical καί). The gospel is about the Savior (objective genitive); he is its content. Who he is and what he came to do and still does for us is the good news, the gospel. The gospel is God's own power to save everyone who believes (1:16). Through it the Holy Spirit imparts faith and keeps believers in faith (10:17). Those who preach the gospel do not preach themselves (2 Co 4:5) but Christ crucified (1 Co 1:23). Anything else is a perversion of the gospel, "a different gospel—which is really no gospel at all" (Gal 1:6,7). This good news about a Savior from sin and death who came to this earth to take our place and save us by his grace is the good news we are preparing to celebrate at Christmas.

The gospel of Jesus Christ is "the revelation of the mystery hidden for long ages past." In secular Greek usage a μυστήριον was a "secret" revealed to initiates in the mystery religions. In New Testament usage μυστήριον refers to a secret that is hidden from human understanding and which God has revealed. Only those who have faith in Christ can comprehend God's mysteries. Paul has used this expression earlier, to describe how the unbelief of the Jews led to the opportunity for the Gentiles to be saved (11:25). He uses it elsewhere to describe the incarnation of Christ (1 Ti 3:16), the death of Christ (1 Co 2:1), God's own purpose to sum up all things in Christ (Eph 1:9), and the change in believers' bodies on the Last Day (1 Co 15:51).

The words "hidden for long ages past" might give the impression there had been no revelation of this mystery in the Old Testament. Paul dispels that impression with the words "revealed and made known through the prophetic writings." The Old Testament was far from silent on this mystery. The prophets had predicted the birth, suffering, death, and resurrection of the coming Savior as well as the ingathering of the Gentiles. Paul has made use of the "the prophetic writings" in this letter directly (1:16; 4:3,9,22) and indirectly (3:21) to prove justification by grace through faith alone.

However, what lies faintly foreshadowed in the Old Testament stands clearly revealed in the New. Only with the coming of Christ did the promise find fulfillment and full fruition. Only in accordance with Christ's command (Mt 28:18-20) did the apostles begin to take the gospel into all the world "so that all nations might believe and obey him." Only in the proclamation of the gospel and the practical teaching of the apostles was the dividing partition between Jew and Gentile permanently broken down.

The apostle's whole discussion of the how and why of divine revelation has volumes to say to the church today. The puny minds of men wish to dissect and discard direct divine revelation in the Bible as so much human baggage and ballast. People crave to find truth through subjective human experience, when God has chosen to reveal it through objective propositional statements, the proclamation about Jesus Christ. Note that there is more than a hint of verbal inspiration here: The prophets wrote about the coming Christ and his church "by the command of the eternal God."

All of this and more is part of the mystery revealed by the Holy Spirit to the eyes of faith, but revealed only through the Spirit's chosen means, God's Word.

v. 27 — —to the only wise God be glory forever through Jesus Christ! Amen.

After committing the Roman believers to God's power for spiritual safekeeping, Paul now praises "the only wise God." This is an especially fitting description in view of what Paul has just said about God's great purpose of salvation in revealing this mystery in history. This naturally draws forth the apostle's adoration of God's wisdom here, as it does elsewhere in the letter (11:33-36) and in his other letters, e.g., 1 Corinthians 2:6-13. Giving glory or praise to our gracious God is the ultimate aim of believers now and in eternity. So the apostle appropriately closes this letter which summarizes Christian cardinal truths by focusing faith's attention on our faithful God.

"The Romans need not fear; whatever tasks they undertake, they shall not undertake in vain. They need but bow in adoration before the God whose wisdom guides all history toward His goal, to the glory of His grace. Faith sees that goal and glory even now and gives God glory through Him in whom God's glory has appeared, through Jesus Christ" (Martin Franzmann, *Concordia Commentary: Romans*, p. 282).

Homiletical Suggestions

As we continue our Christmas countdown during Advent, the last Sunday of the season proclaims, "The time has come!" The Old Testa-

28

ment Lesson reminds us that the time has come *for the fulfillment of prophecy*. The Lord promised David a great name, rest from his enemies, and an eternal kingdom—all promises which had their ultimate fulfillment in his greater descendant, the Messiah. The angel Gabriel's announcement of the birth of Jesus to the Virgin Mary in today's Gospel shows the time has come *for the birth of God's Son*. The Epistle picks up on this theme as the apostle Paul proclaims:

The Time Has Come for the Revelation of God's Mystery!

1. Foretold through the prophets by God's command (v. 26)
2. Proclaimed in the gospel to God's glory (vv. 25,27)

An alternate theme emphasizes the idea of doxology or praise with the parts focusing on God's power and wisdom revealed in the gospel. In order to end with the idea of committing believers to God's power which preserves them in faith, the order in which these ideas occur in the text can be inverted in the sermon parts:

Glorify Our Wise and Powerful God for His Gospel!

1. It reveals his wisdom, once mysteriously hidden (vv. 25b,26a,27)
2. It proclaims his power to save all believers completely (vv. 25a,26b)

CHRISTMAS DAY — THE NATIVITY OF OUR LORD

The Scriptures

Old Testament — *Isaiah 52:7-10*
Epistle — *Hebrews 1:1-9*
Gospel — *John 1:1-14*

The Text — Hebrews 1:1-9

Jesus was the center of everything for the Jewish Christians who are addressed in the letter to the Hebrews. Sad to say, for many of these believers—daily facing the fury of Satan at the hands of persecuting Jews and pagans—Jesus seemed to be the focus of their distress. The author knew how true this was! He wrote his letter to fortify these troubled Christians so that their faith would not crumble. Yes, Jesus and his righteousness *were* at the center of their troubles; they were hard-pressed and abused.

But more than that and of infinitely greater importance, Jesus was at the center of God's plan for their salvation. Jesus was their God, who wondrously became their Brother. Jesus was the Priest who sacrificed himself. Jesus was their strength to endure and their motivation to press on. Jesus was the heart of their faith, their hope, their life. Jesus was everything to them. The writer made all this clear to his struggling friends.

He also makes it clear to us. At a time when the Christmas season and holiday celebration in our society are decidedly Christ-less, we need the reminder that Christ is at the center of Christmas. So, as he begins his letter, the author tells us exactly who this Jesus, this baby boy born in a barn, truly is: the eternal, unfathomable God who took on a human nature to save and exalt sinners.

v. 1 — *In the past God spoke to our forefathers through the prophets at many times and in various ways*

God raised up many prophets in the time before Christ came to begin his ministry. One after the other, in continuing succession, the prophets preached, taught, lamented, sang, warned, promised, and comforted. All this varied activity because God wanted to speak to his people! God's great desire from the time of the Fall onward was to speak to his people about his Son and about the salvation he would accomplish.

v. 2a — *but in these last days he has spoken to us by his Son*

What a miracle of love that God should choose to speak to us directly through his Son! The phrase "these last days" informs us that we shouldn't look for any new revelations, any new prophecies. We don't need any additional information. Nor is God going to start communicating with us in new and different ways, other than through the Scriptures. Jesus Christ, in his person and in the record he caused to be set down in the New Testament, is God's last and fullest word to us. The anarthrous ἐν υἱῷ emphasizes the unique prophetic office of Christ. He speaks about the finished redemption of God.

So we listen closely as God speaks to us about the Redeemer in this book. Specifically, we find the doctrine of the two natures of Christ underlined here. Luther remarked that the two natures are rarely taught with as much clarity and detail as they are in this section of Scripture. It is this truth that gives us so much comfort and joy at Christmas time. When we see how God exalted human nature as the attributes of the Son of God were communicated to the man born of Mary, when we see how God gave hope to humanity by honoring humanity in Christ, then we can rejoice! God did not give up on humanity. Instead he found a way to raise us up from our sin and decay to give us the hope of a glorious and holy life. He asked his Son to take on our human nature and to share the glory of God with it.

v. 2b — *whom he appointed heir of all things, and through whom he made the universe.*

The communication of attributes, that glorious exaltation of Christ's humanity, is expressed when the writer declares, "whom he appointed heir of all things." As true God, Christ had no need to be appointed heir; he was the original owner! But as true man he was appointed heir of "all things," i.e., of the whole creation, which certainly includes all people. We belong to Christ because God appointed him heir and we are his inheritance.

But we are also part of his creation: "Through (him) God created the universe." The Son was the intermediate agent through whom the Father created all that there is. He was with God and was God, John writes in today's Gospel (1:1-14), and so all things were made through him and nothing was made without him. It is also true, then, that we belong to Christ because he is the one who made us.

v. 3a — *The Son is the radiance of God's glory and the exact representation of his being, sustaining all things by his powerful word.*

Ἀπαύγασμα and χαρακτήρ are used only in this verse of the New Testament. Ἀπαύγασμα in its active sense is a radiance or bright shining forth and in its passive sense a reflection. God's Son possesses the glory of God in and of himself and also radiates that glory in order to make it known to us. In Jesus the shining holiness, the bright wisdom and power, the glowing love and mercy of God light up the world so that we can see what our God is like.

In the same way Christ is the "exact representation of God's being." When we look at Christ we see God and everything about God in perfect detail. If we want to see how merciful God is, we look to the Scriptures to see the mercy of Christ. If we want to know about God's power over Satan, we look to the Scriptures to see how Jesus exercised power over the devil and all his evil schemes. If we want to see God's wisdom, we turn to the Scriptures to study the teaching of Jesus. These two phrases help to explain how God speaks to us and makes himself known and knowable to us through his Son.

Τε, the conjunction which indicates close connection between parts, joins the phrase "sustaining all things by his powerful word" to what precedes. This emphasizes that Christ is not less than God because he is the radiance and representation of God. He is God himself and in conjunction with the Father does the work only God can do.

vv. 3b,4 — *After he had provided purification for sins, he sat down at the right hand of the Majesty in heaven. So he became as much superior to the angels as the name he has inherited is superior to theirs.*

Although it is almost hidden away in a preliminary clause, here is the heart of the Christian message. The Son of God took on human flesh and blood for one purpose: to provide purification from sin. This is the Good News of Christmas, and all of the preceding information about the glorious divinity of Christ only serves to set apart and highlight God's gracious love for us. It was the almighty Creator of the universe who favored men and women with a love that was greater than their sin. That's grace. Again we can say that what followed in this text points to the blessings we receive from God's grace. We have a glorious life, free from sin and death, waiting for us in heaven.

A few points to reflect on in regard to this καθαρισμός. Notice that Christ cleansed us of sin. He did not clean up our will, our reason, or our abilities so that we could earn God's favor and blessing through some sort of second-chance effort on our part. It was not our work but

Jesus' work that purified us from sin. It was Jesus by himself who washed away the filth of sin by offering his own body and life as the final atoning sacrifice. Without Christ there is no forgiveness and no purity before God. Without Christ we would be forever unclean and unable to stand in the presence of the holy God. But Jesus did wash us clean. We have been purified, as the temporal clause and Jesus' subsequent exaltation demonstrate.

It should also be noted that purification for sins comes only through faith in Christ. In Acts 15:9 Peter explained this to the Jerusalem Council as he spelled out the truth for Jew and Gentile alike: "God purified their hearts by faith." The one who trusts that Jesus has cleansed him of sin is cleansed, for faith holds on to God's powerful promise in Christ.

The writer goes on to state that this same Jesus who humbled himself and became obedient even to death was also exalted to the highest place (cp. Php 2:9-11). Christ poured out his blood on the cross to purify us from sin. Jesus died. But then God raised him from the dead and exalted him. The writer to the Hebrews explains that after Jesus died and rose again he "sat at the right hand of the Majesty in heaven." Here again we marvel that the human nature was raised up and exalted. As true God, the Son always possessed the power and authority of God. But it is God's great miracle and our great hope that this power and authority was shared with the human nature of Christ.

This point is underscored by the comparison of Christ with the angels. Certainly God is greater than the angels, but it is truly amazing that the man Christ Jesus was exalted to a position far greater than that of the angels! Our human nature, the body and soul that we possess as human beings, was not defeated and destroyed by sin. Rather, in Christ Jesus it was honored and exalted.

So it is wonderful to know that the man Christ Jesus is greater than the angels and has inherited a name far superior to theirs. Angels are servants and messengers, but the man Christ Jesus is LORD. The angels may be flames of fire whose power we can't even imagine, but only Jesus Christ can be called the Mighty God. The angels often appeared in human form, but only God's Son incarnate could truly be called Immanuel. The angels have been sent to serve those who will inherit salvation, but only Jesus Christ was sent to win that salvation for us! In Philippians 2:9-11 Paul offers a beautiful commentary on this verse.

The writer adds five Old Testament quotations to support this point.

vv. 5-9 — *For to which of the angels did God ever say,*
   "You are my Son;
      today I have become your Father"?

Or again,
   "I will be his Father
      and he will be my Son"?

And again, when God brings his firstborn into the world, he says,

   "Let all God's angels worship him."

In speaking of the angels he says,

   "He makes his angels winds,
      his servants flames of fire."

But about the Son he says,

   "Your throne, O God, will last for ever and ever,
      and righteousness will be the scepter of your kingdom.
   You have loved righteousness and hated wickedness;
      therefore God, your God, has set you
         above your companions
      by anointing you with the oil of joy."

With the first three passages (Ps 2:7; 2 Sa 7:14; 1 Ch 17:13; Dt 32:43 LXX) the writer points out that Jesus Christ is superior to the angels both in his divine nature and in his human nature.

The first two passages (v. 5) refer to the mystery of the Trinity and the relationship of the Son to the Father. The Son receives his being from the Father in eternity. The Father is greater than the angels he created. So, too, is the Son.

The third passage (v. 6) certainly refers to the nativity of Christ. At that time the angels sang a song of praise to the little human baby born in Bethlehem: "Glory to God in the highest. . . " The angels called him God Most High and worshiped him as such. And we remember that the angels are very careful to worship God alone (Rev. 19:10).

With the final two quotations of our text (vv. 7-9)—taken from Psalm 104:4 and Psalm 45:6,7—the writer simply compares the angels with Christ. Of course, there is no comparison; Christ is superior. Angels were made to be God's servants and God calls them that. But God praises Christ as the eternal, powerful God of heaven and earth. God praises Christ as the very God, who rules over his people in righteousness. God addresses Christ as God, not as a creature or a servant—or even as an angel.

Two vital points are linked together in this last quotation (vv. 8,9): 1) Christ has been exalted above every name and power, and 2) he has companions (μετόχους, "sharers"). Jesus shares a human nature with us and it is this human nature that has been highly exalted. Moreover, the fact that Christ shares our human nature means that we truly are his "companions."

Putting these two truths together, we realize that Christ's exaltation is our great hope. Where he is, we will be. What his body and soul enjoy in heaven, we will also enjoy. That he was raised up from death to glory means that we will be raised as well. We won't become divine, to be sure, for God has set Christ above us (παρὰ τοὺς μετό– χους σου), but we will share and be partners in his glory. This is our hope and joy as we gaze into the manger at Christmas time. We see a little boy with a body and soul just like our own, and we know that we will share that "body-and-soul" life with him forever.

Homiletical Suggestions

Both the Old Testament and Gospel lessons tell us that God will bring about salvation in the sight of all people. God does not want his salvation to be a secret. He did not work it out in secret nor will he let it remain a secret. God wants to speak to the world about it! Here is one approach to this epistle text:

At Christmas time we send out dozens of greeting cards. Why? For one thing, we want to express our love for friends and relatives. At the same time we often include in our Christmas greetings hopes and wishes for the new year that lies ahead. God sends Christ as his greeting to the world, and in Christ he expresses his love for us and his wishes for our future. That suggests the outline:

Jesus Is God's Christmas Greeting to the World

1. He expresses God's love for us (vv. 1-3a)
2. He expresses God's blessings for the future (vv. 3b-9)

Another way to approach this text and highlight the person of Christ would be to use a familiar carol as the theme:

What Child Is This?

1. This Child is our majestic God (vv. 1-3a)
2. This Child is our Savior from sin (v. 3b)
3. This Child is our hope of glory (vv. 4-9).

Using the same theme and utilizing only verses 1-6:

What Child Is This?

    1. This is God's Son, through whom God speaks to us (vv. 1,2)
    2. This is God himself, working our salvation (vv. 2b-6)

FIRST SUNDAY AFTER CHRISTMAS

The Scriptures

> Old Testament — *Isaiah 45:22-25*
> Epistle — *Colossians 3:12-17*
> Gospel — *Luke 2:25-40*

The Text — Colossians 3:12-17

Since this is the first selection from Colossians in Series B, the preacher will want to keep the entire content of the letter in mind, even if the larger context is not treated directly in the sermon. The letter to the Colossians is one of four letters (with Philemon, Ephesians, and Philippians) which Paul wrote during his first Roman imprisonment. Epaphras had come from Colosse in Asia Minor to visit Paul in Rome. He had expressed some grave concerns about the condition of this troubled congregation, which the apostle had never visited. Paul must counter the destructive ideas of Judaism, legalism, and ritualism on the one hand, and the influence of Hellenistic philosophy on the other. Some form of the latter was promising the Colossians enlightenment and a more complete spiritual life than the gospel alone could offer them.

Both movements negated the very heart of the gospel. Therefore, before writing words of encouragement for sanctified Christian living (chapter 3), Paul first treats the subjects of Christ's supremacy (chapter 1); then freedom from human regulations, with warnings against heresy (chapter 2).

Verses 10 and 11 serve as a link between two sections of encouragement for holy living. The link emphasizes the real motivation for wanting to follow Paul's inspired instructions. The believer wants to live a holy life because the Holy Spirit has given him a "new self . . . renewed . . . in the image of its Creator." This "new self" gladly and willingly accepts the fact that "Christ is all, and is in all." The believer's Christ-centered life strives always to glorify the Savior. That motivational link makes the believer ready to listen to Paul's "therefore," which introduces the text.

> vv. 12-14 — *Therefore, as God's chosen people, holy and dearly loved, clothe yourselves with compassion, kindness, humility, gentleness and patience. Bear with each other and forgive whatever grievances you may have against one another. Forgive as*

the Lord forgave you. And over all these virtues put on love,
which binds them all together in perfect unity.

"Clothe yourselves, therefore" are the words with which the Greek text begins. What is introduced by "therefore" (οὖν) is an inference based on what precedes. New life in Christ means that every day the believer gladly puts on those qualities which characterize the Christian life. But before Paul describes what those qualities are, he again provides the motivation for doing it.

The motivation for wanting to clothe oneself in godly qualities springs from the fact that believers are "God's chosen people, holy and dearly loved." Believers are "God's chosen people" (ἐκλεκτοὶ τοῦ θεοῦ). Peter uses the same word when he calls believers a "chosen people" (1 Pe 2:9). Being chosen people of the Lord God was a concept familiar to Jewish believers (Ex 19:5,6; Dt 14:2; Isa 43:20,21), but Paul now wants Christians from both Jewish and Gentile backgrounds to see that the one true and living God has chosen or elected them to be his own through the one and only mediator of the new covenant, Jesus Christ. This saving mediator brings sinners a new and imputed holiness (Ro 5:19; 2 Co 5:21; He 2:11) which is ours only because the Father chooses to love us dearly in Christ (1 Jn 3:1).

Thus motivated, the believer gladly dons compassion, kindness, humility, gentleness, and patience.

"Compassion" is what the Samaritan felt toward the man who fell among thieves (Lk 10:33). It is what Jesus felt toward the crowds who "were like sheep without a shepherd" (Mk 6:34). It sees the hurt of others and is moved to do something about it.

"Kindness" is a goodness found in God and demonstrated by God in his saving acts. It is also a quality demonstrated by the believer as he forgives his fellowman (Eph 4:32).

"Humility" was demonstrated by the tax collector, who would not even look up to heaven (Lk 18:14) and by Jesus, who became obedient to death (Php 2:8).

"Gentleness" is a characteristic which Jesus ascribes to himself (Mt 11:29), which makes his followers willing to come to him and learn from him. It is a magnetic quality that attracts cautious people rather than polarizes them.

"Patience" is what makes us willing to "suffer long," even as the Lord suffered the pangs of hell for us and continues to tolerate our sinfulness.

Wearing the clothing of these Christian virtues, it is natural for the believer to follow the specific instructions which apply them in verse 13. "Bear with each other," in the sense of putting up with one another's sinfulness. Graciously forgive (χαριζόμενοι) grievances, or causes for complaint, just as God in Christ has forgiven us. The variant readings in verse 13 would not at all change the sense of the closing statement.

Verse 14 highlights the unifying factor that makes it possible for all the other directives to come together. Love (ἀγάπη) is the final piece of spiritual clothing that is put on. Love is described figuratively as "the bond (fetter) of completeness." It is the sash that coordinates the believer's spiritual clothing. It is possible to strive to be the way Jesus was only when we live in Jesus's love.

Paul now moves from individual Christian virtues to collective attitudes and activities that further build up the body of Christ.

vv. 15,16 — *Let the peace of Christ rule in your hearts, since as members of one body you were called to peace. And be thankful. Let the word of Christ dwell in you richly as you teach and admonish one another with all wisdom, and as you sing psalms, hymns and spiritual songs with gratitude in your hearts to God.*

Christ's peace affects relationships among believers. "Rule" comes from a verb which literally means to serve as an umpire at the games. Christ's peace settles things. It determines and announces the outcome. Strife and competition are removed from Christian relationships because the Prince of Peace (Isa 9:6) has brought mankind a peace with God that the world cannot give (Jn 14:27), for Christ has suffered the punishment that brought us peace (Isa 53:5). The believer who accepts the peace treaty signed in Jesus' blood strives to cultivate peaceful relationships within the body of Christ, which has been called to peace. The unity which believers share in the body will not allow them to war against other members of the body, anymore than they would war against the body's Head.

The Christian at peace with his God, with himself, and with other members of the body is in the right frame of mind to have a thankful attitude toward all of God's gifts. He not only sees God's many blessings for body and soul, but also wants God to lead him to appreciate them and receive them with thanksgiving.

The variant readings at the beginning of verse 16 again pose no problem. Christ's word is God's word is the Lord's word. Christ's word is all of Scripture. It is the complete revelation given to us through and by "the Word [who] became flesh" (Jn 1:14). Christ's word is spirit and life (Jn 6:63). It is worth our every effort to let the

Word of God makes its dwelling within us in such a way that we consider its true spiritual riches as beyond value.

When one is living at peace within the body and is living in the Word of God, it is natural that his activities with the other members of the body will promote the spiritual welfare of all. Gatherings of believers focus their attention on teaching spiritual truth (Ac 2:42). This teaching will affect not only the intellect but also the will, as loving admonition to correct erroneous beliefs and sinful actions is given. The teaching and admonition are done by those who have been made wise for salvation (2 Ti 3:15) and who therefore desire to apply God's revealed wisdom in Scripture to themselves and their fellow believers.

As the encouragement in verse 16 continues, it is obvious that Paul has been thinking of activities in which the body of Christ gathers in public assembly. Instruction, as he conceives of it here, is a public activity. So also is the singing of "psalms, hymns and spiritual songs."

The Psalms served as the Old Testament hymnal. Whether a collection of New Testament hymns of praise already existed, we do not know. As the assembled body sings, it expresses heartfelt gratitude to God. That heartfelt gratitude and its expression also affect our personal relationships.

Paul has said so much that affects Christians in so many ways that he evidently feels compelled to wrap up his exhortations with one more all-inclusive word of encouragement before going on to specific instructions for family relationships.

v. 17 — *And whatever you do, whether in word or deed, do it all in the name of the Lord Jesus, giving thanks to God the Father through him.*

Whatever one does "in word or deed" includes all that we say or do. Others do not know our thoughts, nor are they affected by them. But our words and actions do touch others. Everything about the Christian that touches others is to be done "in the name of the Lord Jesus Christ." The name "Jesus" is the full revelation of his saving reputation as he has given it to us in Holy Scripture (Ac 4:12). Every aspect of the Christian life is to be the response of faith which rests on the solid foundation of that saving message. In his life the Christian looks for opportunities to express his Christian faith. All that the believer says and does as a believer expresses that faith in the Lord Jesus.

True faith in the Lord Jesus also gives thanks to God through Jesus. Only through the agency of (διά) Jesus' redemptive work is it possible for anyone to be in a thankful relationship of faith in God, for without Jesus' saving work humanity remains under God's law and deserving of God's wrath. That Jesus put himself under the law in our place from infancy (see today's Gospel) enables us to live for God in thankful faith through Christ. Just as Paul's words in verse 16 imply not only actual songs of praise but also a praise-filled attitude, so also these concluding words imply that the Christian's life consists not only in prayers of thanks but also in a thankful attitude.

Homiletical Suggestions

The Gospel lesson reports the words and actions of Simeon and Anna when Mary and Joseph took the Babe to the temple to fulfill the law's requirements. Jesus was the one who would bring redemption and salvation not only to Israel but even to the Gentiles.

The Old Testament lesson underscores this theme of universal redemption and salvation, for Isaiah extends God's universal invitation in the words, "Turn to me and be saved, all you ends of the earth." The link between these two lessons and the sermon text lies in the fact that this salvation, which is promised to all and received through faith, leads the believer to peace and joy.

The preacher will want to continue the joyful proclamation of the Christmas gospel and not be tempted to preach a sermon based solely on admonitions. Behind all of the conduct that Paul encourages, and motivating it, lies their perfect fulfillment by the Christchild, who came to fulfill the law in our place. Christ's forgiveness, peace, word, and saving name will permeate the sermon with good news of great joy, and God's holy people are urged to respond in faith. Key phrases in the text suggest the first three themes:

Clothe Yourselves in Christ

1. Imitate his holy qualities (vv. 12-14)
2. Seek his spiritual gifts (vv. 15,16a)
3. Offer him a praise-filled, thankful life (vv. 16b,17)

Let Christ's Word Dwell in You Richly

1. Display a Christ-like attitude (vv. 12-15)
2. Live in thankful gratitude (vv. 16b,17)

Do All in the Name of the Lord Jesus

1. Clothe your lives in Christ-like qualities (vv. 12-14)
2. Deal with others in a Christ-motivated way (vv. 15-17)

The following outline, based solely on verse 15-17, continues the Christmas theme:

Cherish the Christchild's Gifts

1. His peace to rule our hearts (v. 15)
2. His word to make us wise (v. 16)
3. His name to give us life (v. 17)

NEW YEAR'S DAY —
THE CIRCUMCISION AND NAME OF JESUS

The Scriptures

        Old Testament — *Numbers 6:22-27*
        Epistle — *Romans 1:1-7*
        Gospel — *Luke 2:21*

The Text — Romans 1:1-7

Paul's letter to the Roman congregation seems to have been written in 57 or 58 A.D., toward the close of his three-month stay in Corinth, near the close of his third missionary journey. He intended to deliver the collection gathered from the predominantly Gentile congregations for impoverished Jewish Christians of Jerusalem. Following his trip to Jerusalem, the Apostle desired to visit Rome and then continue on a mission to Spain (1:11,12; 15:23,24).

The apostle's purposes in writing were to prepare the Roman Christians for his coming visit; to establish them firmly in the Lord's doctrine, so that they might serve as a strong base for mission work to the West; and to bring about harmony and unity between the Jewish and Gentile Christians there. We find that Romans has the following characteristics, in keeping with these purposes: It is the most "systematic" of Paul's letters; it has a strong doctrinal emphasis, concentrating on sin and grace, justification and sanctification; and it makes wide use of Old Testament quotations.

The sermon text includes Paul's salutation and greeting.

v. 1 — *Paul, a servant of Christ Jesus, called to be an apostle and set apart for the gospel of God—*

These words introduce the longest salutation of any of the Pauline Epistles. That may be because Paul was not the founder of this congregation, and he had not as yet visited them.

The Apostle refers to himself as a δοῦλος, one who belongs body and soul to another. He is writing to a congregation that included a fairly large number of slaves. The term was full of meaning in that society. But the Apostle says that he is one of the slaves of Christ Jesus; and, of course, the recipients of his letter were that also. As such a servant, Paul is writing to these people; it is God's idea and will that he send this letter.

The phrase κλητὸς ἀπόστολος reminds us that the call of God and the office of apostle go together. The Lord is the one who called him, the Lord gave him his mission, and the Lord is the ultimate source of his message to them. That is why the message is so valuable. Even though they hadn't met Paul or been taught by him, his message to them in this letter carries God's own authority and is worth heeding.

With ἀφωρισμένος Paul points out that by the Lord's choice and work he has been set apart and placed into the same class with the other twelve apostles. The εἰς clause tells us that the purpose for this setting apart is that he might be dedicated to the cause of the gospel.

v. 2 — —the gospel he promised beforehand through his prophets in the Holy Scriptures

The aorist middle προεπηγγείλατο points out that the good news for which Paul was called and set apart for its proclamation is not something new. God's people living in the Old Testament era had the promise of the gospel. Paul proclaims the fulfillment of that same good news of God's salvation that was so long in preparation. Paul's doctrine coincides exactly with that of the Old Testament.

Διὰ τῶν προφητῶν αὐτοῦ is one of the many references to the fact that God himself is the source for the Holy Scriptures through his inspiration of the holy writers. Here is a clear statement that the good news is God's news.

v. 3 — regarding his Son, who as to his human nature was a descendant of David,

The content of the gospel is the Son of God himself. In this verse we have a precise and concise exposition of the person and work of this Son. First of all, he is the eternal Son of God who had his relationship with the Father before the incarnation, from all eternity. At a certain predetermined point in the history of the world, this eternal Son of God came into the flesh, assuming human nature as a descendant of the royal line of David. Thereby he entered upon the first of two distinct, successive stages of which he became the subject. In other words, he entered his state of humiliation. When he assumed his human nature and entered his state of humiliation, not showing forth or using all of his divine power and glory all of the time, the Son took upon himself the limitations and weaknesses of our human nature without taking on our sinfulness.

v. 4 — and who through the Spirit of holiness was declared with power to be the Son of God by his resurrection from the dead: Jesus Christ our Lord.

Jesus was openly declared to be the Son of God in the next stage of this historical process of which he became the subject, his resurrection. In other words, he entered in upon his state of exaltation, in which he did reveal and make full use of his divine power and glory. We understand ἐν δυνάμει to be the modifier of υἱοῦ θεοῦ. His resurrection demonstrates that he has divine power. The NIV relegates this understanding of ἐν δυνάμει to a footnote: "The Son of God with power."

The contrast between the two states is further carried out by the double use of κατὰ in verses 3 and 4. The κατὰ of verse 3, which refers to Jesus' state of humiliation "as to his human nature," has its corresponding κατὰ in verse 4, which refers to his state of exaltation.

There is considerable discussion concerning the phrase κατὰ πνεῦμα ἁγιωσύνης. It is helpful to note the alternate translation of this phrase in the NIV: "who as to the spirit of his holiness was appointed. . ." This phrase occurs nowhere else in the New Testament, so we need to rely on the context for a proper and full understanding of it. The context is the contrast between Christ's states of humiliation and exaltation. The phrase ἐξ ἀναστάσεως νεκρῶν adds the idea that the "spirit (or Spirit) of holiness" is linked to Christ's resurrection. This verse is not only referring to Jesus Christ according to his divine nature or to the relationship between the Son and the Holy Spirit. It is referring to his holy obedience according to his human nature, in doing the work of salvation. And then it is referring to his exaltation in that very nature (Php 2:6-11; Jn 17:4,5; Heb 2:9). He has been glorified and his glory has been witnessed on earth from the time of his resurrection appearances.

The Son of God is boldly named and entitled at the end of this verse that proclaims his exaltation. He is Jesus, which name establishes his historical identity and purpose. He is Christ, which title declares his official work. He is Lord, which proclaims his authority and power at the right hand of God. This authority and power he now exercises in heaven and earth.

v. 5 — *Through him and for his name's sake, we received grace and apostleship to call people from among all the Gentiles to the obedience that comes from faith.*

Διά points to the fact that through the Lord Jesus Christ Paul and his readers have received the undeserved love of God and the apostleship. Because the Romans are united with Paul and others through the gift of faith, they are also beneficiaries of the work of the apostles, who are among Christ's gifts to his church (Eph 4:11).

The phrase εἰς ὑπακοὴν πίστεως deserves special note. It says that the purpose and result (εἰς) of such a proclamation is "the obedience of faith." The best grammatical explanation for πίστεως seems to be that it is the epexegetical use of the genitive: "the obedience which is faith." Other possibilities are genitive of possession or subjective genitive, either of which would be translated: "faith's obedience." However we look at it, the meaning is clear. Christian faith, worked by God, is essentially trusting obedience. It acknowledges, receives, and appropriates the gospel. It accepts Jesus as Savior, glorifies God's name, and obeys his will. Such is the desired effect of proclaiming the gospel.

The NIV translates πάντα τὰ ἔθνη with the words "all the Gentiles." Even though Paul's was to be an apostleship to the Gentiles, most commentators don't exclude the Jewish nation from the ἔθνεσιν, because Paul did work among Jews in the Gentile cities he visited. There were also Jewish Christians among the recipients of this letter to the Roman congregation.

Since Jesus Christ our Lord humbled himself and became obedient for the salvation of all, it is his name that is served when the gospel is preached. When people are brought to the obedience which is faith, his name is glorified.

v. 6 — *And you also are among those who are called to belong to Jesus Christ.*

Paul includes the Roman Christians among the people who have been called to the obedience which is faith. Ἰησοῦ is subjective, a genitive of agent. Jesus Christ himself is the one who has called them and placed his name upon them.

v. 7 — *To all in Rome who are loved by God and called to be saints: Grace and peace to you from God our Father and from the Lord Jesus Christ.*

On the basis of what he has just said, especially in verse 6, the apostle now addresses his letter to the Roman Christians as people who are loved by God and who are called saints by virtue of that love. In his greeting he uses exclamatory nominatives that are very familiar from his other letters. He calls down upon the Roman Christians the grace and peace which come from the Father and the Son.

Notice the double, unarticulated, object of ἀπό. God our Father and the Lord Jesus Christ are one, equally the source of grace and peace.

46

Homiletical Suggestions

New Year's Day has traditionally emphasized the circumcision and naming of Jesus. The Gospel for the day is Luke 2:21, the brief account of those events on the eighth day after the Savior's birth.

The Old Testament reading, Numbers 6:22-27, is the giving of the Aaronic Blessing, which was to be pronounced upon the Lord's people. In it we hear his "name," his revelation and reputation, as the one who blesses, gives grace, and showers his people with favor and peace. This was the name he wanted to be placed upon his people for their blessing.

The day and the readings suggest this treatment of the text:

The Name Says It All

1. For Jesus Christ (vv. 2-4)
2. For his people (vv. 1,5-7)

Using the same theme, we could also focus on the implications of the Lord's name and reputation for the work of the Savior and of his people:

The Name Says It All

1. It reveals the work of the Savior (vv. 2-4)
2. It reveals the work of his people (vv. 1,5-7)

A third approach:

We Hear an Important Name

1. It focuses our attention on whose we are (vv. 2-4)
2. It focuses our attention on who we are (vv. 1,5-7)

SECOND SUNDAY AFTER CHRISTMAS

The Scriptures

> Old Testament — *Isaiah 61:10—62:3*
> Epistle — *Ephesians 1:3-6, 15-18*
> Gospel — *John 1:1-18*

The Text — Ephesians 1:3-6,15-18

Though Paul's humble admissions of weakness have led some to conclude that he was less than compelling as a public speaker, his writings strongly portray him as a man filled with energy and exuberance that bubbled over from his soul. At the same time, his writings give evidence of a calculated and Spirit-guided choice of words. He has the gift to pack a truckload of meaning in a small bucket of words.

More than a few of the Bible passages stored in our memory banks are, no doubt, from Paul's letter to the Ephesians. They are passages which offer comfort to the troubled conscience as they extend the hand of God's grace in Christ to sinners. They are passages we rely on for our teaching because of the clear presentation of original sin and God's grace. They are passages which lead us to a proper grasp of the doctrine of election. It is a very precious and useful book.

As clear and useful as this book is in teaching us God's truth, it is difficult to determine if there was any one underlying cause which compelled Paul to write the letter. Reading 1:15 may lead us to conclude that Paul had heard such encouraging words about their faith that he was moved to pray for them and share his joy with them. He may also have simply decided it was time to share his joy concerning their faith after discovering that they were distressed by his imprisonment. He may have wanted to encourage them to recognize the grace of God at work in his life and theirs.

After a formal introduction, he begins the body of the letter with a rousing doxology. It rises from his lips as he contemplates the entire work of God for our salvation.

> v. 3 — *Praise be to the God and Father of our Lord Jesus Christ, who has blessed us in the heavenly realms with every spiritual blessing in Christ.*

Though Paul addresses his praise to God the Father, he repeatedly acknowledges that our God has blessed us through the work of

Christ. The phrase "in Christ," or some variation of it, is found in almost all of the first fourteen verses of the chapter.

Paul offers praise to Christ's "God and Father," emphasizing both his humanity (the Almighty is his God) and his divinity (the Almighty is his Father).

With the simple phrase "our Lord Jesus Christ," the inspired writer pulls his readers into the picture to share in the moment of rejoicing. What stirs us to praise is the wealth of blessings that are ours in connection with Christ and his saving work: our election, redemption, and certification as heirs of God's kingdom.

The grammar alone doesn't determine whether this was intended to be a single statement that characterizes God as being well spoken of, or an exhortation to praise God. In the context of listing the blessings God has given, however, it seems that Paul is expressing his desire that God be praised.

v. 4 — *For he chose us in him before the creation of the world to be holy and blameless in his sight.*

The entire multitude of spiritual blessings which are the possession of Paul and the Ephesians (and us) are not the object of some vague and distant hope but a solid and present reality. We can say that with conviction because God chose us before we were born and even before the world was created. "Chose us" is "elected us," built on ἐκλέγομαι: "I pick individuals out of a large number." He chose us out of many people in this world, not because he saw a wholesome inclination in our souls, but rather "in him." God didn't look at what we would be or what we would do, but at what his Son was and what he would do.

God chose us for a purpose: to be holy and blameless. The rest of the letter and the rest of Scripture make it very plain that this can be only "in him." The blessings of election are ours because it was God's will and pleasure to give us these through his Son. Through him we have been adopted as his children.

v. 5 — *In love he predestined us to be adopted as his sons through Jesus Christ, in accordance with his pleasure and—*

Adoption implies that by birth we were not God's children. Certainly our sinful thoughts, words, and deeds show that we are not by nature children of the true and holy God. Yet, the fact that God chose us or "predestined" us before the creation of the world does not violate his essential righteousness or holiness. The demands of the law which had to be satisfied were satisfied through Christ, who kept the law and redeemed us from its curse. It is in him that we were predestined to be adopted as his sons.

The doctrine of election offers comfort from first to last. No matter what trials we suffer or how great our battles against error might be, everything that happens will bring us closer to God's goal for us.

v. 6 — —*to the praise of his glorious grace, which he has freely given us in the One he loves.*

By restoring wayward mankind God enables us to fulfill the role for which we had been created: to glorify him. He is not glorified only in the words of praise which we were predestined to offer. The very fact that we sinners are adopted into his family is a testimony of God's grace. It glorifies God because it shows his love. Our self-righteous sinful nature may lead us to look at some of our fellow believers and express amazement that God's grace would so work to convert even their hearts. Actually, they could say the same about us. Even a quick glance in the mirror of God's law will remind us that God's grace is beyond description and worthy of praise. Rotten and disobedient children though we were, he adopted us through Jesus' blood.

The Christmas season that now draws to a close has also blessed us with clear reminders of God's grace. Instead of giving us what we deserved, he humbled himself to be born under the law to become our Savior. Once again we have knelt beside the manger to praise God for his glorious grace. But our praise doesn't stop there. In our lives we will show our praise by our presence in worship, by showing our trust as we call on his name in our prayers, by gladly honoring his representatives, etc.

vv. 15,16 — *For this reason, ever since I heard about your faith in the Lord Jesus and your love for all the saints, I have not stopped giving thanks for you, remembering you in my prayers.*

After finishing the grand doxology in which he praised God for the panoply of blessings he has given the believers, Paul bubbles over with thanks. His thanksgiving is inspired by the good news he had heard about their faithfulness. Paul was particularly relieved to hear about their faithfulness, because God had revealed that there would be trouble in their future (Ac 20:29,30). How good it was to hear that it had not yet happened. They had faith, which was proved by their loving deeds done for each other.

The only textual variant in this selection is found in verse 15. Some early texts from Egypt have omitted ἀγάπην. Since the texts that include it are both early and widespread, however, and because Paul's words are difficult to understand without it, it seems better to include it.

v. 17 — *I keep asking that the God of our Lord Jesus Christ, the glorious Father, may give you the Spirit of wisdom and revelation, so that you may know him better.*

Commentators expend a bit of ink over the discussion of whether or not Spirit should be capitalized. In the end, they agree that it really doesn't make a great deal of difference in meaning. A person cannot have an inner attitude which reflects true wisdom and revelation without the Holy Spirit's working (1 Co 2:14; 12:3).

By the grace of God through the work of the Holy Spirit, we are no longer among the fools who say there is no God. It was wise Solomon through whom the Spirit revealed the precious reminder, "The fear of the LORD is the beginning of wisdom. . ." (Pr 9:10). It is this wisdom which comes from the Spirit that is so precious to us. With every bit of knowledge we gain about the essence of God, about his plan of salvation, and about the way he carries out his plan, our lives here on earth will be more full and complete.

v. 18 — *I pray also that the eyes of your heart may be enlightened in order that you may know the hope to which he has called you, the riches of his glorious inheritance in the saints.*

The expression "eyes of your heart" is unique, but by no means difficult to understand. In both the Old and New Testaments the heart is presented as the center of intellectual and spiritual life. The unregenerate heart is blind to the truth and filled with decadence. "For out of the heart come evil thoughts, murder, adultery, sexual immorality, theft, false testimony, slander," Jesus said (Mt 15:19). The heart must first receive sight (2 Co 4:6).

When the eyes of our hearts are opened, by God's grace, the result will be that we possess hope. Our hope consists in the assurance that the promises of God for this life and the life to come are real and true. For example, all things work for our good (Ro 8:28); he won't leave us or forsake us (Mt 28:20); when we die, Jesus will receive our spirits (Ac 7:59); he will raise us on the last day (Jn 6:39); we will have glorified bodies (Php 3:21); we will stand accepted in the judgment (Ro 8:33).

This hope reaches its culmination in the wealth of our inheritance. We will have eternal life in the presence of God, perfect knowledge, absence of pain and hunger, etc.

Paul prays that the Ephesians may see this. He knows that when they do, they will be strengthened in their resolve not to trade this inheritance for the worthless wares of the world. Nor will they be discouraged to the point of despair because of his imprisonment.

Homiletical Suggestions

All three readings for the day emphasize the marvelous joy that is ours because of God's grace. The Epistle (our text) resounds with praise for the many blessings that are ours in Christ. This fits well in the Christmas season. We have just celebrated the birth of the Christchild. Through the Apostle Paul, God very succinctly lists spiritual blessings that are ours through the work that the Christchild later accomplished.

This is bound to be an upbeat sermon. These verses convey the comfort the doctrine of election offers. Our adoption into God's family is not based on flimsy hopes but on God's sure promise, through the work of Christ, according to his pleasure and will.

The application might include the encouragement to bring forth the fruits of faith in all areas of life. This fruit would be to the praise of his glorious grace.

Although, in preaching on this text, we wouldn't fail to expound the Scriptural teaching of election, a doctrinal treatise on the subject is not the way to relate these verses to the Christmas event. Maintaining our focus on God's grace "through Jesus Christ" will keep the sermon from becoming a dogmatic presentation.

The second part of the text (vv. 15-18) provides the opportunity to encourage people not to take spiritual blessings for granted. By faithful use of God's Word we give the Spirit the chance to build us up so that we may know the hope of our salvation even better.

A service on the second Sunday after Christmas will still carry much of the Christmas flavor. At the same time, it does mark the end of the immediate Christmas season. With that in mind you might utilize the following outline, which keys on the praise and prayer that comprise the backdrop of the text:

A Christmas Closing Prayer

1. It recognizes our blessings (vv. 3-6,15,16)
2. It recognizes our needs (vv. 17,18)

A sermon that focuses more on our election, but under the theme of God's grace, would be:

Marvel at God's Saving Grace
1. God chose us from eternity (vv. 3,4)
2. He predestined us to live as his children (vv. 5,6,15,16)
3. He called us to eternal life (vv. 17,18)

The following outline brings out the joy that the Apostle Paul expressed as he contemplated these blessings:

We Live in Joy Because of God's Grace
1. God has blessed us with every spiritual blessing (vv. 3-6,15,16)
2. God has given us the hope of eternal life (vv. 17,18)

EPIPHANY OF OUR LORD

The Scriptures

> Old Testament — *Isaiah 60:1-6*
> Epistle — *Ephesians 3:2-12*
> Gospel — *Matthew 2:1-12*

The Text — Ephesians 3:2-12

Epiphany focuses on the truth that God sent his only Son to save all people. And so the gospel goes out to all people, as foretold in Isaiah 60:1-6, the Old Testament reading. This fact is clearly demonstrated by the Magi's arrival at Bethlehem (today's Gospel, Matthew 2:1-12), and by the gospel's spread to Ephesus and beyond.

> vv. 2,3 — *Surely you have heard about the administration of God's grace that was given to me for you, that is, the mystery made known to me by revelation, as I have already written briefly.*

Paul begins this chapter with a thought which he picks up later on (v. 14). Thus, the verses of our text are actually parenthetical. The apostle interrupts himself in order to express the series of truths which constitute our text. These truths give basis for the prayer which he expresses in verses 14-21.

Paul pauses to reflect on the way in which God entrusted him with the administration of his grace. Through the revelation of Jesus Christ himself he received the command, "Go; I will send you far away to the Gentiles" (Ac 22:21). So the Ephesians were among those for whom God entrusted Paul with the gospel.

Paul touched on this οἰκονομία in the previous chapters. "And you also were included in Christ when you heard the word of truth, the gospel of your salvation" (Eph 1:13). "But now in Christ Jesus you who once were far away have been brought near through the blood of Christ" (Eph 2:13).

> vv. 4,5 — *In reading this, then, you will be able to understand my insight into the mystery of Christ, which was not made known to men in other generations as it has now been revealed by the Spirit to God's holy apostles and prophets.*

There are many mysteries which have been revealed to us in the Bible. There are many truths which we could not know if God's Spirit had not revealed them to us. Elsewhere Paul tells us that "the mystery of godliness is great" (1 Ti 3:16). That Jesus truly is God in the flesh is a truth we could not know without the revelation of Scripture. That salvation is by the grace of God and not by works is also a mystery which "God has revealed . . . to us by his Spirit" (1 Co 2:10). Irwin Habeck wrote in his commentary on Ephesians that a mystery "is that which God alone knows but which he then makes known to human beings in order that they in turn might tell it to others."

The mystery about which Paul writes here is that the Gentiles also have been elected for eternal life. This truth had been revealed to the Old Testament people of God. God had told Abraham that through his descendant "all nations of the earth will be blessed" (Ge 22:18).

What Israel had been told the Ephesians had now seen and experienced for themselves. They were living proof that God wants all people to be saved through faith in Jesus the Christ.

v. 6 — *This mystery is that through the gospel the Gentiles are heirs together with Israel, members together of one body, and sharers together in the promise in Christ Jesus.*

As believers the Gentiles are co-heirs, sharing in Israel's inheritance. As members of his church they are members of his body, as Paul elaborates in 1 Corinthians 12. They are no longer partners with the disobedient in this world (Eph 5:6,7), but have a share in the promises of forgiveness, life, and salvation—found only in Christ Jesus.

These blessings are mediated by the gospel. The gospel is the power of God for the salvation of everyone who believes, proclaimed first among the Jews and then also among the Gentiles (Ro 1:16,17).

vv. 7-9 — *I became a servant of this gospel by the gift of God's grace given me through the working of his power. Although I am less than the least of all God's people, this grace was given me: to preach to the Gentiles the unsearchable riches of Christ, and to make plain to everyone the administration of this mystery, which for ages past was kept hidden in God, who created all things.*

Paul never ceased to marvel at the grace of God which had rescued him from devastating the church on earth and from suffering eternal devastation in hell. Like John Newton, known as "The Great Blasphemer" until his conversion, Saul of Tarsus considered himself less than the least of all the saints. All who have looked into the mirror of God's law know how wretchedly wicked they are. How amazing that God graciously reaches out to rescue us!

In addition to all this God calls and equips us to share the unsearchable riches of Christ with the world. Having just celebrated the birth of the Savior, we now pause to contemplate who he is. He is the eternal God, who nevertheless had a birth in time. He is the almighty Lord, who in weakness allowed himself to be nailed to a tree. He is the immortal God, who died to redeem us from sin. He is the ascended Lord, who nevertheless is with us at all times. We cannot fathom his glory. We can never understand him completely.

vv. 10,11 — *His intent was that now, through the church, the manifold wisdom of God should be made known to the rulers and authorities in the heavenly realms, according to his eternal purpose which he accomplished in Christ Jesus our Lord.*

The angels of God had to wait until these days—the days of the church—to see how wise God is. The angels looked over the shoulders of the prophets as they intently studied the Scriptures God had given them to write. They also "long to look into these things" (1 Pe 1:12).

Now the Lord has demonstrated to them how manifold (πολυποίκιλος, variegated, "of many colors") his wisdom really is. The angels witnessed the successes which the apostles enjoyed as they took the gospel to the ends of the earth. Again and again they rejoiced as sinners came to repentance.

Let us make it our business to put smiles on the angels' faces. It is our privilege to share the gospel today! As we do this, God's manifold wisdom will be proven again and again, increasing the joy of saints and angels.

v. 12 — *In him and through faith in him we may approach God with freedom and confidence.*

"We" refers to both Jews and Gentiles. Paul wrote similar words in 2:18. Because we believe the promises of the gospel, we have confidence to turn to God in every situation. We freely call God "Abba." We freely come into his presence without fear because we are dressed in the righteousness of his Son. We boldly look to him for everything we need, confident that he will hear us and give us only that which is good for us.

Homiletical Suggestions

Epiphany celebrates how the baby of Bethlehem has fulfilled the promises of the gospel. In the gospel God has revealed his plan of salvation which is for all people. That which was hidden for so many centuries has now been unveiled for everyone to enjoy.

With emphasis on sharing the gospel with the world the preacher can present the message under the theme:

The Salvation Secret Is Out!
1. God has revealed this secret in Jesus (vv. 2-5)
2. God has revealed this secret for all people (vv. 6-9)
3. God has revealed this secret through the church (vv. 10-12)

FIRST SUNDAY AFTER EPIPHANY
(THE BAPTISM OF OUR LORD)

The Scriptures

> Old Testament — *Isaiah 42:1-7*
> Epistle — *Acts 10:34-38*
> Gospel — *Mark 1:4-11*

The Text — Acts 10:34-38

In the ILCW arrangement of the Church Year this first Sunday after the Epiphany is subtitled, "The Baptism of Our Lord," Mark's account of that baptism being the Gospel of the Day. The Epistle lesson makes reference to the baptism of Jesus—and to his anointing as the Messiah, a reference to the Old Testament lesson from Isaiah.

Acts 10 is the account of the conversion of the Roman centurion Cornelius. God used this event to open the eyes of the early church to understand that God's grace is for all people, that Jesus is the Savior of the world. In the first part of the chapter (vv. 1-7) we are introduced to Cornelius and told of the vision which God gave him, to summon Peter to come to Caesarea. Verses 9-23 focus on Peter and the vision God gave him, to reveal that the "dividing wall" between clean and unclean (and so, Jew and Gentile) was removed. Verses 23-33 recount the actual meeting between Peter and Cornelius, a meeting which leads Peter to speak the words of the text, verses 34-38.

vv. 34,35 — *Then Peter began to speak: "I now realize how true it is that God does not show favoritism but accepts men from every nation who fear him and do what is right."*

Peter is primarily addressing his Jewish brothers in Christ who had accompanied him to Caesarea. Naturally, he is addressing Cornelius and his household, but it is the Jewish brothers who are amazed by what they have seen and heard.

Christians today may be surprised for the opposite reason. The fact that Jesus is the Savior of the Gentile as well as the Jew is so elementary they may wonder what was "wrong" with the early Christians that they expressed such amazement (cf. Ac 11:18). It is important to remember the centuries-old cultural message that had been drummed into Peter and his Jewish brethren. By God's own command Jew and Gentile had been separated. Although the hatred and mistrust that had grown up between Jew and Gentile was (and is) not God's will and does not have his sanction, Peter and the others had been told over and over that Jews did not associate with "Gentile sinners."

This phenomenon is, of course, repeated in various contexts down to the present. Wherever people gather they are likely to make distinctions based on race, creed, habit, culture, or sex that create a real "dividing wall" that expresses itself in much the same way: hatred, mistrust, etc. It is a fact of history that some have even used a perverted "Christianity" to justify these things (e.g., the Ku Klux Klan). The amazement of Peter and the others ought not so much move us to curiosity about them as to careful examination of ourselves, to search our own attitudes toward the unlikely people of the world. Peter's words need to become our own: "I now realize. . . ."

It is important to note two things at this point. First, Peter and the others—as surprised as they were—were rejoicing over this revelation. The wonder they express leads them to praise God. There is not resentment or fear over a loss of status or privilege, but genuine joy over the fact that "God does not show favoritism but accepts men from every nation. . . ."

"God does not show favoritism" is literally, "God is not a προσωπολ-ήμτης." The Greek noun draws on the LXX's translation of the hebraism, "acceptor of faces," which implies partiality. Peter is restating the familiar truth of 1 Samuel 16:7, "Man looks at the outward appearance, but the Lord looks at the heart."

This leads to the second point. In itself this was not something new for Peter. God had not changed his mind or his ways. Peter knew from Scripture that God did not show favoritism (Dt 10:17). But his eyes were now opened to see the Scripture truth in action in a very pointed fashion.

Perhaps those to whom these words are preached need also to learn to truly listen to the Scriptures, especially those portions that are so familiar. God's Word is not merely a dry book of facts, but is "living and active. . . . it judges the thoughts and attitudes of the heart" (He 4:12). As we open our eyes and ears to it in faith, its truth shines more brilliantly and wondrously for our comfort and guidance, Psalm 119:105.

Ultimately, Peter's words are an expression of his wonder over God's wonderful grace. Grace is truly God's free and undeserved love that is not the private domain of the Jew, or the inheritance of the wealthy, or the recompense of the poor, or the birthright of lineage. It is grace. It is a cause for joy that is especially appropriate on the Sunday after the "Gentiles' Christmas," but it is also a message of timely instruction.

A buzzword of recent years in American Christendom is the word "inclusive." Examples of unscriptural "inclusiveness" abound as many try to subvert the Bible's message about sin and the need for repentance, or its teaching about gender roles. They do it for the sake of outward growth or to avoid unpleasant conclusions or unpopular practices. But of course the word can denote a very scriptural message, the true message of Epiphany: God's grace is all-inclusive. Peter's words offer a challenge to the church of all time to be rightly "inclusive" in its preaching, teaching, outreach, and assimilation. If God is not one to show favoritism his ambassadors cannot be, either.

v. 36 — *"You know the message God sent to the people of Israel, telling the good news of peace through Jesus Christ, who is Lord of all."*

Peter now turns to a brief rehearsing of the gospel, reminding them of things they had heard or seen about Jesus. Peter notes that God sent this message to the Jews wrapped up in the person of his Son. It is a message that is here summed up by the word "peace." That peace, of course, is not a worldly peace of any sort (cf. Jn 14:27), but peace with God through the forgiveness of sins. And it is won, proclaimed, and offered through him who is the "Prince of Peace" and the "Lord of all."

vv. 37,38 — *"You know what has happened throughout Judea, beginning in Galilee after the baptism that John preached—how God anointed Jesus of Nazareth with the Holy Spirit and power and how he went around doing good and healing all who were under the power of the devil, because God was with him."*

Peter's words are evidence of how widespread the events of John's and Jesus' ministries were. It would have been inconceivable that those in Caesarea would not have heard the facts about John and Jesus.

But Peter's rehearsal of the facts penetrates beyond mere recitation. The facts are interpreted as the Lord himself urged: ". . . believe [in me] on the evidence of the miracles themselves" (Jn 14:11). "Jesus of Nazareth" showed his credentials as the one whom God anointed (ἔχρισεν, "christened") with the Holy Spirit and power." As those who stood with him at his baptism witnessed, "God was with him."

The Lord Jesus Christ gave evidence of his messiahship by fulfilling what Isaiah prophesied: "Here is my servant, whom I uphold. . . .

I will put my spirit on him . . . , and will make you to be a covenant for the people and a light for the Gentiles" (Isa 42:1-7). The well-known facts of his life and ministry, his preaching, healing, and good works were dramatic evidence that he was Israel's awaited Messiah and the "light to lighten the Gentiles" (Lk 2:32).

It is important in this connection not to skip too quickly over the little word "all" in Peter's recounting of Jesus' ministry. Again, Peter is giving expression to a new-found understanding of some "old" facts he had long known. He had been with his Savior when the Samaritan leper returned to give thanks (Lk 17:11-19). He had heard Jesus' words of gracious praise to the Gentile centurion at Capernaum (Lk 7:9). He had witnessed his Lord's mercy to the Phoenician woman (Mt 15:28). Whatever might have been his thoughts or reaction to these incidents at the time, they now came flooding back to emphasize the marvelous grace of God in Christ for all, Jews and Gentiles. This was and is the gospel.

Homiletical Suggestions

Plainly, this particular text offers up God's universal grace as its main message. We are to join in expressing delight with Peter that God's grace is not restricted or private, but is proclaimed to all on the basis of Christ's unlimited atonement, the gospel of peace.

In our society, as in every society, there is a tension between the private and the public, between what is "mine" and what is "ours." Human beings, even of the fellowship of the household of God, are always subject to the inclinations of the Old Adam to cordon off bits and pieces of life for themselves, to exclude, and to show favoritism. In view of this, the hymn verse is both poignant and impressive:

> Teach us, O Lord, true thankfulness divine,
> That gives as Christ gave, never counting cost,
> That knows no barrier of "yours" and "mine,"
> Assured that only what's withheld is lost.

While the hymnwriter may have gifts and offerings primarily in mind, how much more is this true of the call to share the gospel!

Christians who are predominantly the offspring of the Cornelius branch of the Christian family do well to remember, both in terms of rejoicing and in terms of practice, that we are the people of God by grace. Just as we rejoice that "God has granted the Gentiles repentance unto life!" (Ac 11:18), meaning us, so also we should rejoice and be eager to extend this same grace to all.

With this in mind we could use this outline:

Everyone Is Invited!

1. Our Lord extends his grace to all (vv. 34,35)
2. Through the gospel proclaimed to all (vv. 36-38)

If the preacher desires to utilize the remembrance of Jesus' baptism, the theme could focus on Peter's mention of Jesus' being anointed in his baptism (v. 38):

Rejoice in the Lord's Anointed!

1. Anointed with power for salvation (vv. 36-38)
2. Anointed to extend grace to all (vv. 34,35)

SECOND SUNDAY AFTER EPIPHANY

The Scriptures

> Old Testament — *1 Samuel 3:1-10*
> Epistle — *1 Corinthians 6:12-20*
> Gospel — *John 1:43-51*

The Text — 1 Corinthians 6:12-20

The text is part of a section on Christian living in which Paul treats such issues as the disciplining of an impenitent sinner (5:1-13), taking disputes with fellow believers to civil court (6:1-8), and living in wickedness (6:9-11).

In 6:12-20 Paul instructs us in the proper use of Christian freedom, distinguishing it from sinful license. He addresses the sinful, Christ-dishonoring nature of sexual immorality. He highlights the gospel-created change in the believer's life and calls for the God-honoring use of a Christian's body. This text is filled with helpful lessons for Christians who face a challenge similar to those which the Corinthian Christians faced: how to keep one's beliefs and life pure and strong in a skeptical and immoral culture.

v. 12 — *"Everything is permissible for me"—but not everything is beneficial. "Everything is permissible for me"—but I will not be mastered by anything.*

Paul addresses a distortion of the principle of Christian freedom. Some in Corinth were insisting that their liberty in Christ gave them freedom to commit certain sins, particularly such sexual sins as fornication with prostitutes at the pagan temples.

Paul counters that false claim by quoting the principle of Christian liberty which they were citing and then points out the limits which God places on the exercise of such liberty. We are not free to use our liberty in a way that will not benefit others or that will enslave us.

v. 13 — *"Food for the stomach and the stomach for food"—but God will destroy them both. The body is not meant for sexual immorality, but for the Lord, and the Lord for the body.*

Paul moves on from the general principles he enunciated in verse 12 to the specific matter of πορνεία, unlawful sexual activity. Apparently some in Corinth were justifying their sexual immorality by claiming that it was on a par with satisfying physical hunger, a morally indifferent matter.

Paul counters by pointing out that the two issues are not the same. God did intend that we use food to satisfy physical hunger during our earthly lives. God did not, however, intend our bodies to be used for sexual immorality. He gives us our bodies as instruments through which we can serve and glorify him, instruments which are totally dependent on him for their function. Because God has designed the body for this purpose, Paul contends, our sexual actions do matter morally and spiritually, as expressions of our relationship with God.

v. 14 — *By his power God raised the Lord from the dead, and he will raise us also.*

Paul goes on to demonstrate God's high regard and eternal plans for the body. God raised Jesus' body from the dead and will raise the bodies of all believers from the dead on the Last Day. He sharply distinguishes between the transient things which God will one day eliminate (the stomach and food, verse 13), and the body which he intends to transform and glorify for eternity. His point here is that a body destined for glorious immortality should not be used for degrading immorality.

v. 15 — *Do you not know that your bodies are members of Christ himself? Shall I then take the members of Christ and unite them with a prostitute? Never!*

In the opening question of this verse Paul reminds his readers of a principle they have already learned. In his grace God makes a believer's whole person, both soul and body, a member of Christ's spiritual body, the Church. This intimate identification with the Lord Jesus gives the bodies of believers great dignity and makes them sacred, set apart from sin for devoted service to God.

Paul goes on to ask the Corinthian Christians if they should take the members of Christ from their proper use, honoring God, and make them violate God's will by joining them in sexual union with a prostitute. His answer indicates that such a desecration of the body is out of the question, not even to be considered: "Never!"

v. 16 — *Do you not know that he who unites himself with a prostitute is one with her in body? For it is said, "The two will become one flesh."*

In a third question, Paul asks the Corinthians to consider that the person who joins with a prostitute in sexual relations is expressing a perverted oneness with her. He cites the scriptural truth (Ge 2:24) that people express oneness in a sexual relationship. That oneness is properly expressed in marriage. God intended the marriage union to be the context in which man and woman can rightly have sexual relations, thereby declaring that they have willingly given themselves to each other for mutual assistance and comfort for life.

Paul indicates that sexual relations outside the marriage bond are an illegitimate distortion of the divinely established marriage union, a dishonest, sinful mockery of God-pleasing sexual expression.

v. 17 — *But he who unites himself with the Lord is one with him in spirit.*

Paul proceeds to tell the Corinthian believers that there is a higher, more important union than that expressed in the sexual relation. It is the believer's union with Christ. No relationship is more precious than that between a Christian and the Savior. This priceless oneness with Christ leads God's people to resist and avoid anything which would harm or destroy it.

v. 18 — *Flee from sexual immorality. All other sins a man commits are outside his body, but he who sins sexually sins against his own body.*

Paul now calls for Christian action. The Greek present imperative denotes a continual avoidance of immorality, "constantly be fleeing immorality," as Joseph resisted the repeated advances of Potiphar's wife (Ge 39). The Christian is not to play with sexual temptation, but is to resist it at the beginning by decisively abandoning it in thought and action.

Commentators have understood the second clause of the second sentence in two ways. The majority regard Paul's words, "he who sins sexually sins against his own body," as his way of highlighting the self-gratifying, personally degrading nature of sexual immorality. Some regard the first part of the sentence as quoting some of the Corinthians who justified their sin by claiming that physical acts could not damage the secure "personality" of the saved. They then view the second part of the verse as Paul's rebuttal, in which he states that sexual immorality is a damaging offense against one's entire "person."

v. 19 — *Do you not know that your body is a temple of the Holy Spirit, who is in you, whom you have received from God? You are not your own;*

Paul again uses a rhetorical question to remind the Corinthians of a well-established truth. He asks them to recall that the body of each believer is a temple in which the Holy Spirit lives. Their bodies have become God's sacred dwelling places, devoted to his holy worship and use. Because of the One who lives in them, they could no longer consider their bodies as their own.

v. 20 — *you were bought at a price. Therefore honor God with your body.*

Here is the reason we are not the owners and masters of our bodies. We have been "bought at a price." Jesus Christ has purchased us at the cost of his perfect life and sin-bearing death. As God's possession, we are to use our bodies to bring him honor. We are no longer to serve the cause of sin, but to live holy lives to glorify God before others.

Homiletical Suggestions

The other lessons for the day are 1 Samuel 3:1-10 and John 1:43-51. God called Samuel to be his prophet and judge in order to bring about a spiritual reformation in Israel. In the Gospel, Jesus calls Philip and Nathanael to believe in him, to follow him, and to serve him as his disciples. A connection between the sermon text and these readings appears to be God's call of the believer to render sacred service to him. The first suggested outline carries out that thought, while stressing the intimate and blessed relationship which God has established with his believers.

Our Bodies Belong to God

1. The Savior has purchased them (vv. 15,17,20)
2. The Spirit lives in them (vv. 18,19)
3. The Father will glorify them (vv. 12-14)

Here is an outline which stresses the avoidance of sexual immorality and the reasons why:

Say "No" to Sexual Sins

1. Sexual immorality is sin, not freedom (vv. 12,13a)
2. Your body is meant for honor, not disgrace (vv. 13b-17)
3. Your body belongs to God, not yourself (vv. 19,20)

A similar treatment under another theme:

Safeguarding Words for Soul-threatening Times

1. Know the difference between liberty and license (vv. 12,13)
2. Avoid the danger of self-destroying sin (vv. 15-18)
3. Fulfill the purpose of ransomed life (vv. 19,20)

THIRD SUNDAY AFTER EPIPHANY

The Scriptures

> Old Testament — *Jonah 3:1-5,10*
> Epistle — *1 Corinthians 7:29-31*
> Gospel — *Mark 1:14-20*

The Text — 1 Corinthians 7:29-31

Prominent among the problems in the Christian congregation at Corinth was sexual immorality. In the midst of a cosmopolitan population it was natural that even Christian believers would have many questions about marriage and morality. A center of commerce and culture, fostering the worship of Aphrodite (Venus) with its temple prostitution, Corinth was hospitable to sexual immorality of all kinds. The impact on God's gift of sexual happiness in marriage was devastating.

As children of their times the Corinthian Christians gave evidence of reflecting the arrogance and conceit of their city. Despite having many spiritual gifts, they were immature and unspiritual. Luther notes: "Things got so wild and disorderly that everyone wanted to be the expert and do the teaching and make what he pleased of the gospel, the sacrament, and faith. Meanwhile they let the main things drop—namely, that Christ is our salvation, righteousness, and redemption—as if they had long since outgrown it. This truth can never remain intact when people begin to imagine they are wise and know it all" (LW 35.381).

The entire seventh chapter of 1 Corinthians is devoted to answering questions raised by the Corinthian Christians about marriage and celibacy. After giving some general principles (vv. 1-7) and advice concerning the problems of married believers (vv. 8-24), the Lord's Apostle Paul now turns to the problems of the unmarried. Our text is part of a section which the NET (New Evangelical Translation) heads "To Marry Or Not To Marry." Application is made to all Christians.

v. 29 — *What I mean, brothers, is that the time is short. From now on those who have wives should live as if they had none;*

Speaking here as the Lord's apostle (1:1) and therefore having full authority from the Lord Jesus himself, Paul addresses his readers as "brothers." What a gracious word, considering the multitude of problems in their congregation! Paul still considers them to be fellow believers.

When Paul speaks of "the time" he uses ὁ καιρός, which means "the opportune time." This opportune time is "being shortened, drawn together" (συνεσταλμένος, present passive participle) by the Lord Jesus, who promised: "If those days had not been cut short, no one would survive, but for the sake of the elect those days will be shortened" (Mt 24:22).

The Epiphany Christ wants us to be so focused on his gospel mission, so eager for his return, that nothing gets in the way. Living as servants responsible to God means Christ has top priority even over marriage. No matter how deeply a husband may love his wife, he must always be aware that his first loyalty is to the Lord, and his believing wife also belongs first to the Lord and is bound for glory. Even a Christian with an unbelieving spouse can look past marital difficulties to the true mission of Christians to spread Christ's Epiphany light. He or she can focus on Christ and then love the wife who is difficult to love, or respect the husband who is difficult to respect—out of love and respect for Christ. Such is the power of having "the mind of Christ" (2:16).

v. 30a — *those who mourn, as if they did not; those who are happy, as if they were not;*

The emotional life of a Christian can be a paradox. He weeps while the world rejoices and rejoices while the world weeps. Of such the Lord Jesus says, "Blessed are you who weep now, for you will laugh" (Lk 6:21). When insulted for your faith, he says, "Rejoice in that day and leap for joy, because great is your reward in heaven. For that is how their fathers treated the prophets" (Lk 6:23).

The opportunity of these shining, yet distressing, last days calls for all Christians to remember that our emotions too belong to the Lord. From a prison cell the same Apostle Paul would write: "Rejoice in the Lord always. I will say it again: Rejoice!" (Php 4:4). James 1:2,3 echoes the call: "Consider it pure joy, my brothers, whenever you face trials of many kinds, because you know that the testing of your faith develops perseverance." Only one who believes that our loving Lord Jesus is in complete control can rejoice in trials because of the maturity and completeness of faith which is to follow.

"Those who are happy as if they were not" almost sounds as though Paul were negating our joy in Christ. Yet the Christian in the midst of his rejoicing over God's grace is continually sorrowing over his sins. As the Old Testament writer put it 1,000 years before Jesus' birth, "The heart of fools is in the house of pleasure" (Ecc 7:4). With these shortened days whipping by it is especially important that all of us learn "to number our days aright, that we may gain a heart of wisdom" (Ps 90:12). True wisdom accepts the scathing message of God's law and then rejoices in the glorious good news that all our sins are forgiven.

vv. 30b,31 — *those who buy something, as if it were not theirs to keep; those who use the things of the world, as if not engrossed in them. For this world in its present form is passing away.*

The goal of our Lord was to "shine forth" to the glory of his heavenly Father. Our goal as Epiphany Christians is to "shine like stars in the universe as [we] hold out the word of life" (Php 2:15f). Paul wants to show us how "to live nobly for the Lord without being distracted by other things" (v. 35 NET).

Now Paul really gets at the heart of Christian living in a very materialistic society. For those who have the financial means to buy things, the apostle counsels doing so "as if it were not theirs to keep." Not only can you "not take it with you," but when our Lord comes in his full eternal glory on Judgment Day, "the heavens will disappear with a roar; the elements will be destroyed by fire, and the earth and everything in it will be laid bare" (2 Pe 3:10). Everything we own really belongs to the Lord. It is not ours to keep but ours to share, in order to "use worldly wealth to gain friends for [our]selves, so that when it is gone, [we] will be welcomed into eternal dwellings" (Lk 16:9).

Even Christians with limited financial resources have many opportunities to use modern conveniences and technology. But, bombarded with advertising, it's easy to become engrossed in the "rags to riches" dream. Here again, though, to shine as "the light of the world," as Jesus calls us (Mt 5:14), we can't be hiding the lamp of our faith "under a bowl." We do not want to hustle and bustle about in the mad pursuit of what the world calls "happiness." We have some serious shining to do.

"For the world in its present form is passing away." The day is fast approaching when this shadowy planet will be bathed in the light of him who gives light to the myriad of stars. A thousand suns will dim like candles beside his eternal brilliance. Suddenly it will become brilliantly obvious to everyone that everything was created for God's use and God's glory—computers and jet planes for spreading the gospel, banks and money for financing churches, marriage and romance for illustrating the love of Christ for his church. For those who by faith rejoiced in his light, Christ's final revelation will be grand

and glorious for all eternity. But for those who "loved darkness instead of light because their deeds were evil" (Jn 3:19), terror will let loose in "the darkness where there shall be weeping and gnashing of teeth" (Mt 22:13).

Homiletical Suggestions

The gospel preacher striving for clarity can draw the following connections between this text, the Church Year, and the other two readings for the day: "Epiphany" means "shining forth," as Jesus did when he revealed himself to be the Christ, the Son of God. The message of repentance preached by Jesus and his forerunner, John the Baptist, was carried by Jonah to Nineveh, the capital of Assyrian cruelty. The Holy Spirit blessed the Word preached through Jonah with gracious results. Likewise, Jesus' preaching of repentance (Mk 1:14-20) drew his first disciples away from their families and jobs to become "fishers of men." Married and unmarried disciples of Jesus in these last days will want to "shine forth" by living for God in every way. Our Epistle text tells us how.

Combined thoughts from season and Scripture can be summarized in these ways:

Epiphany Happiness Is to Shine like God

1. In intellect (v. 29)
2. In emotions (v. 30a)
3. In will (vv. 30b,31)

Taking the theme from v. 29a:

The Time Is Short

1. What this means for our marriages (v. 29)
2. What this means for our emotional life (v. 30a)
3. What this means for our use of this world's goods (vv. 30b,31)

70

FOURTH SUNDAY AFTER EPIPHANY

The Scriptures

Old Testament — *Deuteronomy 18:15-20*
Epistle — *1 Corinthians 8:1-13*
Gospel — *Mark 1:21-28*

The Text — 1 Corinthians 8:1-13

Corinth was quite a place. When Aristophanes used the word "Corinthianize," everyone knew exactly what he meant. Corinth's immorality was notorious, even in a Hellenistic world which condoned anything short of incest. The temple of Aphrodite, with its more than 1000 sacred prostitutes, perched atop the Acrocorinth.

But sexual immorality was not the only problem with which the Christians of Corinth had to contend. There were at least twelve temples devoted to a variety of gods and religions, and the sacrifices at their altars led indirectly to a problem for some of the Christian believers. Not all of the meat offered in the many daily sacrifices was burned up. Typically, one part was offered on the altar, a second was given to the offerer for a cultic meal, and a third was given to the priests. What the priests did not eat was taken to the public meat market.

This posed the problem which Paul addresses in our text. Many of the Corinthian Christians had been adherents of the pagan cults before their conversion. Could they continue to purchase meat from the market, meat which had likely been part of a pagan rite, without compromising their faith? Or did that action make them participants in pagan worship? For Jews, using food sacrificed to idols (εἰδωλόθυτον, v. 1) was strictly forbidden. Was the same true for Christians?

The Corinthians had written to Paul about their problem, seeking his advice (cp. 7:1,25). He gives them his answer here and in 14:23—15:1).

vv. 1-3 — *Now about food sacrificed to idols: We know that we all possess knowledge. Knowledge puffs up, but love builds up. The man who thinks he knows something does not yet know as he ought to know. But the man who loves God is known by God.*

Paul speaks first of γνῶσις, a concept of high significance in Corinth and in the Hellenistic world. Some of the commentators debate whether or not this has any connection to the gnosticism which developed later, but such discussion is really beside the point. What is clear is that there were those in the congregation who were proud of knowing about Christian liberty, and they flaunted the liberty they knew was theirs. They ate the meat without giving it a second thought, not knowing or not caring about what effect their actions might have on other Christians.

But "knowledge" is not the whole story. As Carleton Toppe writes in *The People's Bible* commentary on 1 Corinthians, "Even weak Christians may 'know' that idols are really nothing. But head and heart are not always in tune. Knowing about something does not always make us feel right about doing it" (pp. 76,77). Those who were "in the know" needed to understand this, and they needed to temper their knowledge with love.

Note the perfect tense of ἔγνωσται in verse 3 and the comfort this brings—we have come to be acknowledged and recognized by God as his own, and this wonderful situation continues on.

> vv. 4-6 — *So then, about eating food sacrificed to idols: We know that an idol is nothing at all in the world and that there is no God but one. For even if there are so-called gods, whether in heaven or on earth (as indeed there are many "gods" and many "lords"), yet for us there is but one God, the Father, from whom all things came and for whom we live; and there is but one Lord, Jesus Christ, through whom all things came and through whom we live.*

Paul makes two fundamental points: Idols are nothing, and there is only one God (Dt 6:4-9; 1 Ki 18:39; Isa 45:5). Yes, there was the pagan pantheon with which the Corinthians were quite familiar, with Satan and his cohorts hiding behind the faces of those "so-called gods," and human society had its share of rulers ("gods" and "lords"), but the former had no existence and the latter were subordinate to the one true God. The Father is the source (ἐξ οὗ) of all that exists, and the Son is the one through whom (δι᾽ οὗ) it came into existence. Since we live for this one true God, there is no reason per se to be concerned with meat sacrificed to idols.

> vv. 7-9 — *But not everyone knows this. Some people are still so accustomed to idols that when they eat such food they think of it as having been sacrificed to an idol, and since their conscience is weak, it is defiled. But food does not bring us near to God; we are no worse if we do not eat, and no better if we do.*

Nevertheless, there is still a reason to be concerned: "Not everyone knows this." There were new Christians who had only recently been delivered from paganism and brought to faith in the true God. Anything that smacked of idolatry now made them feel uncomfortable. Eating meat sacrificed on pagan altars made them feel that they were once again involved in pagan worship and were sinning against their Lord.

Their subjective feelings are not based in fact, as Paul points out in verse 8. Eating the meat is a matter of indifference that does not affect our standing before God. As such, of course, it would be legalism either to prohibit the practice or to insist on it as a matter of Christian freedom.

> vv. 9-13 — *Be careful, however, that the exercise of your freedom does not become a stumbling block to the weak. For if anyone with a weak conscience sees you who have this knowledge eating in an idol's temple, won't he be emboldened to eat what has been sacrificed to idols? So this weak brother, for whom Christ died, is destroyed by your knowledge. When you sin against your brothers in this way and wound their weak consciences, you sin against Christ. Therefore, if what I eat causes my brother to fall into sin, I will never eat meat again, so that I will not cause him to fall.*

Βλέπετε, Paul says, "Look out!" He then sketches out a scenario which probably was common enough in Corinth. You, one of the knowledgeable ones, receive an invitation to a cultic meal at one of the temples. (Such invitations have actually been found among the papyri.) You accept the invitation and go, knowing that there is nothing inherently wrong with doing so. But as you recline at the table, you are observed by a fellow Christian with a weak conscience. Your action might well cause him to do what his mistaken conscience tells him is wrong. After all, he wants to be "in the know," as well. For him, however, that would be sin—not because the eating itself is sinful but because the decision to do something he thought was wrong is a violation of the First Commandment.

Paul's conclusion is that if food actually causes his fellow Christian to stumble in his faith, he will become a vegetarian! That shows to what lengths a believer will be willing to go when his actions might have a spiritual impact on another believer.

Homiletical Suggestions

If the question Paul addresses in our assigned text would have been on the agenda at the "Corinthian Pastoral Conference," it would have been listed under "Questions in Casuistry." Paul's approach to the question is instructive: First, he lays down principles and then he makes application.

Our people will not face circumstances which are exact parallels to the Corinthian context. They will, however, be confronted with situations where they need to apply the same principles in other matters dealing with the lifestyle of a Christian. This text affords an opportunity to help your people become more adept at applying faith to life.

Dr. Martin Luther dealt with the topic of Christian liberty in his magisterial work of 1520, "The Freedom of a Christian." The two theses he develops succinctly describe the tension we face in answering questions about how to be and behave as God's children when dealing with adiaphora:

"A Christian is a perfectly free lord of all, subject to none. A Christian is a perfectly dutiful servant of all, subject to all" (LW 31.344).

Luther later comments, "Man, however, needs none of these [good works] for his righteousness and salvation. Therefore he should be guided in all his works by this thought and contemplate this one thing alone, that he may serve and benefit others in all that he does, considering nothing except the need and advantage of his neighbor" (LW 31.365). It would be difficult to improve on that as a guide for Christian living.

The following treatment of the text employs Luther's two categories:

We Are Free Servants

1. We understand our Christian liberty (vv. 4-6,8)
2. We restrict our freedom when love requires it (vv. 1-3,7,9-13)

Another approach keys off Paul's statement at the end of the text, using the contrast of knowledge and love, and it would likely discuss the concept of vegetarianism in the introduction:

Are You a "Christian Vegetarian"?

1. Does your head understand that "meat-eating" is acceptable? (vv. 4-6,8)
2. Does your heart cause you to "eat vegetables" for the sake of a fellow Christian? (vv. 1-3,7,9-13)

Another theme has its source in verse 9:

Exercise Your Freedom Carefully

1. God gives you Christian freedom; treasure it! (vv. 4-6,8)

2. God gives you fellow believers; love them! (vv. 1-3,7,9-13)

Finally, the preacher could use a three-part division:

Healthy Helpings from God's Table

1. Light on proud knowledge (vv. 1-6)
2. Light on reckless freedom (vv. 7-12)
3. Heavy on considerate love (vv. 1c,13)

FIFTH SUNDAY AFTER EPIPHANY

The Scriptures

> Old Testament — *Job 7:1-7*
> Epistle — *1 Corinthians 9:16-23*
> Gospel — *Mark 1:29-39*

The Text — 1 Corinthians 9:16-23

Chapter 9 of 1 Corinthians is part of the section which deals with moral issues. Paul speaks of his calling as an apostle. He had the right to seek financial support from the members of the congregation, but he did not exercise that right. He had preached the gospel without cost to them. That was a reminder of the grace of God that is revealed in Christ and his gospel. Paul speaks of the call which compelled him to preach the gospel.

v. 16 — *Yet when I preach the gospel, I cannot boast, for I am compelled to preach. Woe to me if I do not preach the gospel!*

Paul uses the subjunctive of εὐαγγελίζομαι This speaks to the heart of every believer's calling, which is to preach the good news (Mk 16:16). He says that we have nothing to boast of if we answer that call. This balances what Paul had said about being able to boast because he did not accept any pay from the congregation. He could boast before men but not before God. His boasting was not centered in human pride but in the grace of God. In grace God had given him a call to preach. There was therefore an inner compulsion to carry out that call. That compulsion was born of faith.

The expression, "I am compelled to preach" is literally "a necessity lies on me." Since it was the Lord who placed this responsibility on Paul, he was compelled to carry it out.

God's judgment would have rested on Paul if he had not carried out his calling. The gospel becomes an instrument of judgment if we do not believe it and share it (Mk 16:16). Paul did not want to face judgment because of the gospel. He wanted to know its sweet joy and comfort even as he proclaimed it.

v. 17 — *If I preach voluntarily, I have a reward; if not voluntarily, I am simply discharging the trust committed to me.*

Paul's statement in verse 16, "I am compelled to preach," suggests that Paul might regard the second condition of verse 17 ("not voluntarily") to represent the reality in his case. In any case, since he was entrusted with the stewardship of the gospel, he does not look for any honor or glory for simply doing his duty.

v. 18 — *What then is my reward? Just this: that in preaching I may offer it free of charge, and so not make use of my rights in preaching it.*

Was there a reward for Paul, then? Yes, there was. It was that he had the blessed opportunity to share the gospel with others. He was doing so without any kind of pay from those who received it. He would have had a right to expect support. Those who preach the gospel have a right to live from it. Paul, however, was grateful that he did not need to exercise that right. It gave him an opportunity to reflect God's grace in a special way. There could be no question about his motivation. He was acting in faith in response to God's grace. May that be true of us, whether we are receiving support in our gospel ministry or not.

v. 19 — *Though I am free and belong to no man, I make myself a slave to everyone, to win as many as possible.*

Paul speaks at length about Christian freedom in his letter to the Galatians (5:1-15). Here we can see that he had a keen understanding of how the Christian exercises that freedom. It is not used to indulge the sinful nature (Ga 5:13). It is used in joyful service to the Lord. Paul belonged to Christ, being redeemed by his blood. He was not under obligation to any person. He did not need to impress anyone. He was not bound to serve anyone. His only allegiance was to Christ.

In the exercise of that freedom, however, he gladly made himself a slave to everyone. He looked upon himself as a servant of everyone he met. Though he knew that it is only the Holy Spirit who can win the hearts of the people, he was so totally involved in his gospel ministry that he viewed himself as winning souls for Christ. He was bound to bring the word of life to others.

v. 20 — *To the Jews I became like a Jew, to win the Jews. To those under the law I became like one under the law (though I myself am not under the law), so as to win those under the law.*

Ἐγονόμην, aorist, is used here to stress the action. Paul sought to identify with his own people as fully as possible. He was free from the condemnation of the law. He was free from the observance of the many customs and festivals that the Jews observed. Nevertheless, he understood what it was like to have a conscience which still bound one to these observances.

The people viewed in both parts of this verse are the same people. They are viewed first according to nationality and then according to religion. Paul knew from bitter experience what it was to be in bondage to the law. He had been a Pharisee, trying to save himself on the basis of the law.

Now he recognized what a futile effort it had been. By God's grace he had been called to free others from that plight. He knew that it could only be done through the working of the Holy Spirit in the gospel.

We need to make every effort to understand where the Jews are today in their religious life. The better we understand, the more prepared we will be to speak to their real needs.

v. 21 — *To those not having the law I became like one not having the law (though I am not free from God's law but am under Christ's law), so as to win those not having the law.*

Now he turns to his dealings with the Gentiles, all who are outside the family of Israel. They did not have the written law. They did have the law in their hearts, as Paul points out in his letter to the Romans (2:14,15). Their consciences bore witness to that law and their thoughts accused—or even defended—them. Their life, however, was different from that of the Jewish people who lived under the written code. So, Paul knew that he had to use a different approach. He sought to understand the Gentile people and identify with them as fully as he could.

Paul appears to say the exact opposite of what he has said in the previous verse. He says that he is not free from God's law. We understand this to mean he still uses the law as a guide, the "third use" of the law. He was not free from this. As the fruit of his faith he sought to live according to God's holy law.

He explains in what sense he is still under God's law: "[I] am under Christ's law." To be under Christ's law is seeking to live according to the great law of love, motivated by the gospel. "By this all men will know that you are my disciples, if you love one another" (Jn 13:35). As Paul says elsewhere, "Love is the fulfillment of the law" (Ro 13:10). In love he sought to win people of every nation for the gospel.

v. 22 — *To the weak I became weak, to win the weak. I have become all things to all men so that by all possible means I might save some.*

The question has been raised concerning this verse whether Paul is speaking of believers or unbelievers. There is no good reason to exclude either one. He has spoken about weak believers earlier in this letter (8:9). These weak were already "won." They had faith, even though it was weak. Paul, however, did not want to see them lose that faith. So, he identified with them and sought to bring that word to bear in just that way which would serve to strengthen them.

The weak outside of the church are those who are given to all sorts of sinful weaknesses which keep them in unbelief. They need to be approached in a way which understands why they yield to their sinful weaknesses. They need to hear the law to know that their sin separates them from God. They need to hear the gospel so that they can be converted and saved.

Here Paul uses σώζω (save) instead of κερδαίνω (win). Again, he certainly knew that it is the Lord who saves and not he. He was so deeply concerned, however, about the salvation of others that he looked upon it in this very personal way. Would that we had such concern at all times for the salvation of others! Do we seek to become all things to all men so that we can by all means win some?

v. 23 — *I do all this for the sake of the gospel, that I may share in its blessings.*

We might say that Paul again answers the question he had asked about receiving a reward (v. 18). His first concern was to share the gospel with others so that they might be saved. He also had a concern for himself. We can hardly have a healthy concern for the salvation of others unless we are concerned about our own salvation at the same time. Paul explains in the verses that follow how a minister of the gospel needs to strive in order that he does not lose its blessings. Every believer needs to be involved in the same struggle. There is victory in the Lord Jesus and in his gospel.

Homiletical Suggestions

This text would be very suitable for a pastoral conference. It also serves well to encourage personal evangelism on the part of God's people.

The Epiphany season gives us opportunity to focus on our Savior's appearance in the world as our Savior from sin. The Old Testament lesson pictures our hopeless and helpless condition without a Savior. The Gospel lesson points to the Lord Jesus as our great healer. He is the only one who can lift us out of despair and give us hope.

Drawing on some of the main thoughts of the text, we suggest this approach:

What Compels Us to Preach the Gospel?

1. We have a sacred trust (vv. 16,17a)
2. We can see a desperate need (vv. 19,20-22)
3. We have a gracious reward (vv. 17b,18,23)

If a two-part sermon is preferred it can be formulated in this way:

What Compels Us to Speak the Gospel?

1. God's call (vv. 16-18)
2. Man's need (vv. 19-23)

If you prefer to take a theme from the text, use the words of verse 22:

"I Have Become All Things to All Men"

1. God calls us to do this (vv. 16-18)
2. He promises rich fruits (vv. 19-23)

SIXTH SUNDAY AFTER EPIPHANY

The Scriptures

> Old Testament — *2 Kings 5:1-14*
> Epistle — *1 Corinthians 9:24-27*
> Gospel — *Mark 1:40-45*

The Text — 1 Corinthians 9:24-27

The ninth chapter of Paul's first letter to the Christians at Corinth contains the apostle's frank discussion of his gospel ministry. In verse 15 Paul states his purpose in refusing compensation for his work among the Corinthians. He wanted no strings attached to the gospel he proclaimed. The apostle didn't want these Christians to get the impression that they were, in any way, buying the good news of Jesus. The gospel was God's gift to them, given solely out of the Lord's grace. Paul's purpose in carefully dispensing the gospel was to win as many people as possible.

But the apostle also recognized another important reason for his unselfish, disciplined action. He, too, wanted to make sure that he would share eternally in the life his Savior had won for him. In preaching the gospel unselfishly, Paul was not only making a statement about the priceless nature of the gospel, he was also testifying to his own faith and the gospel's work in his own heart. Paul lived the way he did for his own spiritual benefit as well as for the benefit of the gospel and those who would hear it.

> v. 24 — *Do you not know that in a race all the runners run, but only one gets the prize? Run in such a way as to get the prize.*

The apostle compares the Christian's life under God to a race. A person finishes a race unsatisfactorily if he runs in a half-hearted manner. So also God's children endanger their race of faith if they fail to view it as a serious exercise. The Christian's race of faith requires total commitment, with the prize of eternal life in mind.

The picture of the race employed by Paul was well known in his world. Most larger Greek cities had stadiums with race courses. The city of Corinth even had its own Isthmian Games, which were held every other year and were second only to the Olympic Games in importance.

Paul never speaks of the prize of life as something he is earning by his own work. The picture he presents is that of a child of God running toward that which already exists and has already been won by virtue of Jesus' perfect life and death. In his letter to the Philippians (3:14) Paul expresses this same thought: "I press on toward the goal to win the prize for which God has called me heavenward in Christ Jesus."

The present imperative (τρέχετε) expresses an action which is to take place continuously. Christians are to keep on running and always run their race of faith in Christ Jesus.

v. 25 — *Everyone who competes in the games goes into strict training. They do it to get a crown that will not last; but we do it to get a crown that will last forever.*

Paul begins to describe the type of race which God calls his children to run. In verse 27 the apostle will more fully explain the kind of self-control needed by the runner. The point in this verse is that self-control ("strict training") is essential for any kind of victory.

Self-control was essential in securing the perishable crown (a wreath of laurel or wild olive leaves) given to runners in Paul's day. Christians will recognize that self-control is much more essential when looking forward to the imperishable prize which God offers.

As in verse 24, the apostle's emphasis in this verse is not necessarily on the struggle, but on the prize. The runner who forgets what he's running for will also forget his training needs. The child of God is to live every day with the memory of Jesus' victory over sin and death. Every day the child of God directs faith's focus toward the crown of righteousness (2 Ti 2:8), the crown of eternal life (Rev 2:10), which Jesus won and will give to those who love him (Ja 1:12).

v. 26 — *Therefore I do not run like a man running aimlessly; I do not fight like a man beating the air.*

Paul's race of faith toward the crown of life is run in a focused and directed way. He is not "all over the track," distracted by cares and pleasures and false goals. Nor, changing the picture to another event in the games, does he waste his energy and strength by swinging wildly. Though he speaks in the first person singular, there is an implicit exhortation to his readers to follow his example.

v. 27 — *No, I beat my body and make it my slave so that after I have preached to others, I myself will not be disqualified for the prize.*

Like the athlete who disciplines his body for the contest, Paul subdues the impulses of his sinful nature, which wants to use his body in the service of sin. He is not a slave to his passions. Rather, he trains his body to serve him in the contest.

God's Word instructs, "For if you live according to the sinful nature, you will die; but if by the Spirit you put to death the misdeeds of the body, you will live" (Ro 8:13). By the power of God's Spirit living in them, Christians say "No" to sin and "Yes" to the Lord and his saving will for their lives.

Μή πως ("lest") introduces a negative purpose clause: The reason for saying "No" to the sinful nature is to avoid being disqualified. Again, what God has done and has won is that which motivates and enables the Christian to run the race in the way described here.

It is clear from the text that Paul was in no way writing of the Christian meriting salvation through the discipline of the body. Rather, he encourages God's people to be what God has made them in Jesus. The child of God strives to live and love unselfishly, in imitation of the Savior who lived and loved and died unselfishly for all. A lack of such thankful living would show that the gospel has been rejected, and the prize of eternal life has been lost.

Homiletical Suggestions

The Old Testament and Gospel readings are companion lessons in that they both relate God's miraculous healing of individuals afflicted with leprosy. The sermon text is encouragement to run the race and fight the fight for which Jesus has freed us from the leprosy of sin.

Appearing near the end of the Epiphany season (almost two months after the Christmas Festival), this text issues a much-needed reminder of Christ's purpose in coming to this earth. The Lord has called us heavenward in and because of Jesus Christ. The life which we have been given in Jesus is more than seasonal. While indifference to the gospel seems to be so commonplace, God's saving love revealed in Jesus gives us more than ample reason to run our race of faith with seriousness of purpose and self-discipline.

The following outlines emphasize the actions to which the text encourages us:

Keep Your Eyes on the Goal

1. The prize has been provided by God's grace (vv. 24,25)
2. The race is run with God's power (vv. 26,27)

Are You Ready for the Contest?

1. It's a contest for an eternal prize (v. 25),(26,27)
2. It's a contest which requires consistent effort (vv. 24,26,27)

SEVENTH SUNDAY AFTER EPIPHANY

The Scriptures

> Old Testament — *Isaiah 43:18-25*
> Epistle — *2 Corinthians 1:18-22*
> Gospel — *Mark 2:1-12*

The Text — 2 Corinthians 1:18-22

The Apostle Paul was not a stranger to controversy. Throughout his life as a Christian he encountered one difficulty after another. In many cases the reason for his troubles was his faith. Other times it was his background. His dramatic turnabout from Christ-hater to Christ-lover aroused suspicion in the hearts of many. People regularly examined and weighed the apostle's words and actions, looking for false or selfish motives which would discredit him and his ministry. That was the case when he wrote 2 Corinthians.

Paul's opponents were trying to create controversy over the apostle's change of travel plans. At one time he had planned to visit the Christians in Corinth on his way to Macedonia (v. 16). Circumstances, however, led him to change those plans. His enemies pounced on that revision of his itinerary and claimed that it was evidence of a much more serious problem than simply a character flaw like fickleness.

They said the apostle's words, especially in the area of religious truth, could not be trusted, that he was unstable in his theology. In the verses under consideration the apostle defends his ministry and message and uses the personal attack against him to underscore God's faithfulness and his reliable word.

v. 18 — *But as surely as God is faithful, our message to you is not "Yes" and "No."*

Word order in the original language is always important, and πισ-τός at the beginning of this verse points out the central thought. Faithfulness describes God's entire dealing with this human race. He is Jahweh, the God of free and faithful grace. He is faithful in what he says and in what he does. Truer words were never spoken than when Balaam said, "God is not a man, that he should lie, nor a son of man, that he should change his mind. Does he speak and then not act? Does he promise and not fulfill?" (Nu 23:19).

Paul gets right to the heart of the issue and states that not only is God faithful but so is the message which God gave him. When Paul

84

preached and taught God's Word he wasn't guilty of talking out of both sides of his mouth. He didn't adjust his theology to the times or circumstances or his audience. He preached a steady, faithful message about a faithful God.

v. 19 — *For the Son of God, Jesus Christ, who was preached among you by me and Silas and Timothy, was not "Yes" and "No," but in him it has always been "Yes."*

The emphatic position of τοῦ θεοῦ stresses the deity of Jesus Christ and thus the divine authority of Paul's gospel. Paul also shows that his message is consistent with that of two other reliable preachers who served the Corinthian congregation, Silas and Timothy.

This is further proof of God's faithfulness. God can use different messengers at different times to speak to people, and the message can be the same. That was the case with the presentation of the Word to the Corinthian congregation. God had said many things to the people through various speakers and, when everything was evaluated, the message was entirely consistent. That faithfulness of the Corinthians' preachers was a reflection of the Corinthians' God.

v. 20 — *For no matter how many promises God has made, they are "Yes" in Christ. And so through him the "Amen" is spoken by us to the glory of God.*

Paul now centers on the amazing faithfulness of God. He points the reader in the direction of God's promises. Those promises fill page after page in Scripture. They begin in Genesis and continue all the way to Revelation. In the Word God makes promises ranging from the present to the future, from care of the body to care of the soul, from what we would consider the insignificant things of life to the extremely important things of life.

Unlike the proverbial political candidate, God does not ignore or renege on his promises. When he promises, he carries it out. And his greatest promises are fulfilled in Christ. In Christ all of God's promises are "Yes"; the promises are kept.

When people respond with God-given faith to God's promises, it's as if they offer up an "Amen" to him and all his promises. Ναί is a word of certainty. Like ἀμήν, Jesus used it in repetitive form to introduce some of his most important statements, to assure his listeners that what he was about to tell them was truthful, beyond the shadow of a doubt. This kind of certainty in God's promises can only be the result of God's working in a person's heart. That certainty finally comprises the heart and soul of Christian faith: "Faith is being sure of what we hope for and certain of what we do not see" (He 11:1).

This verse provides a good opportunity for the preacher to review the purpose of an "Amen" spoken or sung by the congregation following the worship leader's prayer. "Amen" is more than a musical interlude or a liturgical custom. The congregation's "Amen" is its ownership of the prayer spoken for them. More than that, it expresses certainty that the prayer offered for them is heard by God and will be answered by him in the best way and at the best time. Similar things can be said about the "Amen" which concludes a sermon.

The verses which follow show that this certainty comes from God.

vv. 21,22 — *Now it is God who makes both us and you stand firm in Christ. He anointed us, set his seal of ownership on us, and put his Spirit in our hearts as a deposit, guaranteeing what is to come.*

Paul gives God the credit for the believer's certainty in the word and its promises. Βεβαιόω has the meaning "to make firm, confirm, strengthen." All those things God does for a person's faith on an ongoing basis, as the present participle indicates. God confirms and strengthens a person's faith through his gospel in Word and Sacrament.

After speaking of God's present care for the believer, Paul goes back in time to when the believer first came to faith.

Χρίσας, "anointing," describes that time. The word recalls what happened in biblical times when a person was inducted into office. Oil was poured on his head, designating him as one whom the Lord had chosen for specific work.

The believer's anointing takes place at baptism. The application of water and the use of God's word wash away sin and bring the individual into God's family by working faith in Jesus Christ. As in the case of Jesus' baptism, the believer's baptism also sets him apart for service to God. As a child of God the believer not only receives blessings from God; he is also entrusted with the responsibility of living life in God's way. See Ephesians 2:8-10.

Paul uses a second, even more descriptive, word to describe God's involvement in the believer's life. Σφραγίζω means "mark with a seal." It's the word used in Matthew 27:66, when Pilate marked Jesus' tomb with a seal. Such a seal shows ownership and warns of consequences if the seal is tampered with.

When the Holy Spirit brings people to faith through the gospel, he "marks them with a seal." The seal is not an outward one which can be seen. Rather, it's an inward one. The outward identifying mark of the believers—mentioned in Revelation 14:1—is purely symbolic, but attests to the Spirit's work of identifying Christians.

The Holy Spirit's presence in the believer's heart not only provides proof of ownership, it also produces certainty about the future. Through Christ God has given believers many blessings in this life, but God promises to bless believers in the future. The Holy Spirit's presence in a Christian's heart amounts to a down payment by God on future blessings. The fact that the Holy Spirit dwells in Christians in this life is proof of God's desire to bless them even more in the future. The future blessings the apostle has in mind are part of the glorious life which awaits the children of God in heaven. In eternity the "full payment" of God's promises will be made.

Homiletical Suggestions

Much of our society today places little value on the spoken word. That's because people have seen how good intentions and promises often go unfulfilled. They say, "Put it in writing, and then I'll believe you." People need not say that to God, because he has already put his promises in writing. More than that, he has already put the fulfillment of his promises into writing. It's all there in the Bible.

The text provides insight into God's remarkable faithfulness. Considering that Epiphany 7 is midway between Christmas and Easter, the preacher would do well to review and preview those events in Jesus' life. A look back at Advent and Christmas will show the worshiper that God was faithful in fulfilling all his promises of sending a Savior into the world. A look ahead to Lent and Easter will enable the worshiper to see that God made many more promises to the world regarding the death and resurrection of his Son; he fulfilled them all, too.

The fact that God has a flawless record in prophecy and fulfillment indicates that he speaks clearly and truthfully at all times. That suggests as theme and parts:

With God There Is No Double-talk

1. He speaks clearly through Christ (vv. 18-20)
2. He speaks of timeless blessings (vv. 21,22)

A second outline includes an opportunity to speak of the gospel ministry:

See God's Great Faithfulness

1. In the preaching of his representatives (vv. 18,19)
2. In the working of his Son (v. 20)
3. In the giving of his Spirit (vv. 21,22)

EIGHTH SUNDAY AFTER EPIPHANY

The Scriptures

> Old Testament — *Hosea 2:14-16,19,20*
> Epistle — *2 Corinthians 3:1b-6*
> Gospel — *Mark 2:18-22*

The Text — 2 Corinthians 3:1b-6

Our text picks up Paul's defense of his ministry in Corinth. Some there had questioned Paul's ministry and apostolic authority. In defending himself, Paul wanted to make sure he was not misunderstood. He was not on some "ego trip," out to exalt himself by belittling his critics. Paul had a glorious ministry. As he shared God's Word and will with them, he spoke with divine authority. As Paul now defends his ministry, his confidence is in the Lord who sent him. He wants the Corinthians to understand that. Instead of focusing on Paul, the man, their eyes should be on the Lord who gave this man his ministry and authority.

v. 1 — *Or do we need, like some people, letters of recommendation to you or from you?*

Letters of recommendation or introduction were a familiar and common practice in apostolic times (cf. Ac 18:27; Ro 16:1,2; 1 Co 16:3). Expecting a no answer (μή), Paul asks if he needs such a letter—to or from them.

By asking if he needs a letter of recommendation to them Paul is appealing to their hearts and to what they personally know about him. Letters of recommendation are for strangers—and Paul was certainly no stranger to them! He had lived and worked among them for a year and a half (Ac 18:11). Paul wants these Corinthian Christians to recall that time and remember how he had conducted himself and his ministry while in Corinth. He had not been out to make a name for himself. "I resolved to know nothing while I was with you except Jesus Christ and him crucified" (1 Co 2:1-5).

Paul didn't need a letter of recommendation to them. Nor did he need one from them! Gently but firmly Paul asserts his apostolic authority. One who has been officially sent by the Lord God Almighty needs no further credentials or approval. Paul's authority and ministry were not based on any letter of recommendation from them or anyone else. His ministry and its authority were built on the divine call he had received from his Savior.

There was no need for such formal letters of recommendation for as Paul continues:

v. 2 — *You yourselves are our letter, written on our hearts, known and read by everybody.*

"You yourselves" brings out the emphatic ὑμεῖς. "You Corinthians—you are our letter." They are Paul's letter written on Paul's heart.

Letters of recommendation are just that. They are meant to inform others about the person being recommended so that they receive and welcome him. Paul needs no such letter. He has something better than a piece of paper with some glowing words written on it. Paul lets his ministry speak for itself. It was open for inspection by anyone and everyone.

What was Paul like as an apostle and pastor? How did he carry out his ministry? Just look at how he conducted his ministry in Corinth! They were certainly no "ideal" congregation. With their doctrinal (even such a basic doctrine as the resurrection!) and moral problems, with their petty bickering and cliques, they had certainly caused Paul plenty of heartache and headache. But there was no bitterness, no anger, no malice in Paul's heart. Instead, they were on his heart and in it! What love, patience, support Paul had showered on them! He was not ashamed of them. He confidently pointed to them as his letter of recommendation.

v. 3 — *You show that you are a letter from Christ, the result of our ministry, written not with ink but with the Spirit of the living God, not on tablets of stone but on tablets of human hearts.*

With two participial phrases Paul further explains how they are his letter. The NIV paraphrases the first part of this verse to put the participles φανερούμενοι ("you show") and διακονηθεῖσα ("the result of our ministry," literally "[a letter] having been served by us") into good English.

Paul had previously called these Corinthians "our letter." He had been their pastor. They were the result of his faithful stewardship of God's Word. But the glory and the credit really don't belong to Paul. He was simply the "pen" used to write this letter. They were really Christ's letter, written by the Holy Spirit. Through Paul's ministry of God's Word and sacraments Jesus and the Holy Spirit had been at work in their hearts and lives.

Did Paul need, like some people, a letter of recommendation? Look at the letter he has! A letter not written on paper with pen and ink but written by the Holy Spirit on human hearts. What a letter! Perhaps some of them had been immoral people, idolaters, adulterers, male prostitutes, homosexual offenders, thieves, greedy people, drunkards, slanderers, or swindlers (1 Co 6:9,10). Now, however, they were "washed, sanctified, justified in the name of the Lord Jesus Christ and by the Spirit of our God" (1 Co 6:11). People like that now joined together as "the church of God in Corinth" (1:1). People who had been slaves of Satan, bowing down to the gods of sex, self, money, etc., now worshiping the living God and his Son as their beautiful Savior. What a letter—what a ministry—Paul had!

Yet none of this went to Paul's head:

vv. 4,5 — *Such confidence as this is ours through Christ before God. Not that we are competent to claim anything for ourselves, but our competence comes from God.*

There is a tightrope that every servant of the Lord must walk in his ministry. On the one side is the hazard of being overwhelmed by the problems and cares of day-to-day ministry. On the other side is the danger of acting like the "savior" of the congregation—thinking it all depends on the minister and what he does. Paul here shows us how to walk that fine line. The two hazards are not that far removed from one another.

There is no denying that the ministry is hard, demanding work. Let no one misunderstand that! All is not roses. No congregation is perfect—nor any pastor! There are and there will be problems. There is sin and discord. There is frustration, disappointment, agony, and grief. Paul understood that. He had gone through that himself! Just look at the problems he had there in Corinth and in the other congregations he had served. But there is no need to give up and call it quits.

The servant of the Lord must despair in his ministry—despair of himself, his own abilities, talents, strength, stamina. No person of and by himself is capable or qualified to carry out such a calling. Who am I to handle and rightly divide the Word of truth (2 Ti 2:15)? Who am I to guard and oversee—to be a shepherd of the church of God, which he bought with his own blood (Ac 20:28)? I see how imperfect my faith and life is, I see how little I really understand God's holy Word, I see people looking to me, coming to me for comfort, guidance, direction from God. Who am I? Where is the faithful shepherd who has never been plagued by such thoughts?

"But our competence comes from God." The Lord's servant must despair of himself, but not of the God who called him into the ministry. With his eyes on his Lord, leaning on his Lord, looking to his

God for the strength, guidance, wisdom, understanding he needs—
such a servant can minister with the utmost confidence.

v. 6 — *He has made us competent as ministers of a new
covenant—not of the letter but of the Spirit; for the letter kills,
but the Spirit gives life.*

Here is where Paul's confidence lay: in the God who called him
into the ministry and in the means which God had given him to do
his ministry. Here also is our competence and confidence.

God has made us ministers of "a new covenant." Through his
prophet Jeremiah (31:31-34; cp. He 8:7-13; 10:11-18) God spelled out
the terms of this new covenant. It centered around this, "I will forgive their wickedness and will remember their sins no more." God
has entrusted us with a gospel-centered ministry. Our ministry is
above all else a preaching of repentance and forgiveness of sins in
the name of our crucified and risen Lord Jesus (cf. Lk 24:47).

With striking contrasts Paul describes the difference between the
old and new covenants, between law and gospel. The law is literally
a covenant "of letter" (no article in the Greek, emphasis on quality)
and it "kills." The gospel is "of spirit" (again no article, "spiritual")
and it "gives life." We do not agree with the NIV's capitalization in
translating πνεῦμα, but it does not present a problem, since it is the
Spirit who gives the gospel its spiritual quality and gives life
through it.

The law has a role in our gospel-centered ministry. It prepares the
way for the good news of the gospel. The law with all its fine points
and demands crushes the sinner, damns him, kills him and any hope
of meriting eternal life in heaven. The law demands conformity and
offers no compromise. It can to a certain extent change or shape outward obedience, but it cannot change the heart. How depressing and
discouraging it would be to be a minister of the old covenant!

The gospel—that is good news! God in love sending his own Son
to be the Savior of a world of sinners. Jesus in love living for us an
absolutely sinless life—and giving us all the credit for it! Jesus in
love taking all the blame for everyone's sins and being punished in
our place. Relish and savor the terms of this new covenant of the
gospel: full, free forgiveness of all sins, peace with God, eternal life
in heaven, the privilege of prayer, God's abiding presence in our daily lives, the precious promises of his Word, etc. Oh, what a glorious
ministry we have as ministers of this new covenant! Through it the
Spirit makes alive those who are dead in sin. Through it the Spirit
makes us a new creation, makes saints out of sinners, children of

God out of slaves of Satan. Through it the Spirit gives us a new heart, freeing and empowering us to live for God's glory.

The gospel in Word and sacraments—that is the ministry and means God has entrusted to us. The gospel, not gimmicks. The sacraments, not statistics and surveys.

Homiletical Suggestions

A careful and prayerful study of these verses will provide the preacher with the opportunity to review his ministry. These verses take our attention off our problems and difficulties and refocus it on the gospel. The gospel—that's what the ministry is all about! What a glorious ministry! A responsibility to be sure, but a special privilege and honor.

It's not just pastors and teachers who need to take time to step back and review their ministries in the light of God's Word. The people they serve need to do the same thing. What do they have a right to look for and expect—even demand—from their called servants? These verses say much about the called ministry and the relationship between the called servant and the people he serves. With these verses the pastor can review his ministry with "his" people.

Your Pastor Reviews His Ministry

1. My relationship with you in the congregation (vv. 1-3)
2. My relationship with the Lord who has called me (vv. 4-6)

Since people often have a tendency to judge the church by its pastor, the sermon can deal with that in this way:

Don't Look at Me!

1. Look to the Lord who has called me (vv. 4-6)
2. Look at what the Lord does through this ministry (vv. 1-3)

We are still in Epiphany season. The sermon can reflect this:

The Epiphany Continues

1. That's why God has established the gospel ministry (vv. 4-6)
2. Consider the results of this ministry (vv. 1-3)

THE TRANSFIGURATION OF OUR LORD —
LAST SUNDAY AFTER EPIPHANY

The Scriptures

Old Testament — *2 Kings 2:1-12c*
Epistle — *2 Corinthians 3:12—4:2*
Gospel — *Mark 9:2-9*

The Text — 2 Corinthians 3:12—4:2

In 1 Corinthians, written from Ephesus, Paul had dealt with many different problems. He had indicated his intention to visit the church there soon. He planned to remain in Ephesus until Pentecost, and then travel through Macedonia and so down to Corinth (1 Co 16:5-9). But the riot of the silversmiths at Ephesus (Ac 19:23—20:1) forced Paul to leave sooner. He sent Titus to Corinth so that Titus could report back to him on the progress of the Corinthian believers. He expected to meet Titus at Troas but was disappointed when he didn't find him there (2 Co 2:13). Instead, he found him in Macedonia, with a mixed report about conditions in Corinth. Paul's gratitude at good news was balanced by anguish over bad news as he wrote this letter to prepare the believers in Corinth for his planned visit.

Paul writes to the Corinthians about the change in his plans—but no change in God's plans! He writes about forgiveness for the sinner. He writes extensively about the gospel ministry—before and after his report and encouragement regarding the offering for famine victims in Jerusalem.

3:12 — *Therefore, since we have such hope, we are very bold.*

Paul had stated that the ministry of Moses was glorious (vv. 7-11). Paul calls Moses' law preaching "the ministry that brought death" (v. 7) and "the ministry that condemns men" (v. 9). But that glory of the law faded away. The glory of the gospel ministry, however, does not fade away.

The hope that Paul speaks of is the certain hope of this gospel ministry. He calls it "the ministry of the Spirit" (v. 8), "the ministry that brings righteousness" (v. 9). He cites the greater glory "of that which lasts" (v. 11). Since we have the certain hope that our gospel ministry is glorious and lasts into eternity, "we are very bold."

v. 13 — *We are not like Moses, who would put a veil over his face to keep the Israelites from gazing at it while the radiance was fading away.*

In the previous paragraph (2 Co 3:7-11), Paul has recalled the incident of the veil of Moses (Ex 34:29-35). When Moses spoke with God, his face would shine. As Moses then repeated what God had said to the Israelites, the people saw that Moses' face was shining. After he finished speaking, Moses would put a veil over his face so that the people could not see that this glow faded away.

Paul contrasts Moses' action with the boldness of the New Testament gospel ministry. "We are very bold. . . not like Moses." We do not need to put a veil over our faces, because the glory of the gospel ministry does not fade away. This "gospel boldness" is an important fact for every preacher to remember. "If anyone speaks, he should do it as one speaking the very words of God" (1 Pe 4:11).

v. 14 — *But their minds were made dull, for to this day the same veil remains when the old covenant is read. It has not been removed, because only in Christ is it taken away.*

Πωρόω is to cover with a callous, to make the skin hard. It is also used of hearts becoming hard. Their minds were made dull, hardened, so that the truths of God's Word could not sink in. "Their minds" refers first to the Israelites at Moses' time, and then to the same kind of Israelite at Paul's time. The words Moses brought to them from God were finally rejected. So also at Paul's time many refused to see the great truths of the gospel.

Paul says that these people are reading the Old Testament with a veil before their eyes. That makes it very difficult for them to understand what God is saying to them. The veil before their eyes is not made of cloth, but of their legalistic mindset. Unbelieving Israel sees only rules and regulations in all of God's words. That is all they can find there. God's Word remained a closed book to them, because they could not see Christ there. Only in Christ and through faith in Christ could this veil be removed from their eyes.

v. 15 — *Even to this day when Moses is read, a veil covers their hearts.*

Of all the writers of the Old Testament, Paul has been speaking of Moses because Moses played an especially important role in God's revelation. God dealt with him "face to face" (Nu 12:6-8; Dt 34:10-12). Whenever any part of the Old Testament was read, the veil of legalism covered the hearts of the unbelieving Jews. They did not see Jesus in those Old Testament passages. All they saw were rules and regulations. Nor did they even read these rules and regulations properly. "Even though Moses is read, yet the veil which he put over his

face is never lifted, so that they cannot understand the Law spiritually, and how great things it requires of us, and how severely it curses
and condemns us because we cannot observe or fulfill it" (*Concordia
Triglotta,* p. 955). Such blindness is not limited to Israel: Thomas
Alva Edison once said, "I have never had time, not even five minutes,
to be tempted to do anything against the moral law, civil law, or any
law whatever."

v. 16 — *But whenever anyone turns to the Lord, the veil is taken
away.*

This verse is listed in the UBS text as an allusion to Exodus 34:34,
"But whenever he entered the Lord's presence to speak with him, he
removed the veil until he came out." Moses wore the veil over his face
between the time he finished speaking to the people and the time he
reentered the Lord's presence. He did not wear the veil while he was
listening to the Lord.

Paul applies this removal of the veil to faith. Whenever anyone
turns to the Lord in repentance and faith, the veil is taken away so
that he can see God's salvation in Christ. Paul knew this from his
own experience. After his conversion he spent a number of years
restudying the Old Testament, seeing Jesus everywhere.

v. 17 — *Now the Lord is the Spirit, and where the Spirit of the
Lord is, there is freedom.*

The Holy Spirit has opened our hearts so that we understand and
believe what God says about our salvation (cf. 1 Co 2:9-14). The Holy
Spirit, who opens our hearts to the gospel, gives us freedom from the
legal mindset, freedom from the veil, freedom to see all the great
things God has done for us in Jesus.

v. 18 — *And we, who with veiled faces all reflect the Lord's glory,
are being transformed into his likeness with ever-increasing
glory, which comes from the Lord, who is the Spirit.*

Paul and his fellow ministers of the gospel do not wear a veil over
their faces. They reflect the radiant message of the gospel, the message given to them by God. The minister of the gospel who listens to
God's gospel daily will reflect God's gospel to those he meets.

Furthermore, ministers of the gospel "are being transformed into
his likeness"; they are becoming more and more like the One whose
glory they reflect. The word translated "likeness" is εἰκών, commonly
used for the image of God. Through the gospel we are regaining the
image of God lost in the Garden of Eden. The present μεταμορφούμεθα
signifies a continuing process: "are being transformed."

"Ever-increasing glory" renders ἀπὸ δόξης εἰς δόξαν, from glory to glory. The whole ministry of the gospel is surrounded by the glory of God. Once again, none of this comes from the minister, or from Paul, or from Moses. All of it comes from the Lord, from the Spirit.

4:1 — *Therefore, since through God's mercy we have this ministry, we do not lose heart.*

What minister of the gospel doesn't need such encouragement? We did not become ministers because of our good character, or our surpassing gifts, or our hard work. We became ministers of the gospel through God's mercy. God had mercy on us and entrusted his glorious message to us "jars of clay" (2 Co 4:7).

We do not lose heart. The ministry of preaching the gospel to a people who are "obstinate and stubborn" (Eze 2:4) can involve many things that could lead preachers to lose heart. The words of God we speak do not meet the reception they deserve, nor do we meet the reception God's spokesmen deserve. Things go wrong. Our efforts seem unsuccessful.

And then we remember that it is "through God's mercy" that "we have this ministry." We do not have this ministry because we went out and acquired it for ourselves, but because God, in his mercy, put us here. Therefore, we do not lose heart, but instead go back to doing what God told us to do: Preach the gospel.

v. 2 — *Rather, we have renounced secret and shameful ways: we do not use deception, nor do we distort the word of God. On the contrary, by setting forth the truth plainly we commend ourselves to every man's conscience in the sight of God.*

Faithful ministers of Christ "are very bold" (3:12). They "reflect the Lord's glory" (3:18). "We do not lose heart" (4:1). Therefore we do not use methods unworthy of the gospel, act or speak deceptively, twist the meaning of the Word. Paul has more to say about ministerial ethics in the last chapters of this letter. Instead of deceiving, Paul says, we set forth the truth of God's Word plainly. That has been Paul's point in discussing the veil. The veil kept the Old Testament believers from seeing that the radiance on Moses' face faded away. New Testament ministers of the gospel, however, do not wear a veil. They have nothing to hide. Obedience and faith are not forced on people. Rather, "we commend ourselves to every man's conscience in the sight of God." Our task is simply to proclaim the gospel message. We trust that God will work through his words on every hearer's conscience to work faith in every hearer's heart.

96

Homiletical Suggestions

The preacher will encounter difficulties in presenting this text, since very little of the background information can be taken for granted. The story of the veil of Moses is little known, and Paul's comments on this incident are not simple. The doctrine of the ministry may not be well understood by all hearers. These difficulties, however, make it all the more important and necessary to preach on it.

The glory of the Lord, manifested in Jesus at his transfiguration, is central in this outline:

The Glory of the Lord in His Congregation

1. Proclaimed without a veil (3:12-16)
2. Seen with believing hearts (3:16-18)
3. Expressed in faithful witness (4:1,2)

Since the apostle is extolling the gospel ministry, a sermon on the ministry would be in order, even while the preacher keeps the day's Transfiguration theme in mind:

The Glory of the Gospel Ministry

1. It clearly reveals God's salvation (3:12-16)
2. It graciously makes us partakers of God's salvation (3:16—4:2)

ASH WEDNESDAY

The Scriptures

> Old Testament — *Joel 2:12-29*
> Epistle — *2 Corinthians 5:20b—6:2*
> Gospel — *Matthew 6:1-6,16-21*

The Text — 2 Corinthians 5:20—6:2

After receiving a somewhat favorable report from Titus about conditions in Corinth, Paul wrote a letter in late summer of 57 A.D. The positive results of that letter had been counterbalanced by continuing attacks on the apostle's ministry. He skillfully rests the defense of his ministry on the fact that he serves God's glory by proclaiming the treasured message of Christ's reconciliation of the world. Those who criticize Paul's ministry also despise the very gospel of Christ dying for the world.

> 5:20 — *We are therefore Christ's ambassadors, as though God were making his appeal through us. We implore you on Christ's behalf: Be reconciled to God.*

The Greek places greater emphasis on the relationship between Christ and his ambassadors than does the NIV. "For Christ," begins the sentence in the original. The focus then is on the Author of this ministry, and the ambassadors are placed in the role of willing service to their King. Just as an ambassador would seek the joint benefit of his homeland as well as the nation where he serves, so Paul seeks first to serve his Savior and thus the highest spiritual good of his readers. The pastor preparing his sermon can be mindful of the fact that he does not serve by contract, nor at the beck and call of a gathering of people. Rather, he serves as Christ's ambassador to dying souls who need to hear the gospel.

Paul begs his readers to accept the reconciliation won by Christ. (On his use of "we" see 1:1). The inspired apostle evidences his heartfelt desire for the readers to receive the victory won by Christ. The pleading is made in behalf of Christ, as his servant. It is not simply Paul's personal wish.

καταλλάγητε is the aorist imperative passive of καταλλάσσειν. It is nearly impossible to translate this into English without having some active sense intrude. The Holy Spirit is careful in his choice of words as they apply to the invitation to faith, the conversion of the unbeliever. We do well to remember the scriptural doctrines expressed in the Formula of Concord: 1. . . . that in spiritual things the understanding and reason of man are altogether blind . . . , 2. . . . that the unregenerate will of man is not only turned away from God, but also has become an enemy of God. 3. God the Holy Spirit, however, does not effect conversion without means, but uses for this purpose the preaching and hearing of God's Word . . . (*Concordia Triglotta*, p. 787).

v. 21 — *God made him who had no sin to be sin for us, so that in him we might become the righteousness of God.*

The translation is a bit weaker than the original here. Christ is described as τὸν μὴ γνόντα ἁμαρτίαν, "the one who knew not sin." This Christ "God made. . . to be sin for us." The one who didn't even know sin was effectively made to be sin itself in our stead, for our benefit.

In considering this great exchange we must keep the wealth of Scripture's descriptions of Christ in our minds. James wrote (Ja 1:13): "For God cannot be tempted by evil, nor does he tempt anyone." At the same time the writer to the Hebrews says (4:15): "For we do not have a high priest who is unable to sympathize with our weakness, but we have one who has been tempted in every way, just as we are—yet was without sin." While Jesus of Nazareth experienced temptation, his soul was never dirtied by even a passing positive consideration of any temptation. His resistance to evil remained absolutely firm. He remained unreachable to Satan and his devilish forces. (Cf. 1 Peter 2:22.)

Yet, he who is absolutely pure was made sin itself in payment for our sins. In the culmination of his work of redeeming the world Christ would not only bear the load of sin upon the cross, but he would be judged to be sin for the sake of the world. This is the thought expressed in Galatians 3:13, "Christ redeemed us from the curse of the law by becoming a curse for us. . . ."

Christ's anguish is captured in Matthew 27:46, "My God, my God, why have you forsaken me?" Our text does not call to mind some cool, cost-free exchange of man's sin for God's righteousness.

> "Ye who think of sin but lightly,
> Nor suppose the evil great,
> Here may view its nature rightly,
> Here its guilt may estimate" (TLH 153:3).

6:1,2 — *As God's fellow workers we urge you not to receive God's grace in vain. For he says, "In the time of my favor I heard you, and in the day of salvation I helped you." I tell you, now is the time of God's favor, now is the day of salvation.*

Paul continues his address and invitation to his readers with the thought that he and Timothy are their fellow workers. While their connection to God is easily seen in this matter, συνεργοῦντες includes the fact that Paul and Timothy are also helpers to the Corinthians themselves. Their role as God's helpers is also for the benefit of the Corinthians.

Since grace is so frequently misunderstood, Paul's simple definition, as he provides it in Romans 11:8, cannot be stressed too often: "And if by grace, then it is no longer by works; if it were, grace would no longer be grace." This is God's undeserved kindness in sending Christ to be our Savior. This is not an "infused" grace, which gives man sufficient motive and ability to complete his own salvation with works which merit God's approval. Scripture knows no such grace.

God's grace would be received in vain if it were diluted with even the smallest portion of work-righteousness. The Judaizers of Paul's day insisted that though salvation was from Christ, one had to firm up that salvation by the performance of the old ceremonies and rules. The old problems of dietary restrictions and the practice of circumcision have been replaced in our day by conditioning salvation on either outward performance or inward experience.

Lutherans should be quick to recognize that those who either diminish or delete the means of grace do not have a good handle on grace itself. We would be receiving grace in vain if we looked to Christ as the source of our salvation and yet looked to our lives or our emotions as sources of assurance that we have salvation. We would be receiving grace in vain if we conditioned the gift of forgiveness on an emotional acceptance of that forgiveness or a specific external response to it.

Ever so carefully Paul brings the Word of God to his hearers and his hearers to the Word of God. He truly is a helper to all involved. He goes on to explain why he is so intense in this work: The day of salvation has come.

The text which began with Paul's ambassadorship for Christ is emphatically punctuated by the thought that the time for this blessed salvation is now. Quoting one of the many Messianic portions of Isaiah (49:8), Paul neatly ties the prophetic utterance to the continual fulfillment found in the Christ once sacrificed for the salvation of the world. The eternal nature of our salvation is made ours only in time, the time of grace granted us by God. Those who reject Christ and his salvation in this life will not be given any second chance. Those who think that a later date will be more appropriate for the serious matters of their souls' salvation will be sadly disappointed when the opportunity to hear the gospel of Christ is snatched away from them by their untimely death. Our people, too, are tempted at times to think that the time for placing Christ first in their lives is still in the distant future.

Homiletical Suggestions

In the season of Lent we are given special opportunities to see the great sacrifice that Christ made to reconcile the world to God. The great cost of our salvation will lead believers to place God's unconditional grace as the highest priority in their lives.

"Now is the day of salvation." With these exhilarating verses we are launched into the Passion Season. The young preacher may feel overwhelmed at the thought of sermons twice a week. The veteran shepherd may feel his years as his workload is compounded by the inevitable Lenten funeral. Each step of the somber journey to the cross reminds us of our sinfulness—in sharpest contrast to the purity of the sinless Lamb of God. Yet, in him and in his cross is the great certainty of our salvation. There God's love for us is expressed to the fullest.

The three readings for the day are tied together with the thought of sincerity in faith. With sincere devotion we worship with our heads bowed in repentance, our hearts filled with the assurance of sins forgiven. Only God will recognize all that is done to his glory in lives dedicated to the King of kings. We will not seek the fleeting praise of our fellowmen. Suggested outlines:

Hear Paul's Urgent Call

1. A call to reconciliation (5:20)
2. A call signed in blood (5:21)
3. A call that cannot wait for an answer (6:1-3)

An Ash Wednesday Invitation for All

1. Accept God's gift (5:20—6:1)
2. Use the day of grace (6:1,2)

FIRST SUNDAY IN LENT

The Scriptures

>Old Testament — *Genesis 22:1-14*
>Epistle — *Romans 8: 31-39*
>Gospel — *Mark 1: 12-15*

The Text — Romans 8:31-39

The words of this text represent a climax in Romans. Since this lesson is not part of a *lectio continua,* the preacher will need to do some work to bring his hearers with him to appreciate this high point. Background information needn't be dull or lengthy. Witness how briskly Paul walks his readers through the weighty topics of universal condemnation and universal justification in the first five chapters of this letter. Witness how well he understood the particular sins and temptations of each group in the congregation: the Jews who thought they were "one rung up" on everyone else because they had the law, the Gentiles who thought they weren't to blame because they had been ignorant pagans. Make those first chapters live for yourself and your congregation.

As Paul took up the subject of sanctification in 6:1, he didn't open his discussion with such a dull theological term. Rather, he began with two rhetorical questions which immediately involved his readers: "What shall we say then? Shall we go on sinning that grace may increase?" He forcefully asserted that being justified changes the way we live right here and now. And that argument reaches its conclusion with the series of rhetorical questions contained in our text:

>v. 31 — *What, then, shall we say in response to this? If God is for us, who can be against us?*

To introduce the text properly, we must decide what Paul (ταῦτα) is referring to in his opening question. He could be referring to everything he has written up to this point. Our life and confidence certainly depend on God's entire message to us. Or he could be referring to all of chapter 8, which begins with the marvelous truth, "Therefore, there is now no condemnation for those who are in Christ Jesus" (8:1). Or, more likely, he's looking back on the immediate context of verses 28-30, where he declares that God's people are foreknown, predestined, justified, and glorified. God works all things for the good of those same people.

Paul's second question is based on a simple conditional statement: Since "God is for us," therefore no one "can be against us." God is on our side with more than just kind feelings. He has acted on our behalf with his salvation, and he will continue to do so.

v. 32 — *He who did not spare his own Son, but gave him up for us all—how will he not also, along with him, graciously give us all things?*

There is no doubt that God will give "all things"—taken in the sense of Matthew 6:33, all the spiritual and temporal necessities of life—to the people he loved and saved. Jesus is the guarantee of that, because his sacrifice gave us the right to be God's beloved children.

This verse also brings God's people face to face with the importance of the Lenten message. Our confidence in life is based on the message of Lent, that God did not spare his own Son, but gave him up for us all.

vv. 33,34 — *Who will bring any charge against those whom God has chosen? It is God who justifies. Who is he that condemns? Christ Jesus, who died—more than that, who was raised to life—is at the right hand of God and is also interceding for us.*

Here is another opportunity to draw the important picture of the courtroom and θεὸς ὁ δικαιῶν. That justification took place when Jesus died, but our confidence doesn't stop there. That same Jesus is now alive, at the right hand of God, and interceding for us. Who would dare speak against us!

And yet there are many who speak against God's people, shaking our faith, causing us to doubt our faith and our Savior. It would be good to mention in the sermon who these accusers are. For the Roman Christians their accuser was the sinful world of Jews and Judaizers, philosophers and governors. Although our religion enjoys legal status today, Jesus people are still a "little flock," hated by the world (Lk 12:32; Jn 15:18-25). A few specific examples of the media's antipathy toward Christianity would make the point well.

But it would be wrong to pass by this verse without mentioning the two most effective accusers of God's people, Satan and our own hearts (cf. 1 Jn 3:19,20; Rev 12:10). Because of our sinful nature and the *opinio legis* we are often more inclined to think of sin and punishment than to think of grace and God's forgiveness. We are often our own worst accusers, thinking we ought to suffer rather than to hear God's verdict of "not guilty."

vv. 35-39 — Who shall separate us from the love of Christ? Shall trouble or hardship or persecution or famine or nakedness or danger or sword? As it is written: "For your sake we face death all day long; we are considered as sheep to be slaughtered." No, in all these things we are more than conquerors through him who loved us. For I am convinced that neither death nor life, neither angels nor demons, neither the present nor the future, nor any powers, neither height nor depth, nor anything else in all creation, will be able to separate us from the love of God that is in Christ Jesus our Lord.

It is important (and in a way ominous) to note in these glorious verses that God never promises to bring heaven to earth. In fact, the quotation from Psalm 44:22 indicates that God's people have always faced hardship and persecution and always will. But the glory here is that in the midst of what others measure as disaster "we are more than conquerors." For an explanation of the Christian's victory, see Paul's words at 1 Corinthians 15:54-57.

We are "more than conquerors" because God's plan was that suffering should bring salvation, and that the Christian's suffering should bring maturity, purity, and blessing. Only consider Jesus' beatitudes (Mt 5:3-12), which promise that we will be blessed when we are poor in spirit, mourning, hungering for righteousness, persecuted, insulted, and slandered. Christ and his love turn hardships into blessings. Can anything separate us from that love? Certainly not the Lord, who says: "Never will I leave you, never will I forsake you" (Heb 13:5).

It might be helpful for your hearers to identify with the troubles Paul mentions in verse 35: Literally, θλῖψις ἢ στενοχωρία is "pressure or narrowness," (we still speak of being in "dire straits"). Διωγμός is pursuit or persecution; followed by "famine and nakedness; κίνδυνος, "being at risk;" and for some, like Paul, "the sword." But even in death we are more than conquerors.

Notice that Paul's second list (vv. 38,39) begins with death. There is nothing in life or beyond it, no being—good or evil—in the spiritual realm, no time in the present or future, no powerful force, no place so high or low, nothing at all in all creation that can separate us from the love of God which he has proved to us in Christ Jesus our Lord.

Homiletical Suggestions

The clear message in the three lessons for the First Sunday in Lent is the conquering power of Christ. In the Gospel Mark relates

Christ's victory over Satan in the wilderness. In the Old Testament lesson we see Abraham passing the test of his faith, relying completely on the grace and promises of God. Our Romans text calls on people to realize the powerful grace of God in their lives:

God Is for Us!

1. He gave us his Son (vv. 31,32)
2. He declared us righteous (vv. 33,34)
3. He loves us to eternity (vv. 35-39)

This text also answers those skeptics (and immature Christians) who see Christianity as a religion only for the hereafter but not for the here and now, suitable for death-bed conversions but not for day-to-day living. We can proclaim:

The Gospel Is for Here and Now

1. Right now we have a Savior (vv. 31,32)
2. Right now we have forgiveness (vv. 33,34)
3. Right now we have the victory (vv. 35-39)

A final note: Preaching on a text such as Romans 8:31-39 may give a preacher "great text anxiety," the plaguing worry that the mere reading of such a powerful Scripture may be the high point of the sermon, that much explanation will only be distraction. Why not keep exposition to a minimum and simply offer the truths for appropriation in a practical way?

SECOND SUNDAY IN LENT

The Scriptures

>Old Testament — *Genesis 28:10-17*
>Epistle — *Romans 5:1-11*
>Gospel — *Mark 8:31-38*

The Text — Romans 5:1-11

Paul's letter to the Romans was written to Christians who, for the most part, were not personally acquainted with the Apostle. Acts and the Epistles make it clear that people were often traveling to and from Rome on business. So, although Paul had not established this church in Rome and had not yet visited there, these Christians had learned about Paul's work from business people or others who had met him or been informed of his work.

Paul, too, had received reports about the Christian church at Rome (1:8). He was familiar with its strengths and weaknesses. He was well acquainted with the problems that often existed where Jews and Gentiles were members of the same church. Strict observance of the Mosaic Law might be advocated by Jewish members. Contempt for or indifference toward those who were sensitive about that law might characterize some Gentile members. Knowing what he did about these Roman Christians, Paul wrote this letter. We can understand why he laid great stress on the significance of the Mosaic Law, while at the same time stressing our freedom from its demands and its penalties.

Although the text is long, it is a unit and it is well to treat it as such homiletically. Verses 6-11 serve as an explanation of verses 1-5 and underscore the truths set forth in the first five verses.

>vv. 1,2a — *Therefore, since we have been justified through faith, we have peace with God through our Lord Jesus Christ, through whom we have gained access by faith into this grace in which we now stand.*

It is always important to teach and remind and review the foundational doctrine of our faith, that we are justified through faith. The NIV does well to take δικαιωθέντες as causal: "Since we have been justified." The passive reminds us that it is something that was done to us by God. That this is ἐκ πίστεως Paul has shown in the previous section (3:21—4:24).

Because we are justified we now have peace in the presence of (πρός) God. No sinner can stand in the presence of God and live (Ex 33:20). But by faith in what Jesus did for us on the cross, our sins, which would bring our certain death before God, have been removed.

Now, washed clean of our sins (Rev 22:14) and wearing Jesus' robe of righteousness (Isa 61:10), we have direct and permanent access to God and his grace. This right is given to all who trust in the justifying work of Christ. Thayer (*A Greek-English Lexicon of the New Testament*) describes this access in this way: "That friendly relation with God whereby we are acceptable to him and have assurance that he is favorably disposed toward us" (Eph 2:18; 3:12).

Of great comfort, assurance, and hope is the truth that God tells us we now currently and permanently stand in his grace. This comes out in the perfect active indicative ἑστήκαμεν."

> vv. 2b-5 — *And we rejoice in the hope of the glory of God. Not only so, but we also rejoice in our sufferings, because we know that suffering produces perseverance; perseverance, character; and character, hope. And hope does not disappoint us, because God has poured out his love into our hearts by the Holy Spirit, whom he has given us.*

In the closing statement of verse 2 Paul begins his description of the Christians' response to all that God has done for us. Our response is καυχώμεθα, we joyfully boast. This is not glorying in our own accomplishments. This is a joyful boasting in what God has done and what he promises to all who trust in Jesus. Other passages which reflect this type of "boasting in the Lord" are Psalm 34:2 and Psalm 44:8.

Because we have been declared innocent and have been set free from our sins, we can boast in the hope of enjoying God's glory in heaven. While we live in the tents of our bodies which, like this world, are decaying from the results of sin, do we fully understand or appreciate the glory that will be ours in heaven? We can begin to do that by not letting the "little things" in life get us down. We can do that by setting our minds on things above, always remembering that heaven is by far a better place.

Paul says that we also boast in our sufferings. θλῖψις is an inclusive word which means pressure, hardship, persecution, or anything else that troubles us and causes us to suffer. Paul says we boast about sufferings because suffering produces perseverance, the ability to cope and endure, no matter how difficult the situation.

As we learn to persevere and our faith passes test after test of troubles, that perseverance produces true Christian character or

Christ-likeness in us. Then we too, when we are insulted, will not re-
taliate and when we suffer will make no threats (1 Pe 2:23). Then we
will thank God for our sufferings which test and prove—thus
strengthening our faith—and we will commit ourselves to our faithful
Creator (1 Pe 4:12-16).

Finally, suffering and persevering and character building will
come full circle and produce even greater hope in us concerning our
eternal future with God. This hope, Paul promises, will not leave us
disappointed. God continually pours out his love for us into our
hearts through the gospel which Paul expounds in verses 6-11. As the
Holy Spirit works through that gospel in Word and sacrament, he
confirms in our hearts the truth of God's message and the trustwor-
thiness of the hope that message creates.

vv. 6-8 — *You see, at just the right time, when we were still powerless, Christ died for the ungodly. Very rarely will anyone die
for a righteous man, though for a good man someone might possibly dare to die. But God demonstrates his own love for us in
this: While we were still sinners, Christ died for us.*

Now Paul proceeds to explain further and to nail down what he
has said in verses 1-5. He elaborates specifically on how God's love
produces persevering, character-building, confident hope in us. He
sets law and gospel side by side, correctly distinguishing between
them. We were powerless, ungodly, unrighteous, corrupt sinners.
And *yet* Christ died for us, that is, in our place. There was nothing in
us or about us that would move him to do such a thing. Not only were
we incapable (ἀσθενῶν) of doing what God requires for salvation, we
were actually ungodly and impious (ἀσεβῶν). We were God's enemies,
whose sinful minds were hostile toward God, not wanting or desiring
anything God wanted for us or from us (v. 10; Ro 8:7; Ge 6:5; 8:21).
Yet, for those who hated God and actually fought against him, Christ
stepped in and let their punishment be put on him (Isa 53:5).

In the context ὑπέρ has the meaning of "instead of" or "in the place
of" someone else. Jesus was our substitute, taking our place and suffering the punishment of death we deserve for our ungodly sinfulness. A good illustration of this use of ὑπέρ can be seen in Paul's comment to Philemon concerning the apostle's desire to have Onesimus
serve Paul in Philemon's place (Phm 13).

Christ dying for sinners is the fullest demonstration of God's love
we could ever have. God gave up his only Son to pay the price of our
sins. There could never be a greater demonstration of love. As we
look at the cross during Lent and are reminded that our sins brought

Christ to that place, we should also be reminded of the width and length, the height and depth of God's love for us, demonstrated on that cross in the death of his Son.

> vv. 9-11 — *Since we have now been justified by his blood, how much more shall we be saved from God's wrath through him! For if, while we were God's enemies, we were reconciled to him through the death of his Son, how much more, having been reconciled, shall we be saved through his life! Not only is this so, but we also rejoice in God through our Lord Jesus Christ, through whom we have now received reconciliation.*

In verses 1-5 Paul has described what we have and what we can boast about, thanks to what God in Christ has done for us. Then, in verses 6-8, he told us how that came about, describing the magnitude of God's love for us. Now, in verses 9-11, he assures us of the absolute certainty of our eternal salvation.

Paul uses simple logic that any reader can follow, reasoning from the greater to the lesser. If someone saves you from a burning building, certainly he will also provide you with clothing and shelter. "Look at this," Paul is saying. "If the judge has declared you 'not guilty,' then certainly you will also be spared from his wrath and punishment."

Paul comes full circle to the very first thing he asserted in verse 1, using the same word and form (δικαιωθέντες) he used there. "Since we have now been justified." It is an established fact. God did it for us through the death of his Son for ungodly sinners. Since this fact has been established, we can be absolutely certain that we will also be saved from God's eternal wrath. When Judgment Day dawns we have absolutely nothing to fear. We are safe in Christ Jesus.

In verse 10 Paul builds on the logic he has used in verse 9. If the death of God's Son can make God's enemies his friends, then certainly the fact that God's Son lives forever will guarantee salvation from his wrath to all who have been made his friends.

Again and again, Paul stresses the contrast between what we were and what God has made us. How utterly incapable we are to help or contribute to our salvation and the great price that was required to accomplish it! We were hostile enemies of God. God made us his friends. Καταλλάσσειν means to make a change in status, to replace enmity with friendship. Κατηλλάγημεν is passive, demonstrating that this change in status was something done to us by God, not something we did or cooperated in. That change in our status before God gives us reason again to boast confidently and joyfully in God through our Lord Jesus Christ, who made this καταλλάγη possible.

Homiletical Suggestions

The Old Testament lesson for this day shows us God's promise to Jacob that his Savior God would never leave or forsake him, but would accomplish his plan of saving him and all people through the Promised Seed. The gospel is Jesus' prediction and reminder to his disciples that he must suffer and die as a part of God's plan for saving the world.

Lent is about the change in our status before God, which Christ earned for us and which we have received by faith. Lent should certainly be a time for us to confess that it was our sins that nailed Jesus to the cross. But Lent also can and should be a time of confident rejoicing in what God has done for us through his Son.

Emphasize, as Paul does, the extraordinary nature of the blessings of justification as revealed in the story of Lent:

The Blessings of Lent Are Amazing!

1. Because they are so abundant (vv. 1-5)
2. Because they are so undeserved (vv. 6-8)
3. Because they are guaranteed (vv. 9-11)

An outline that emphasizes the confident and joyful boasting to which Paul urges us would be:

Lent Is a Time to Rejoice

1. In the wealth that is ours by faith (vv. 1-5)
2. In the God who lavishes this wealth on us (vv. 6-11)

THIRD SUNDAY IN LENT

The Scriptures

> Old Testament — *Exodus 20:1-17*
> Epistle — *1 Corinthians 1:22-25*
> Gospel — *John 2:13-22*

The Text — 1 Corinthians 1:22-25

The four verses of the Epistle text for this day are part of a longer section of 1 Corinthians in which the Apostle Paul talks about God's wisdom in comparison with the wisdom of the world. It would be well worth the preacher's time and effort to reread the first two chapters of the letter before studying the text itself.

As people search for answers to life's big questions, they will look for those answers either according to man's way of thinking or according to God's way. While God's way may seem "too simple" or even "foolish" to the sinful human mind, it turns out to be the only way to arrive at real answers—the only right answers—to the important questions of life, especially how we are to be saved and have eternal life. Verses 22-25 deal with the crux of the matter as Paul asserts, "We preach Christ crucified."

v. 22 — *Jews demand miraculous signs and Greeks look for wisdom.*

Jews and Greeks are mentioned in this verse as representatives of all those who are different from the "we" of verse 23, who preach Christ crucified. While Jews and Greeks differ from each other, they are in a class together when it comes to refusing to accept the message of the cross.

The Jews demanded miraculous signs or marks by which the Messiah was to be distinguished from other prophets and recognized. The Old Testament had indicated what those signs would be, and Jesus fulfilled them all. The Jews, however, with their twisted view of what the Messiah was to be, were not looking for signs of grace and mercy but for spectacular signs from heaven, which would equip their Messiah to be an earthly, political king.

The Greeks look for wisdom. The ancient Greeks were famous for their love of wisdom. They were impressed by human philosophy and systems of thought based on logic, using sound reasoning to develop conclusions. But the wisdom they were looking for did not begin with "the fear of the Lord," which, the Scriptures remind us, is the beginning of wisdom.

It is interesting to note that both verbs in this verse are in the present tense. They continue to ask for signs and look for wisdom, but as their search goes on, they never reach anything that truly satisfies, that completely answers the big questions of life so that they can have peace. That's because their search does not lead them to Jesus, the only source of true peace and contentment, the only answer to life's questions that really works.

v. 23 — *but we preach Christ crucified: a stumbling block to Jews and foolishness to Gentiles.*

In contrast to the Jews and Greeks and anyone else who depends on human ways to come up with answers, Paul and all others who have found their answers from God preach Christ crucified. The verb is κηρύσσειν, meaning to announce or proclaim as a herald. Again, he uses the present tense. We are proclaiming God's message. Since God has revealed to us the message that really works, that really saves, that really answers those big questions of life, we don't need to spend time in futile searching. We can proclaim it so that others may hear and be saved.

The heart of the message is Christ crucified, ἐσταυρωμένον. Here we have a perfect participle, indicating that while the action is completed, the effects continue to the present. Think of the many times this fact is emphasized in the Letter to the Hebrews, for example, 7:27, "He sacrificed for their sins once for all when he offered himself."

But this very thing, the proclamation of Christ crucified as God's way of saving sinners, is a stumbling block (σκάνδαλον) to Jews. This word is a later form of σκανδάληθρον, which was the movable stick in a trap or snare. When an animal bumped it, it would ensnare itself by triggering the trap. So the Jews, by refusing to accept Christ crucified as their Savior, would ensnare themselves in a trap leading to eternal death.

To the Gentiles (the broader term is used here instead of "Greeks") the message of Christ crucified is foolishness. In 1 Corinthians 2:14 Paul says, "The man without the Spirit does not accept the things that come from the Spirit of God, for they are foolishness to him, and he cannot understand them, because they are spiritually discerned." To the natural human way of reasoning, it is stupid to think that God should send his Son to take on human form to help us, and especially that he should die and that his death should make any difference to me and my chances for life after death. Obviously, Paul's words apply also to the New Age thinkers of today and others who want us to look inward to find the god within. According to that type of philosophy, the message of Christ crucified—and especially of Christ crucified as the only way a person can be saved from sin and eternal death—is nothing but foolishness.

v. 24 — *but to those whom God has called, both Jews and Greeks, Christ the power of God and the wisdom of God.*

"The called" are those whom God has called by the power of the gospel. Through the gospel they have been invited to believe the good news of Christ crucified for their sins. By the grace of God the message has had an effect in their hearts, so that through Spirit-worked faith they may inherit eternal salvation in God's kingdom of grace and glory.

"Among those who are called are both Jews and Greeks." This makes it clear that in verse 22 Paul was not excluding all Jews and all Greeks from God's kingdom. Those whom God has brought to faith view Christ as the power and wisdom of God. A person's attitude toward Jesus Christ depends on his relationship with him. To those whom God has called to faith, Jesus Christ is God's power and his wisdom personified. He is the Word of God made flesh, who by his crucifixion accomplished for us what we could never do by ourselves—he saved us from the punishment of our sins so that we may be at peace with God and have the sure hope of eternal life with him. Only God's wisdom could plan this, and only God's power could make it work.

v. 25 — *For the foolishness of God is wiser than man's wisdom, and the weakness of God is stronger than man's strength.*

The word translated "foolishness" in most English versions is τὸ μωρόν. The usual abstract term "foolishness" is ἡ μωρία. Perhaps we can understand τὸ μωρόν as "the foolish thing God did," which in context would be permitting the crucifixion of his Son. So also τὸ ἀσθενές, which is usually translated "the weakness of God" (while the Greek abstract noun is ἡ ἀσθενεία), could be understood as "the weak thing God did." Perhaps Paul used these two neuter words so that no one would misunderstand "foolishness" and "weakness" as actual attributes of God.

This foolish thing God did is wiser "than men." It is beyond anything human beings could ever conceive or dream of. We could plan and dream and devise any number of schemes by which a person could attain oneness with God, as ancient and modern philosophers have done and will continue to do, but never would we come up with the plan that God did. Likewise, the weak thing God did—the crucifixion of Christ certainly appeared to be an act of weakness in the eyes of men—is stronger "than men." On our own we are powerless to save ourselves, but God demonstrates his divine power to save in this seemingly weak act.

Homiletical Suggestions

The malady in this text would be to look for answers to life's questions in the wrong places, such as in outward signs or in human wisdom. The goal would be trusting in Christ crucified as the power and wisdom of God, the only way for us to be saved and therefore the only real and effective answer to those big questions of life. These thoughts lead to a couple of possible basic outlines:

We Preach Christ Crucified

1. The power of God (vv. 22a, 23a, 24a, 25b)
2. The wisdom of God (vv. 22b, 23b, 24b, 25a)

Another outline centers on the idea of man's search for answers to the important questions of life:

Looking for the Answers to Life's Big Questions

1. You won't find them in man's wisdom or strength (vv. 22,23)
2. God reveals them to us in the cross of Christ (vv. 24,25)

A third possibility allows the preacher to focus on each individual's attitude toward Jesus Christ and what he did for us. This would fit in well with the thoughts of the Lenten season as we consider in detail the sufferings and death of our Savior:

What Do You Think of Christ Crucified?

1. Stumbling block and foolishness? (vv. 22,23)
2. Or power and wisdom of God? (vv. 24,25)

FOURTH SUNDAY IN LENT

The Scriptures

> Old Testament — *Numbers 21:4-9*
> Epistle — *Ephesians 2:4-10*
> Gospel — *John 3:14-21*

The Text — Ephesians 2:4-10

As we move farther into Lent, the cross looms ever larger before us. It was on that cross that the love and mercy and grace of God reached their climax. The Old Testament and Gospel readings for this day hold the cross before us very vividly. Our text is an instructional preview of Good Friday. It affords a "behind the scenes" glimpse at what motivated God to sacrifice his Son and his Son to go the way of the cross. The words "grace" and "Christ" appear as key words in these verses.

In the first three verses of Ephesians 2 Paul reminds believers of their former unspiritual condition. It is not a pretty picture! He describes their former state with phrases like "being dead in transgressions and sins," "following the ways of the world," "gratifying the cravings of the sinful nature," when they were "by nature objects of wrath." What follows in our text stands in sharp contrast to what used to be. God's grace has made the difference.

> vv. 4,5 — *But because of his great love for us, God, who is rich in mercy, made us alive with Christ even when we were dead in transgressions—it is by grace you have been saved.*

Notice first of all Paul's superlative expressions. He talks about "rich in mercy," "great love," and later "the surpassing abundance of his grace" (v. 7). God's mercy is the richest mercy of all, and his love is the deepest love of all, even without these adjectives. Paul uses the adjectives to remind us of this.

"Love" is the broadest of the three and includes the other two. God's love defies comparison. It is not mere sentiment or words. It acts. In verses 5 and 6 Paul calls to mind what God's love prompted him to do.

"Grace" is God's love extended to guilty sinners. In Christ grace pardons the guilt of sin. It does this despite the sinner's unworthiness.

"Mercy" goes out to the wretched and the miserable. Where grace deals with the cause—guilt, mercy deals with the consequences—the wretched spiritual death in which all sinners lie.

Notice the emphatic position of ὄντας. It appears ahead of ἡμᾶς νεκρούς to stress that we were completely dead in sin. We were spiritual corpses, with absolutely no spark of spiritual life in us. In love, however, God breathed spiritual life into us. We were made alive in Christ. On the basis of Jesus' resurrection, through faith in him, we are spiritually alive. (Cf. Romans 6:1-10 and Colossians 2:13f.)

Paul invites us to share his awe and amazement. How can God love what is unlovable? How can he lavish so much love on those who by nature hate him? "It is by grace you have been saved." Preachers and hearers alike have heard much about God's love and mercy over the years. Complacency and indifference are a constant danger. May God help each of us to share Paul's awe and amazement when we contemplate the grace of our God!

Χάριτί is also in emphatic position. Our salvation is solely the result of God's grace. Paul will reinforce this idea in verse 8. The perfect σεσωσμένοι assures believers that their salvation is both an accomplished fact and a continuing possession.

vv. 6,7 — *And God raised us up with Christ and seated us with him in the heavenly realms in Christ Jesus, in order that in the coming ages he might show the incomparable riches of his grace, expressed in his kindness to us in Christ Jesus.*

For those who still struggle in the church militant it may sound strange to hear Paul say that God has "seated us with (Christ) in the heavenly realms." He speaks of a future event as though it were already a completed action. The Scriptures speak in this way on other occasions, (Jn 17:4; Php 3:20; Col 3:1,3). This is a testimony to God's faithfulness and to the certainty of what he has promised. What he promises for the future is as good as done and present.

Why has God glorified us with Christ? He wants to demonstrate his love and mercy to others. He is not content to merely talk about his grace. He wants to keep on demonstrating it. Whether "in the coming ages" refers to eternity or to future generations in the history of the world really makes little difference. God's grace will shine forth for time and eternity. The beacon of grace will draw many people to it. The Christian can also easily find evidences of God's grace when he surveys God's gracious dealing in his own life. That also holds true for congregations and other groupings of believers. God's grace is there for all to see, though not all recognize it.

Χρηστότης contains the idea of properly assessing a need and then filling that need with a timely, appropriate gift. Sometimes well-intentioned people give gifts for which the recipient really has no use.

That cannot be said about the gift of God's grace. It is a gift for which every sinner, whether he realizes it or not, has a desperate need.

vv. 8-10 — *For it is by grace you have been saved, through faith—and this not from yourselves, it is the gift of God—not by works, so that no one can boast. For we are God's workmanship, created in Christ Jesus to do good works, which God prepared in advance for us to do.*

Paul underscores the theme of his message by repeating it: we are saved by grace! Right now we are "the saved ones." There is no waiting, no trial period, no background check. We possess salvation right now. This time, however, Paul adds "through faith." Faith is the hand that receives all the blessings of God's grace. Yet even this saving faith is not our own doing. It is a gift given by God, worked in us by the Spirit. The credit, the glory, the praise all belong to God. He, he alone, has worked out our salvation.

How fitting that Paul should refer to all this as the gift of God. Think of occasions when gifts are given. Seldom does one receive a gift from a total stranger. They usually come from those who know and love us. A true gift is not given conditionally, with strings attached. It is given freely as an expression of love and friendship. Likewise the gift of salvation is given by One who knows us well and loves us dearly, and it is given unconditionally.

Likewise, gifts are not earned. Paul was keenly aware that work-righteousness is deeply ingrained in the natural man. This is a condition to which Christians can easily revert if they let down their spiritual guard. While good works do play a part in the Christian's life, they are totally, absolutely excluded when it comes to our salvation. Paul doesn't hedge. His words are emphatic: "And this not from yourselves, it is the gift of God—not by works. . . ." In the area of justification works and faith are opposites. Relying on works would rob God of the glory that is his. It would render his grace ineffective in our lives.

In his zeal to condemn work-righteousness, let the conscientious preacher never exclude good works from the life of the Christian. Verses 9 and 10 together show that while works are excluded in justification, they are expected in sanctification. Those works are the Christian's loving response to God and his grace. We not only say our thanks to God; we live it every day.

Here, too, notice the grace of God. He not only enables us to do good works (Heb 11:6), but he also gives us the opportunities for service. Those opportunities will vary according to our station in life. Such opportunities for service are not confined to spectacular or unusual things. Everyday, routine chores also offer avenues for glorifying God (1 Co 10:31).

Ποίημα sometimes connotes a work of art. As a touching poem brings glory to the poet or a fine painting brings glory to its painter, so a Christian's life should bring glory to God. Our lives should be reflections of his grace. God has made us what we are.

Homiletical Suggestions

These verses show up in at least three different pericope series, appearing once in Epiphanytide, once during the Sundays after Easter, and once during the Trinity Season. The text offers enough latitude to fit into any of the three. At first glance, however, it might seem a bit out of place as a Lenten selection. There are, after all, no direct references to the cross or the sacrificial work of the Savior. Yet one cannot talk about God's love and grace without pointing to the cross. There is the greatest evidence of God's grace to sinners.

All of the following outlines incorporate "grace" in the theme.

God's Grace Makes the Difference

1. For eternity (vv. 4-6)
2. For this life (vv. 7-10)

Marvel at God's Amazing Grace

1. Marvel that his love is so deep (vv. 4-7)
2. Marvel that his salvation is so free (vv. 8-10)

By Grace You Are Saved

It is:
1. Extended to us (vv. 4-6)
2. Shown to all people (v. 7)
3. Reflected in our lives (vv. 8-10)

FIFTH SUNDAY IN LENT

The Scriptures

> Old Testament — *Jeremiah 31:31-34*
> Epistle — *Hebrews 5:7-9*
> Gospel — *John 12:20-33*

The Text — Hebrews 5:7-9

Hebrews was written to people in danger of losing their faith. The threat of persecution and the temptation to return to Judaism combined to put these people in spiritual jeopardy. The letter encourages them to cling to Jesus and not go back to the empty forms of the law. The writer constantly reminds his readers that Christ is better than the Old Testament forms, which only foreshadowed him.

He still speaks to us today. Like those of the Hebrew Christians, our lives are filled with temptations. As they needed encouragement to hold to Christ and reject the emptiness of work-righteousness, so do we.

In the section of Hebrews in which we find our text, the holy writer speaks about the high priestly office of Jesus Christ. Again we are reminded of how much better Jesus is as high priest than anyone found in the Old Testament.

v. 7 — *During the days of Jesus' life on earth, he offered up prayers and petitions with loud cries and tears to the one who could save him from death, and he was heard because of his reverent submission*

"During the days of Jesus' life on earth" is idiomatic English for the Greek "who in the days of his flesh." This phrase points to Jesus in his state of humiliation. This was the time when he took the form of a servant. He humbled himself in taking on human flesh. Because of it he was subject to human emotions.

When we read, "he offered up prayers and petitions with loud cries and tears to the one who could save him from death," we are reminded of the great struggle that went on inside of Jesus. He offered up δεήσεις or requests and ἱκετηρίας. The latter are understood literally as olive branches borne by supplicants, and came to mean humble or lowly pleading. The NIV renders it "petitions."

He offered these prayers and petitions with loud cries. Although Jesus prayed to his heavenly Father many times, these words obviously point to the struggle he had in the Garden of Gethsemane. Although he was a stone's throw from his disciples, they could hear him praying—hence the expressions "loud cries." Because of his divine nature Jesus knew precisely what was coming. He could see the torture, the mocking, the suffering, and the dying quite vividly. The events of Good Friday would be no surprise to him. But Jesus was also fully human and his human nature recoiled in horror at the thought of what was coming.

In a limited way we can imagine what Jesus went through. Suppose it was revealed to you that some terrible catastrophe would strike in the next week. Imagine that you knew in advance that you would be stricken by a terrible disease or suffer a crippling accident. The fearful anticipation might well destroy the strongest person. The stress which Jesus suffered was even worse because he knew that he would suffer for all the sins of the world. It is little wonder that he prayed that the cup might be taken from him. He told the disciples, "My soul is overwhelmed with sorrow to the point of death" (Mt 26:39).

Jesus took his agony to his heavenly Father in prayer. He went to the right person, "the one who could save him from death." God could have spared his Son from death. Jesus himself had twelve legions of angels at his disposal (Mt 26:53).

His prayer in Gethsemane was "heard because of his reverent submission." The superficial reader may think that Jesus' prayer was not heard, because he actually did suffer and die. But the real thrust of his prayer was, "Not as I will, but as you will." That prayer was heard because of Christ's reverent submission, his εὐλαβεία. Literally, it means taking a good hold on, handling carefully. In this context it represents the piety of Jesus, his careful handling of the Father's will.

God answered his prayer, not by sparing him from suffering and death but by giving him the strength to overcome the inclinations of his human nature. Luke 22:43 tells us that an angel from heaven appeared and strengthened him. Moments later Judas arrived with the armed crowd. No longer sorrowful to the point of death, Jesus boldly stepped forward and said, "Rise, let us go. Here comes my betrayer" (Mt 26:46). God the Father had indeed answered the prayer of his Son!

vv. 8,9 — *Although he was a son, he learned obedience from what he suffered and, once made perfect, he became the source of eternal salvation for all who obey him.*

Lenski points out that υἱός in this sentence is in the predicate position without the article. Hence, it can be translated, "Although he was THE Son." Jesus was the Son of God, the almighty Second Person of the Trinity. One might think that he would therefore never need to learn anything. But here we are told that he learned obedience from what he suffered and was made perfect.

To be rejected is the notion that Jesus went through a moral transformation and that he was made morally perfect. He was born without the stain of original sin. This same Epistle declares in 4:15, "He was tempted in every way, just as we are—yet was without sin." Rather, Jesus was made perfect (τελειωθείς) in the sense of reaching the goal. His goal was to die for the sins of the world. That goal was accomplished and Jesus became the source of eternal salvation.

On the cross Jesus was abandoned by God. Thus it can be said that he suffered the agony of hell. He suffered more than any other person. He suffered as our substitute and put himself in our place to serve as our great High Priest. He stands before God as our Advocate, pleading our cause (1 Jn 2:1).

Therefore he has become the source of eternal salvation. He is our only hope. Jesus is the way, the truth, and the life (Jn 14:6). He is the only mediator (1 Ti 2:5). His is the only name given by which we can be saved (Ac 4:12). Any attempts to find a back door into heaven are fruitless and worthless. Jesus is the only gate (Mt 7:13). Those "who obey him" are those who trust him as the one who obeyed in our place.

The thoughts of verses 8 and 9 appeared earlier in Hebrews. We read in 2:10, "In bringing many sons to glory, it was fitting that God, for whom and through whom everything exists, should τελειῶσαι (make perfect) the author of their salvation through suffering." Jesus reached the goal through suffering in order to bring us into God's kingdom. Would any of us make our children suffer to benefit someone else? Hardly! But such is the love of God.

Homiletical Suggestions

The text is useful for preparing the congregation for Holy Week and, in particular, Good Friday. The words focus more on the meaning and impact of Christ's suffering than on the facts of his suffering. His suffering was substitutionary. He suffered so that we would not. The suffering and death of Jesus makes him the source of eternal salvation. This is the basis and the content of the new covenant spoken of in Jeremiah 31:31-34, the Old Testament reading.

Another application is in the area of obedience. Just as Jesus obeyed his heavenly Father, so also we obey. We have the obedience which is faith. By the power of the Holy Spirit we are able to obey the directive to place our trust in Jesus. In the Gospel reading, John

12:20-33, we hear the obedient Son say: "Father, glorify your name." Jesus was the Son of God; yet he obeyed his Father's will. How do our lives of obedience compare to that?

A suggested treatment of the text:

Jesus—the Only Source of Eternal Salvation

1. Through his submission (v. 7)
2. Through his suffering (vv. 8,9)

If you use verse 10 in the text, Christ's glorification can be included:

Learn about Jesus, the Great High Priest

1. For you he obeyed (v. 7)
2. For you he suffered (vv. 8,9)
3. For you he was glorified (v. 10)

SIXTH SUNDAY IN LENT — PALM SUNDAY

The Scriptures

> Old Testament — *Zechariah 9:9,10*
> Epistle — *Philippians 2:5-11*
> Gospel — *Mark 15:1-39*

The Text — Philippians 2:5-11

In this portion of his Letter to the Philippians Paul is encouraging his readers to live in harmony and humility with one another. In the verse preceding our text he tells them, "Do nothing out of selfish ambition or vain conceit, but in humility consider others better than yourselves. Each of you should look not only to your own interests, but also to the interests of others" (2:3,4). We don't know whether pride and selfishness were a particular problem for the congregation at Philippi. But we do know that such attitudes are a part of sinful human nature. An encouragement toward humility and service is always in place. Paul points to Christ as the perfect example of humility.

v. 5 — *Your attitude should be the same as that of Christ Jesus:*

It is worth noting that φρονεῖτε is the only imperative in this section. The verses that follow were written to illustrate this initial exhortation to have the same attitude that Christ Jesus had. Christians are to imitate Christ's humility in the way they treat one another. This thought launches Paul into a detailed treatment of the humiliation and exaltation of Christ.

v. 6 — *Who, being in very nature God, did not consider equality with God something to be grasped.*

In Jesus' humiliation we have the ultimate example of selflessness. Jesus is "in very nature God." He is God! But he did not consider his equality with God something "to be grasped" (ἁρπαγμόν = robbery, booty). In Paul's day, when a victorious general returned from war, he would publicly display the spoils of battle for his own personal gain and glory. Christ did not use his equality with God in this way. Although he possessed divine power and glory, he did not make a public show of it and use it to gain earthly fame and fortune.

v. 7 — *But made himself nothing, taking the very nature of a servant, being made in human likeness.*

Instead of using his power and glory for his own gain, Christ "made himself nothing." Literally, he "emptied himself" (ἐκένωσεν). He did not empty himself of his deity. He emptied himself of the full and constant use of his divine power and glory. He set it aside and became like an ordinary man. Except for occasional glimpses of his glory (e.g., his miracles, his transfiguration) Jesus looked like any other man. Just looking at him you would never have known he was God. He looked more like a poor servant. He was like a king who hides his royal garments beneath a beggar's cloak.

v. 8 — *And being found in appearance as a man, he humbled himself and became obedient to death—even death on a cross!*

Here Paul describes the depths of humiliation to which Christ went. Crucifixion was the meanest, most despised kind of death there was. It was a death reserved for the worst criminals and slaves. It was an extremely painful death. Even more significantly, it was a kind of death cursed by God (cf. Dt 21:23; Gal 3:13). Christ died as one cursed by God! Why did Christ do all of this? Why did he hide his power and glory?

Why did he humble himself even to the point of death on a cross? He did it for us! He humbled himself so that he might save us. Only after he had accomplished this did Jesus' humiliation come to an end and his exaltation begin.

v. 9 — *Therefore God exalted him to the highest place and gave him the name that is above every name,*

In his state of exaltation Christ is like the king who has dropped his beggar's cloak and revealed his royal robes. He no longer uses his divine power in only limited ways. He now fully exercises his divine power and majesty as he rules over all things.

The exalted Christ has been given "the name that is above every name." No name is more important and highly honored than his. His is the only "name under heaven given to men by which we must be saved" (Ac 4:12). Only through faith in Jesus' name can sinners be saved.

vv. 10,11 — *that at the name of Jesus every knee should bow, in heaven and on earth and under the earth, and every tongue confess that Jesus Christ is Lord, to the glory of God the Father.*

In heaven the saints and angels are now bowing before Jesus and confessing his name as they worship him. On earth believers bow before him and confess his name, although imperfectly because of their sins. Even those under the earth, the demons and the damned in hell, will one day have to bow to Jesus and confess that he is Lord when he comes again on Judgment Day.

Homiletical Suggestions

The verses of this text could be approached in two different ways. One approach would be to divide it between verses 8 and 9. The following theme divides the text in this way and gives the sermon a Palm Sunday flavor:

What Kind of King Is This?

1. A King who humbled himself to save us (vv. 6-8)
2. A King who is now exalted for our homage (vv. 5,9-11)

The introduction to the sermon could describe Jesus' entrance into Jerusalem on Palm Sunday. In some ways Jesus appeared very much like a king (e.g., palm branches placed on the path before him). In other ways he did not look like a king (e.g., riding on a lowly donkey). But he is the king who saved us and whom we are to imitate.

Another approach to the text would be to use Paul's exhortation in verse 5 as the theme for the sermon:

Follow Jesus' Example of Humility

1. Jesus humbled himself to save us (vv. 6-11)
2. Let us humble ourselves to serve him (v. 5)

MAUNDY THURSDAY

The Scriptures

> Old Testament — *Exodus 24:3-11*
> Epistle — *1 Corinthians 10:16,17*
> Gospel — *Mark 14:12-26*

The Text — 1 Corinthians 10:16,17

One of the remarkable things about the way in which the Bible discusses what we might call the "mysteries of faith" is that it never really tries to explain to us how these things can be. We never hear God explaining just how he created the world from nothing, or how he can be three Persons and yet one God, or how his Son can be fully divine and fully human at the same time. Instead, God simply presents these truths to us and uses the pages of Scripture to focus our attention on what they mean for us and for our salvation.

This short section of 1 Corinthians discusses another of these mysteries of faith—the Real Presence in the Lord's Supper. Again, we don't find Paul trying to explain just *how* it can be that Christ's body and blood are really present along with the bread and wine. Instead, he treats it as a "given" and then uses that truth to explain something else.

His main point in this part of chapter 10 is the danger of participating in the activities and sacrifices at the local pagan temples. See verse 14: "Therefore, my dear friends, flee from idolatry." In the two verses of our text he uses the truth about the Holy Communion to illustrate his point. In so doing, he helps us to see what the sacrament means to us by showing us what God is sharing with us and what we share with one another.

v. 16 — *Is not the cup of thanksgiving for which we give thanks a participation in the blood of Christ? And is not the bread which we break a participation in the body of Christ?*

This is the only place where the NIV uses "thanksgiving" to translate εὐλογία. The literal meaning is "good speech," like the Latin "benediction," and is most often translated "blessing." Thus, most other versions translate, "the cup of blessing." Thanksgiving is not a concept foreign to the scriptural meaning of the Lord's Supper. Jesus did give thanks (εὐχαριστέω) before he distributed the elements. For that reason the Lord's Supper may properly be called the "Eucharist." "Blessing," however, is the better translation here.

The "cup of blessing" was the name given to the last of three cups shared by all in the Passover meal. The "bread that we break" probably refers to the portion of unleavened bread that was saved after the Passover meal. It was probably before the last cup, at the conclusion of the meal, that Jesus shifted the focus of the evening away from the blood of the Passover lamb and to his body and blood.

The word translated "participation" is κοινωνία, a word that is often used to describe the blessings that God shares with us or that Christians share with one another. Older versions translated "communion" here, to picture something that was shared "in common." In other places the word describes the "fellowship" that believers have because they share in God's salvation.

Here, Paul is making the point that when we receive the bread and wine in the Sacrament, we are actually sharing in Christ's body and blood. Implicit in that is God sharing with us the blessings of forgiveness, life, and salvation which Christ earned for us when he gave his body and poured out his blood on the cross.

Notice again that Paul makes no attempt to explain what he is saying. He uses the simple verb ἐστίν. He didn't say, "Doesn't this cup signify. . . ?" Nor does he say, "Doesn't this bread become . . . ?" He simply takes God at his word and believes that God uses the Sacrament to share with us the wonderful spiritual food of his body and blood.

v. 17 — *Because there is one loaf, we, who are many, are one body, for we all partake of the one loaf.*

Because God gives each communicant the same bread ("loaf" in verse 17 and "bread" in verse 16 both render ἄρτος), each is also sharing the same blessings in the Lord's Supper. That makes us all, no matter how many or diverse we are, part of the same body (ἓν σῶμα). See chapter 12 for more about what it means to be "one body" in Christ.

Paul uses the "loaf" picture here to point the connection between the blessings God shares with us (vertical κοινωνία) and what we share with one another (horizontal κοινωνία) in the Supper. Both are happening. God is sharing with us and we are sharing together with one another.

Paul makes the connection in order to lead to his conclusion in verse 21 about participating in the ceremonies of the local pagan temples. Just as taking part in the Lord's Table connects you to him and to everyone who shares in God's blessings of salvation with you, so also taking part in idol worship would connect you to that idol and to those who worship it. The blessings that we receive from God and share with one another are so important that Paul doesn't want anybody to lose those blessings by participating in a false worship.

Homiletical Suggestions

The Holy Spirit has already done a considerable amount of work even before you step into the pulpit on Maundy Thursday. Those who have followed the Passion history during the midweek Lenten services have already reviewed the events that took place in the upper room and on the hill called "the Skull." The pre-service music and the hymns will have already called to mind the love of God, who caused those events to happen. The Scripture readings will have reviewed the Old Testament picture of the Lamb without spot and blemish, and Mark's account of the Last Supper.

This sermon text will allow you to build on that foundation by reminding your hearers of the blessings that our Lord brings to them in the Sacrament they are about to receive. Verse 17 will also allow you to speak about the κοινωνία we have with each other as we partake of the Sacrament together. This emphasis might be especially important for those Holy Week worshipers who haven't taken advantage of the fellowship of believers very often during the rest of the year. Paul's point about fellowship with demons provides an opportunity to speak about closed communion as well.

The various translations of κοινωνία suggest the following outlines:

The Lord's Supper Is an Opportunity for Sharing

1. Christ shares his body and blood with us (v. 16)
2. We share the blessing of fellowship with one another (v. 17)

Let Us Meet at the Lord's Table

1. For fellowship with God (v. 16)
2. For fellowship with one another (v. 17)

Let Us Join in This Communion Supper

1. It strengthens our relationship with Christ (v. 16)
2. It celebrates our relationship with one another (v. 17)

GOOD FRIDAY

The Scriptures

> Old Testament — *Isaiah 52:13—53:12*
> Epistle — *Hebrews 4:14—5:10*
> Gospel — *John 19:17-30*

The Text — Hebrews 4:14—5:10

4:14 — *Therefore, since we have a great high priest who has gone through the heavens, Jesus the Son of God, let us hold firmly to the faith we profess.*

Only sinners need a priest to represent them before God. Only God could provide a great high priest able to atone for sin. In this text the writer makes clear that Jesus' person and work are such that they warrant calling him "a great high priest."

He is great because he "has gone through the heavens." Jesus does not carry out his priestly office in an earthly sanctuary, as did Aaron and his successors, but in the presence of God himself. And he does that as "Jesus the Son of God." The juxtaposition of the human and divine names calls attention both to the Savior's personal greatness and to the state of humiliation in which he carried out his office.

"The faith we profess" is the NIV's paraphrase of τῆς ὁμολογίας, "the confession," objective faith, what we believe. It is the saying back to God of the same thing which he has said to us. "Let us hold firmly to" the word of the gospel in which God has revealed this great high priest to us.

4:15 — *For we do not have a high priest who is unable to sympathize with our weaknesses, but we have one who has been tempted in every way just as we are—yet was without sin.*

Our High Priest's greatness is evidenced in his ability to sympathize with our weakness. His perfection does not lead him to imperious rejection of those who are weak. Instead, he sympathizes with human weakness (though it does not say he sympathizes with human sin). Our Savior is able to do that because he himself has experienced the hardship of being righteous in a sinful world. Especially the temptations at the beginning of his public ministry made clear that the Son of God not only endured temptation but triumphed over it.

As the Gospel for Good Friday makes clear, only after enduring the bitterest sufferings could Jesus say of his earthly work as our

High Priest, "It is finished" (Jn 19:30). Neither the writer nor the evangelists psychologize or speculate about how the sinless one could be truly tempted, nor about how temptation could be real for One who, as God, could not sin. They simply state the facts, and the faithful preacher will do likewise.

> 4:16 — *Let us then approach the throne of grace with confidence, so that we may receive mercy and find grace to help us in our time of need.*

When Isaiah saw the throne of God, his response was, "Woe to me! I am ruined" (Isa 6:5). As a sinner among sinners, he feared that seeing the throne of the thrice-holy God would result in his death. Instead, he was graciously granted forgiveness. Here, too, God's throne is the "throne of grace."

Χάρις, ἔλεος and εἰρήνη are all eternal attributes of God. But only through the mediation of Jesus the Son of God, the Great High Priest, can sinners know of them and approach God with confidence to receive them. His effectiveness as an intercessor does not rest upon being exempted from human weakness, but on enduring human weakness and triumphing over it as the God-Man. He will there grant mercy and grace to those who are in need.

Verses 14-16 thus show why we have the confidence to approach the throne of God's grace: not because we are already perfect but because we have a Great High Priest who can sympathize with us, who is able to be the Mediator between God and men. On Good Friday we consider the full extent of that mediatorial, priestly work, in which our Great High Priest offered the sacrifice of himself for our salvation. The cross is the proof of our High Priest's faithfulness, which moves us to come to him with the assurance that with him we will find mercy (cf. Ps 130:4).

> 5:1-3 — *Every high priest is selected from among men and is appointed to represent them in matters related to God, to offer gifts and sacrifices for sins. He is able to deal gently with those who are ignorant and are going astray, since he himself is subject to weakness. This is why he has to offer sacrifices for his own sins, as well as for the sins of the people.*

Chapter 5:1-10 is an elaboration or explication of 4:14-16, introduced by γάρ. "Every high priest," whether from Aaron's line or not, "is selected from among men." For him to sympathize with men, he must himself be human. Moreover, his office is to represent sinful men in their dealings with God. Once again, the necessity for a medi-

130

ator assumes the sinfulness of mankind, a point made explicit in "gifts and sacrifices for sins." The mediatorial nature of the priesthood is evident in ὑπὲρ ἀνθρώπων . . . τὰ πρὸς τόν.

In the Old Testament it had been Aaron and his descendants who offered those sacrifices in their priestly office. Those sacrifices had been types, possessing value only because they proclaimed and portended the sacrifice which the Great High Priest has now offered in the fulfillment on the cross. Nothing is taken away from the Old Testament priests, but granting them all that is theirs shows Jesus to be all the greater.

Verse 2 brings out another feature of Jesus' priesthood. His own experience of temptation makes it possible for him to deal gently with those who are ignorant and going astray. Jesus was not ignorant; nor did he go astray. But having endured temptation, he is able to deal gently with his weaker brothers who do stray because of their weakness and ignorance.

As verse 3 shows, the sinfulness of the high priests in Aaron's line necessitated that they first sacrifice for their own sins before sacrificing for those of the people (Lev 16:6,15-17). Jesus, the sinless Great High Priest, had no need to make such a sacrifice for himself before sacrificing his own life for our sins. His sacrifice was entirely for us (2 Co 5:21; Gal 3:13). There is an implicit appeal to the Hebrew Christians to turn to such a Great High Priest for help in their ignorance and error. The same appeal is made to us.

5:4 — *No one takes this honor upon himself; he must be called by God, just as Aaron was.*

No matter how able and dedicated he might be, a self-appointed high priest could have no assurance for himself and could give no assurance to others that his priestly mediation was acceptable to God. A high priest appointed by God has the assurance both for himself and for those in whose place he ministers that his office is pleasing to God. He is thus the true mediator, able both to sympathize with sinful men (vv. 1-3) and to fulfill the will of God (v. 4).

5:5,6 — *So Christ also did not take upon himself the glory of becoming a high priest. But God said to him, "You are my Son; today I have become your Father." And he says in another place, "You are a priest forever, in the order of Melchizedek."*

Jesus possessed the qualification for the high priestly office as stated in verses 1-4. He was called by his Father to that office. That the office is foremost in the writer's mind is shown by his choice of the title "Christ" rather than the personal name "Jesus."

The writer cites two Psalm verses to demonstrate his point. The question of the precise import of Psalm 2:7 here, as well as in its earlier appearance in 1:5, is much debated. Bengel seems to be the most helpful when he writes, "The apostle does not mean that then, when the Father said: You are my Son, the Father conferred the honor of the priesthood upon the Son; for the *generation* is certainly prior to the priesthood; but he declares that the Son, who is able to do nothing from himself, but is always in the Father's power, and what the Father wills, that alone he does, and what the Father gives, that alone he accepts, has also received from the Father *the honor of the priesthood,* for which no one except the Son himself was fit."

The Psalm citation is meant to emphasize that the Messiah was called to his office by God. It is not meant to date that calling.

It was this divine appointment which fitted him to be a priest forever in the order of Melchizedek. Melchizedek combined in himself the offices of priest and king, offices which were kept separate in Israel under the Old Testament regulations. He was also acknowledged by Aaron's ancestor, Abraham, as greater than himself when Abraham paid Melchizedek the tithe.

Like that of Melchizedek, Christ's priesthood is not less because it is exceptional; it is greater. That was good reason for the Hebrew Christians not to think of returning to the Aaronic priests and the temple cultus. It also deters us from any thoughts of turning to any of the various sects and cults which have proliferated in our time. Nowhere else will we find a Great High Priest, anointed (χριστός) by God as "a priest forever," who has made or could make such a sacrifice for our salvation.

5:7,8 — *During the days of Jesus' life on earth, he offered up prayers and petitions with loud cries and tears to the one who could save him from death, and he was heard because of his reverent submission. Although he was a son, he learned obedience from what he suffered.*

"In the days of his flesh" takes us from the contemplation of the Great High Priest in glory to the way in which he carried out his ministry in his state of humiliation. In that time his work was one which was so difficult that he was able to carry it out only "with loud cries and tears." Καίπερ ὢν υἱός made his temptations more acute because he knew that his Father could deliver him with twelve legions of angels, that he could avoid all this suffering, that to carry out his mission he could not make use of that aid. It was that conflict that led to the "petitions and cries" in Gethsemane. Δεήσεις are entreaties.

132

ʿΙκετηρίαι are the prayers of a suppliant who, in dependence on another, begs for assistance. In his supreme moment as man and our High Priest, even Jesus' sinless soul recoiled from the awful death which lay before him—yet remained sinless in perfect obedience.

The proof of his obedience is the fact that he was heard. The cup was not taken away; he was given the strength to drink it without fear (Lk 22:43). "The obedience" (note the definite article) to which the writer refers here is the obedience which he carried out in the days of his life on earth. Paul parallels this thought in Philippians 2:6,8.

5:9,10 — *And, once made perfect, he became the source of eternal salvation to all who obey him and was designated by God to be high priest in the order of Melchizedek.*

"Made perfect" does not refer to Jesus' moral perfection. It refers rather to his having carried to completion (τέλος) the work which he had been given to do. Without carrying out the sacrifice of the cross, Jesus would not have been a source of salvation. To have been Prophet and King would not have been enough; he had to be High Priest as well, offering the sacrifice which was able to do away with sin once and for all (7:27; 9:12; 10:10).

The salvation which our High Priest has obtained is now graciously conferred on all who obey him. The word "obey" needs to be kept free of all moralizing, as if faith saves because it is a work. Ὑπακούω has the primary idea of submissive hearing. "Pay attention to" or "listen to" perhaps capture the idea better than "obey." Faith listens to Jesus as the Great High Priest, who has offered the sacrifice for our salvation, and since "faith comes by hearing" (Ro 10:17), salvation is received through faith which believes the gospel in which Christ is preached to us (Ro 1:16,17).

Verse 10 ties up the point made in verse 1, where it is stated that every high priest is chosen to represent men in matters relating to God. In verse 10 God himself greets the Son as the one who has completed his work as "High Priest in the order of Melchizedek." This verse thus forms an assurance for the reader: this High Priest has been both sent by God to carry out salvation and publicly hailed by God as the one who has carried out his priestly work to perfection.

Homiletical Suggestions

The three Scriptures for the day present prophecy, fulfillment, and commentary on the fulfillment (the Epistle). The rich content of these readings supplies the preacher with an abundance of material.

The structure of 5:1-10 is chiastic (Robert Jewett, *A Letter to Pilgrims,* p. 83):

a) a high priest must be sympathetic (vv. 1-3);

    b) a high priest must be divinely appointed (v. 4);

    b) Jesus was divinely appointed (vv. 5,6);

a) Jesus is sympathetic (vv. 7,8).

Therefore, **c)** Jesus is the perfect source of atonement (vv. 9, 10).

These structural points are important to keep in mind when one considers how the text might be divided for homiletical purposes. An analytical outline would be quite difficult. Some form of synthesis will probably serve best. For example:

We Have a Great High Priest

1. He is great in his person (4:14; 5:7-9)
2. He is great in his office (4:14,15; 5:1,4, 8-10)
3. He is great in his work (4:14,16; 5:7-9)

We Have a Great High Priest

1. He is appointed by God (4:14; 5:4,5)
2. He is able to sympathize with us (4:15; 5:1-3,7,8)
3. He is perfect in his qualifications (4:14,16; 5:9,10)

EASTER SUNDAY — RESURRECTION OF OUR LORD

The Scriptures

Old Testament — *Isaiah 25:6-9*
Epistle — *1 Corinthians 15:19-28*
Gospel — *Mark 16:1-8*

The Text — 1 Corinthians 15:19-26

The text is a portion of Paul's powerful resurrection chapter. The Corinthian congregation had plenty of problems both within and from the surrounding godless society. They were experiencing everything from shameful factionalism and temptations of immorality to a lack of Christian discipline and disorder in worship. The apostle addressed each of those issues and more in the first fourteen chapters of this letter. But now came what could have been the most dangerous and eternally disastrous problem: "How can some of you say that there is no resurrection of the dead?" (v. 12). Some in the Corinthian congregation denied that human beings who die will experience physical resurrection.

To counter that misconception the apostle marshaled a powerful series of incontrovertible truths. He began the chapter by riveting their attention on facts which they had accepted and believed. Christ died for our sins. This was no chance event but a fulfillment of God's own promises recorded in the Scriptures (v. 3). Christ was buried and raised on the third day. This, too, was no chance event, but the fulfillment of God's own promises recorded in the Scriptures (v. 4). In addition, Jesus' resurrection was not a figment of someone's imagination. It was not a fairy tale, not a fabrication by disappointed followers, nor even a slightly altered but well-meaning "spin" on the truth. Christ's resurrection was and is an irrefutable fact. Hosts of people had seen him alive again and bore witness to that reality (vv. 5-7). Paul was not pulling the wool over the Corinthians' eyes nor making this up, because, though he certainly didn't deserve or even ask for it, the risen Lord had also appeared to him (vv. 8-11).

To deny the reality of the resurrection, which was the stated problem (v. 12), flies in the face of all the reliable, unalterable, and undeniable evidence (vv. 13,15ff.). Also, if Christ had not been raised from the dead, then we have no proof, no guarantee that he did pay for all our sins. Then we have nothing to believe in, no faith, no hope. Then human beings who die stay dead forever and are lost forever! (vv. 14,17-19).

That brings us to our text for Easter Sunday. In this paragraph the apostle restates the undeniable reality of Jesus' resurrection, and then vividly and emphatically demonstrates that that truth is the wellspring from which two great benefits flow to believers.

v. 19 — *If only for this life we have hope in Christ, we are to be pitied more than all men.*

If someone gave this passage only a cursory perusal, he might be tempted to take it out of context and understand it as if Paul were saying, "Watch out for materialism, because if you pin all your hopes on this earthly life and things of this world, you will be greatly disappointed and you ought to be pitied. You can't take it with you." That is, indeed, an appropriate biblical warning (cp. Lk 12:15).

But that is not what Paul is saying here. He is not offering a warning about materialism and temptations from things of this earthly life. There are three reasons why we know this: 1) the context; 2) the inclusion of ἐν χριστῷ with "hope," which indicates that Paul is talking about spiritual life, our relationship with God; 3) if he were talking about earthly life, he would have written ἐν βιῷ τούτῳ instead of ἐν ταύτῃ ζωῇ. Ζωή is not just physical life but *real* life, that is, a living relationship with God. God wants us to have a living and close relationship with him now, during our earthly existence. But his ultimate plan is to extend that relationship into eternity.

In this verse Paul explicitly states the sad results if the claim by some in Corinth were correct. If there is no such thing as resurrection from the dead, then we can enjoy God's love now, we can appreciate God's power and guidance for our earthly life, we can honor him now, and we can focus on his mercy and majesty to cope with present sufferings. But then that's it. Then there is no future hope. If there is no resurrection of the dead, our relationship with God has a terminus. Praise God, that is not the case!

v. 20 — *But Christ has indeed been raised from the dead, the firstfruits of those who have fallen asleep.*

With an emphatic νυνί, an adversative δέ, and a terse subject and verb, Paul trumpets the triumphant truth, "Christ has indeed been raised from the dead." As he stated earlier in the chapter, no one can undo the historical evidence. Some might deny it; some might not believe it. But unbelief does not change the reality of Jesus' resurrection.

With a striking and vivid appositive the apostle proclaims one of the blessings that flow to believers because of Jesus' resurrection. Jesus is "The firstfruits of those who have fallen asleep." Ἀπαρχή takes us to Israelite agricultural life and its link with their worship. When an Israelite offered God the first grain from his harvest, that not only signaled his thanks and his acknowledgment of God as the source of blessings, it also served as a pledge and promise of more to come.

As surely as God raised his Son from the dead as the firstfruits, so surely the rest of the harvest of souls will follow. This vivid picture carries a powerful message of certainty and assurance. By speaking through his apostle and calling his Son "the firstfruits," God is giving us a sure and certain guarantee. We, too, will rise (Jn 14:19).

We also find comfort in Paul's use of sleep as a metaphor for death. For just as sleep does not end a person's existence, neither does death. At death, a believer's soul keeps right on living with God. Incredibly, Christ guarantees more than life with him as immaterial beings. There will be a resurrection for our bodies.

Paul adds the next verses by way of explanation (γάρ):

vv. 21,22 — *For since death came through a man, the resurrection of the dead comes also through a man. For as in Adam all die, so in Christ all will be made alive.*

Note the implications of θάνατος and νεκρός. Νεκρός means being in the state of lifelessness. Θάνατος here carries with it the sense of death as a punishment for sin. It includes all the misery which afflicts the world as a result of rebellion against God. As in Romans 5:12-21, these verses herald the sad news of imputed sins with death as the consequence—and the good news of imputed righteousness with eternal life as the consequence.

Verse 22 restates the contrast of verse 21, which was expressed in the nouns. Verse 22 points out the contrast in the verbs. Ἀποθνήσκουσιν is present tense. Sin doesn't just lead to a distant future punishment. Our inherited sinful nature puts on all the corruption that flows from it, puts us into a constant state of dying. The use of the future of certainty, ζωοποιηθήσονται, reveals why the restatement of verse 22 is an important follow-up to verse 21. For, in Christ we not only will experience rising from a state of lifelessness (v. 21), but also real life and real living (ζωή) in a close relationship with God instead of separation from God (θάνατος) as a punishment for sin.

With these two verses the apostle underscores the message of certainty and assurance in verse 20. The consequences of sin are a reality some might deny, but denial and unbelief cannot change the fact.

Yet, as sure and certain as death is, so certain and sure is the resurrection from the dead. God's promise is sure!

v. 23 — *But each in his own turn: Christ, the firstfruits; then, when he comes, those who belong to him.*

Excitement and joy fill our hearts as Paul's arguments hit home. He has countered the error that said, "No resurrection." We can have hope, not only in a relationship with God for this life, but in a relationship with God forever. But when will this happen? When will the bodies of the dead be raised? Paul says, "When he comes," that is, at Jesus' παρουσία, on Judgment Day. At that time the bodies of those who have fallen asleep in him will rise and rejoin their souls.

"Each in his own turn" does not mean that some who have died will get ahead of others in the glorious final resurrection. The apostle counters that concern in greater detail in 1 Thessalonians 4. Here he asserts the simple truth that the firstfruits come first and are followed by all the rest of the harvest, by "all those who belong to him."

vv. 24-26 — *Then the end will come, when he hands over the kingdom to God the Father after he has destroyed all dominion, authority, and power. For he must reign until he has put all his enemies under his feet. The last enemy to be destroyed is death.*

Picking up on the παρουσία of verse 23, Paul says, εἶτα τὸ τέλος, "Then the end." On Judgment Day everything will be completed and fulfilled.

But someone may wonder, "Isn't Christ's work complete? Why does the apostle modify "the end" with the two ὅταν clauses? What does Paul mean when he says that on Judgment Day Christ will "hand over the kingdom to God the Father after he has destroyed all his enemies"? Jesus Christ has indeed taken the sting out of death (vv. 56,57), but death (personified in verse 26) still raises its ugly head. For the believer in Jesus death is not a punishment for sin, but it still happens. But on Judgment Day, and then forever after, "There will be no more death or mourning or crying or pain" (Rev 21:4), for the old order of things will have passed away.

In fact, all the enemies of Christ will be utterly and ultimately wiped out on that day. "Dominion, authority, and power" refer to all the evil and dark forces of Satan and his cohorts, temptation and sin (Eph 6:12; Col 2:15). The devil's power has been broken. But God allows him to operate like a dog on a leash to remind us that this world is not the be all and the end all of our existence. What comfort we have, however, in these verses! While the evil forces of dominion, authority, and power still cause trouble for us in our earthly life, "It is necessary (δεῖ) that Jesus reign. God the Father has entrusted the Son with his kingdom.

That does not mean that God the Father has lost interest in us nor that he in some way lacks the desire or ability to care for us. No! It means that in his love and wisdom God the Father has given us the great comfort of the continuing presence of our risen and living Lord Jesus (Eph 1:21; Heb 1:3). This is the second great benefit of Jesus' resurrection, the comfort of the presence and power of our victorious Lord. The first, recall, is the certainty of our resurrection.

On the last day Jesus will "hand over the kingdom to God the Father." That does not mean he will no longer be interested in us. It means that he will be able to report to the Father, "All that you gave me to do is done."

"All his enemies under his feet" highlights the completeness of his victory. His (and our) enemies are conquered and subdued, never to rise again.

The ILCW selection includes verses 27 and 28. They offer a further explanation of verse 24 and describe the relationship of the first and second persons of the Trinity. On the one hand, this is a mystery that surpasses all human understanding. On the other hand, we know that God the Son is "equal to the Father as to his deity, less than the Father as to his humanity," as the Athanasian Creed asserts. We marvel at this relationship and acknowledge it with awe.

Homiletical Suggestions

Easter is rightly viewed as the pinnacle of the Church Year. What a privilege to be able to stand before God's people (and many visitors) to proclaim the certainty and joy we have in our risen Lord. In any Easter sermon appropriation gets the upper hand over application. "Christ is risen! He is risen indeed—for you!"

That is the case with this marvelous Easter text! Because Jesus has been raised from the dead, we have the certainty that we will rise again. Meanwhile, we rejoice that our victorious Lord reigns over us. The suggested outlines reflect these two blessings. Carrying the thought of certainty:

The Risen Lord Gives Us Certainty

    1. A sure and certain deliverance (vv. 19-23)
    2. A sure and certain victory (vv. 24-28)

Deriving the theme from the thought of "hope" in verse 19:

In the Risen Lord We Have a Living Hope

    1. A living hope in his guarantee (vv. 19-23)

    2. A living hope in his victory (vv. 24-28)

Borrowing words from verse 20 for the theme:

Christ Has Indeed Been Raised from the Dead

    1. As the Firstfruits he gives us certainty (vv. 19-23)

    2. As the Conqueror he gives us victory (vv. 24-28)

SECOND SUNDAY OF EASTER

The Scriptures

First Lesson — *Acts 3:13-15, 17-26*
Epistle — *1 John 5:1-6*
Gospel — *John 20:19-31*

The Text — 1 John 5:1-6

The First Epistle of John does not read like many of the other New Testament letters. The style of John's letter almost defies an orderly, structured analysis. Yet, his intertwining themes present such simple truths. God is light, so walk in the light. God is love, so show that love. Jesus is the Christ, so be assured.

In writing, John desires to comfort all believers with thoughts of eternal life in Christ "to make our joy complete" (1:4) and to give guidance for daily living. More directly, John avows, "I write these things to you who believe in the name of the Son of God so that you may know that you have eternal life" (5:13). This echoes the section of today's Gospel by the same author, which states: "But these are written that you may believe that Jesus is the Christ, the Son of God, and that by believing you may have life in his name" (Jn 20:31).

Specifically, this text comforts Christians with proof that they are members of God's family and have overcome the world through faith in Christ. The Holy Spirit's testimony spurs believers toward loving acts of sanctification and away from immorality.

v. 1 — *Everyone who believes that Jesus is the Christ is born of God, and everyone who loves the father loves his child as well.*

Two primary truths stand out in verse 1. Together they efficiently describe the believer's justification and sanctification. The first identifies God the Father as the source and cause of conversion for each believer. Membership in God's family is not awarded as a *post facto* result of deciding for Christ. Rather, faith and a new birth occur in the same moment as our Father in heaven draws each soul into his kingdom. The identifying denominator in God's family is trust in Jesus of Nazareth. He is truly the one chosen by his heavenly Father to be the Messiah of the world.

The second truth is expertly interpreted by the NIV so as to avoid an awkward English expression. Literally John says, ". . . Everyone who loves the one giving birth also loves the one who has been born from him." The Greek text in verse 1 advantageously directs our attention to John's three forms of γεννάω. It means "give birth to," or "become the father of." God's children naturally love their spiritual siblings. Their lives produce the fruitful evidence.

Although ἀγαπάω has a very general meaning in classical Greek, this Christian love-word has a specialized usage in the New Testament. It focuses on God's gracious love for the people of his world and the Christian's loving way of life in God's world.

v. 2 — *This is how we know that we love the children of God: by loving God and carrying out his commands.*

Our immature nature sometimes causes us to pigeonhole love for God and love for his children into separate compartments. John reminds us that love for God is always directed simultaneously toward his children, the ones to whom he gave birth. The parameters for showing love are drawn only by God's commands. The wisdom of these words is tested and proved by daily experience.

God's commands can be simply summarized: "And this is his command: to believe in the name of his Son, Jesus Christ, and to love one another as he commanded us" (3:23). Jesus' reply to the questioning teacher of the law is succinct: "'Love the Lord your God with all your heart and all your soul and all your mind.' This is the first and the greatest commandment. And the second is like it: 'Love your neighbor as yourself'" (Mt 22:37-39).

Living in love requires continual life-long growth. Note the use of the present tense in the main verbs. The next verse assures us that this lifestyle is not impossible or possible only for "super-Christians."

vv. 3,4 — *This is love for God: to obey his commands. And his commands are not burdensome, for everyone born of God overcomes the world. This is the victory that has overcome the world, even our faith.*

Here is the progression of thought so far: How do we love the children of God? By loving God. How do we love God? By obeying his commands.

People who are *of* the world" may complain that God's commands are too heavy to bear, squelching all the joy in their lives. Technically, unbelievers are correct. God's law has the power to crush everyone. This fact, however, does not lend credibility to the complainers. Vigorously opposing the worldlings, John emphatically states that God's commands are not burdensome—that is, to those who are properly equipped to bear the load. Those fitted with faith know the difference. The all-powerful Christ yokes himself to each believer and immediately makes obedience to God's will light and easy (Mt 11:28ff.). Those who are merely "*in* the world" are mighty conquerors in God's army (Ro 8:37ff.).

Habakkuk says, "The righteous will live by his faith" (2:4). This passage not only identifies faith as the receptor of God's pronouncement of acquittal, but it also shows how Spirit-driven faith effects sanctification in a Christian. God working in us is more powerful than the devil working in the world. "You, dear children, are from God and have overcome them, because the one who is in you is greater than the one who is in the world" (4:4).

Since we obtained faith through the means of grace, this is our priority: Remain in the word of God! "I write to you, young men, because you are strong, and the word of God lives in you, and you have overcome the evil one" (2:14).

Inseparably connected to our faith in God are our actions in God. Faith and actions coexist. "Whoever lives in love lives in God, and God in him" (4:16). "Dear children, let us not love with words or tongue but with actions and in truth" (3:18).

v. 5 — *Who is it that overcomes the world? Only he who believes that Jesus is the Son of God.*

Only those who confess with their hearts, lives, and lips that Jesus defeated sin, the devil, and the world are declared victors over the world. Whether a believer has a large or a small faith in Christ, the determining point is the all-surpassing greatness of what the Son of God accomplished for us—the forgiveness of sins. To have forgiveness is to have every blessing of God.

The κόσμος is this planet of sin-infected humanity ruled by Satan, the prince of the world. Though we may suffer in the world now, we shall leave it all behind when we join the victory parade on Resurrection Day.

This verse certainly speaks against those who desire to overcome without Christ. Many attempt to show how spiritually powerful they are with their pietistic, sanctimonious lives. This attitude has pervaded much of American Christianity, where broadcast booths and bookstores permeate our culture with spiritual self-help and how-to ideas. Centuries ago, Luther wrote aptly for our society: "(Yet) when faith is excluded, let no one presume to gain a victory over sin and death. . . . This one text condemns all the books and braggart preachers that have taught methods and rules of conquering (sin)" [WA 20.775f.]. Without faith in the Son of God, there is no victory, only total failure and unending defeat. We are nothing without Christ.

v. 6 — *This is the one who came by water and blood—Jesus Christ. He did not come by water only, but by water and blood. And it is the Spirit who testifies, because the Spirit is the truth.*

Some interpreters intimate—without much justification—that "water and blood" signify Baptism and the Lord's Supper, since these are means of Christ coming to us. Others feel this verse alludes to Christ's pierced side, from which flowed blood and water. These interpretations are hard to exclude, since valuable thoughts may be drawn out of them.

A third, less strained, interpretation fits even better: "Water and blood" refer to two momentous events in Christ's earthly life, his baptism and his crucifixion. The Lamb of God's baptism at the Jordan River marked the beginning of his ministry. Jesus' Father and the Holy Spirit testified that day of his worthiness to be anointed into his ministerial office. Christ's bloody crucifixion at Calvary marked the culmination of his three years of ministry. His spilled blood was accepted as a full payment for the debt of sin levied against the world. Christ had to come by water and blood since both were required by the Father's prophecy.

This interpretation is based on the substantived aorist participle, ὁ ἐλθών, which emphasizes unspecified, untimed action. We are to concentrate on the "happenedness" that Christ "came," and not on the means of Christ's continual coming to us in the sacraments. If John had used a present participle, then the sacramental interpretation would be more justifiable.

The connection between verse 6 and the preceding verses is that a believer's faith needs absolute proof of Christ's purchase of eternal life. In the Scriptures he has presented us with his life and death—water and blood—as unassailable evidence. We accept the truthful testimony of God's Spirit, who moved us to believe the written record of God's salvation story (cf. 5:9, Jn 14:16ff.,26).

Homiletical Suggestions

Sermons preached on the Sundays after Easter often focus on two main emphases: 1) the victorious risen Lord Jesus and 2) victorious Christian living. This particular text allows full development of both themes, so that the preacher can correlate the life of Christ to the life of the Christian. We can point to the Spirit's direct testimony, in the inspired Scriptures, of the historicity and facticity of Christ's victory over sin, death, and Satan. For instance, Peter's sermon in the first lesson (Ac 3:13-15, 17-26) depends on his Spirit-breathed recollection of historical fact. In addition, the preacher can cite the believer's faithful works of love as indirect proof of victory over the world. Many examples of quiet, ordinary faithfulness or of astounding acts of love and courage can underscore the proof of our victory.

The sermon may focus on the victory of God's family:

Children Born of God Are Victorious in Battle

1. They believe in the One who came by water and blood (vv. 1,6)
2. They faithfully obey God's command (vv. 2-4)
3. They overcome the world by faith (vv. 4,5)

Another possibility, less directly derived from the text but implicit in it, focuses on love's victory. Borrowing a popular phrase, the preacher can count the ways that:

Love Conquers All

1. The Father's love won his family for eternity (vv. 1,6)
2. The children's love overcomes the world each day (vv. 2-5)

THIRD SUNDAY OF EASTER

The Scriptures

> First Lesson — *Acts 4:8-12*
> Epistle — *1 John 1:1—2:2*
> Gospel — *Luke 24:36-49*

The Text — 1 John 1:1—2:2

What a wealth of material is provided for us in this text from St. John's first letter! He was writing to believers who were threatened by a gnostic heresy. He was writing to encourage them in their faith, to encourage them not to give in to the false ideas propounded by the heretics. In so doing, he gives us encouragement to solidify the fellowship we have with our God and with our fellow Christians. And he reminds us to live a life of repentance because we have a Savior who has atoned for all of our sins. With such a reminder he has also given us ample motivation to share our faith with others.

> 1:1-4 — *That which was from the beginning, which we have heard, which we have seen with our eyes, which we have looked at and our hands have touched—this we proclaim concerning the Word of life. The life appeared; we have seen it and testify to it, and we proclaim to you the eternal life, which was with the Father and has appeared to us. We proclaim to you what we have seen and heard, so that you also may have fellowship with us. And our fellowship is with the Father and with his Son, Jesus Christ. We write this to make our joy complete.*

At first glance we notice the somewhat awkward way in which John begins this letter. When we work through the Greek we note that John is using this awkward construction to emphasize the work of Christ Jesus.

What is the proper interpretation of the phrase τοῦ λόγου τῆς ζωῆς, "the word of life"? Some have understood this to refer to Jesus. Others have preferred to take this phrase as referring to the gospel. Either interpretation is valid, and neither excludes the other. If we refer to Jesus as the word of life, we are following John's usage in chapter one of his Gospel. "In the beginning was the Word, and the Word was with God, and the Word was God" (Jn 1:1). He also refers to Jesus as the source of life: "In him was life and that life was the light of men" (Jn 1:4).

John had been a witness to Jesus. He had heard, seen, and touched the Savior. He was now proclaiming those facts about Jesus for the benefit of his readers. Through Jesus there is life, life with God now through faith, and life with God forever in heaven.

Those facts concerning Jesus are also the word of life, the gospel. When we proclaim Jesus as the Word of life, we are proclaiming a message which offers and gives spiritual life and eternal life. It is well to use both interpretations of the phrase τοῦ λόγου τῆς ζωῆς because they are so closely connected. Priority, however, should go to the understanding of Jesus as the Word of life, since this is the primary way in which John uses λόγος in his writings.

Now, what is the purpose of proclaiming Jesus Christ and his works in the gospel message? The goal is fellowship. Κοινωνία is more than just a close association with someone. It is something closer than the relationship between spouses. It is that special spiritual relationship established between the true God and those who have saving faith in Jesus Christ. Through faith we are united with the divine, in receipt of all God's blessings.

The goal of our proclamation is fellowship with the true God, and fellowship with one another. It is good to note how we recognize that special relationship with one another. We do so on the basis of the Word, Jesus Christ, and the word, the gospel. There is no other basis for religious fellowship.

Once fellowship with God is established and fellowship with our fellow Christians is recognized there is reason for joy. The ἡμεῖς and ἡμῶν readings in verse 4 are preferred. When there is fellowship among Christians, it is no longer "you" and "I;" it is now "we." The establishment of true Christian fellowship means that you and I, believers, have become "we." We rejoice in this, and our joy is complete. The perfect passive participle denotes completed action with the results of the action continuing in the present.

> 1:5—2:2 — *This is the message we have heard from him and declare to you: God is light; in him there is no darkness at all. If we claim to have fellowship with him yet walk in the darkness, we lie and do not live by the truth. But if we walk in the light, as he is in the light, we have fellowship with one another, and the blood of Jesus, his Son, purifies us from all sin. If we claim to be without sin, we deceive ourselves and the truth is not in us. If we confess our sins, he is faithful and just and will forgive us our sins and purify us from all unrighteous. If we claim we have not sinned, we make him out to be a liar and his word has no place*

in our lives. My children, I write to you so that you will not sin.
But if anybody does sin, we have one who speaks to the Father in
our defense— Jesus Christ, the Righteous One. He is the atoning
sacrifice for our sins, and not only for ours but also for the sins
of the whole world.

John has introduced his letter (1:1-4). Now he begins his message
proper. His message is simple. "God is light; in him there is no darkness at all." Again we hear echoes of John 1. God is pure, without sin,
always reflecting what is right and good. There is nothing in him
that smacks of evil or falsehood. The οὐδεμία added to the negative
οὐκ tells us there is not even a hint of darkness in God.

Since that is the case, there are certain attitudes and actions we
will want to avoid and others we will want to embrace. John begins a
series of five "if" statements. In each one he uses the subjunctive in
the protasis followed by the indicative in the apodosis. In so doing,
John is not accusing his readers of having fallen into the sins mentioned. If he had wanted to do that he would have used εἰ plus the indicative. Instead, he uses ἐαν with the subjunctive to soften his statements. He is not charging his readers with actually holding the false
attitudes referred to. In fact, he includes himself in each one of these
statements. May we be careful to follow the same approach as we
preach.

The first pairing of statements deals with actions. To claim to
have fellowship with God, to be in the light of Christ, means nothing
if our actions say the opposite. If we walk in the darkness we are doing more than slipping into an occasional sin. We are walking
around in a sinful lifestyle, going about in a way clearly opposed to
the light of God.

Rather we want to walk in the light, living so that it is clear we
have rejected sinful lifestyles and attitudes. We want to be reflecting
the light of Christ. Then we have the assurance of being in fellowship
with God, and of having the comfort of cleansing in Christ's blood.
John is not telling us that we will live without sin. He is telling us not
to get trapped in sin and thereby break fellowship with God.

The second pairing of statements deals with our words. To deny
the presence of sin in ourselves is to deceive ourselves. It may seem
as though John is being redundant when he says, ἐαυτοὺς πλανῶμεν
καὶ ἡ ἀλήθεια οὐκ ἔστιν ἐν ἡμῖν. But there are two thoughts here.
Not only are we fooling ourselves if we deny the presence of sin. We
have also lost the truth, that is, the truth of God's Word telling us
that we are sinners.

The solution is honest confession of sin. The promise is this: our faithful God will not abandon penitent sinners, but will comfort us with his forgiveness. We know God is a just God. He who forgives us does not simply excuse sin. He justly punished sin in his Son, and so he is just in cleansing us of those sins.

Verse 10 shows the danger of denying the presence of sin. We make God out to be a liar. God leaves no doubt in his Word about the presence of sin in our lives. To say we are perfect people who don't ever break any of God's commands is to deny what God has spoken about us in his Word. That is denying God and it forfeits the blessed assurance of the gospel: "His word has no place in our lives."

In 2:1 John addresses his readers directly. What he writes encourages us to steer away from sinful thoughts, words, and actions. We want to be shining with the light of God at all times. We must be realistic, however, and John is. We still have a sinful nature. We will fall into disobediences against our God. When that happens, John reminds us, we have help.

We have a παράκλητος. In his writings, John uses this word to refer to both Jesus and the Holy Spirit. Here, it refers to Jesus. He is the intercessor or mediator for sinners. On the basis of his righteous life, he still pleads our case before his Father. Everytime we sin, he is interceding for us in heaven.

The reason he does this is because of what he did here on earth. John takes us right back to the cross. Jesus intercedes because he is the ἱλασμός for every sinner. By becoming sin for us when he was offered on the cross (2 Co 5:21), Jesus has atoned for our sins. God is satisfied that our sins are sufficiently punished, and for Jesus' sake he no longer counts them against us. Because of the atonement, we are no longer fearfully peering at God through a wall of sin. Jesus, as our mediator, gives us the assurance that the wall has been removed. Since Jesus did what he did for the whole world, the atonement he won forms the basis of our proclamation to a world of sinners.

Homiletical Suggestions

This text offers a number of possibilities for preaching. Using the whole text, we key off the idea that we Christians can make claims for ourselves on the basis of Christ's work. We won't claim to be without sin, but we will claim to be in fellowship with God through our Savior's work and the sanctifying effort of the Holy Spirit. In keeping with the season, we can say:

Stake Your Claim on the Risen Christ

1. Declare your fellowship with him (1:1-4, 2:1,2)
2. Demonstrate your fellowship with him (1:5-10)

One can also use shorter portions of the text. Working with 1:5—2:2 gives the opportunity to preach on a life of repentance, as well as the need to prove that repentance with a life of Christian actions and attitudes. This section offers much encouragement and comfort, especially when we consider that John speaks three times of the forgiveness God offers in Jesus Christ. For this outline we key off the word "truth."

Stick with the Truth

1. Lying gets you nowhere (1:6,8,10)
2. Admit your sins (1:5,7,9)
3. Walk in the light of Christ (2:1,2)

The verses of John's introduction (1:1-4) give the opportunity to preach on the subject of fellowship, especially the way we recognize and practice religious fellowship among Christians. John, in dealing with the gnostic heresy, was concerned that people would lose not only their fellowship with God, but also with one another. The following outline might work:

Rejoice in Our Blessed Fellowship

1. With the Father and the Son (1:1,2,3b)
2. With one another (1:3a,4)

150

FOURTH SUNDAY OF EASTER

The Scriptures

> First Lesson — *Acts 4:23-33*
> Epistle — *1 John 3:1,2*
> Gospel — *John 10:11-18*

The Text — 1 John 3:1,2

John wrote his letters to Christians in Asia around 90 A.D., from Ephesus. He wrote to strengthen the pure and growing faith he saw reflected in the lives of his "dear children" in spite of the attacks of false teachers. His first letter is to unspecified readers; his second to a church, the "chosen lady;" and his third to one Gaius, a fellow worker and leader of another congregation.

John wrote in the firm expectation that Jesus was returning. Christians should be ready for Jesus' return at any moment. Already the last of the signs Jesus had given was being accomplished. Many antichrists, those who denied that Jesus is the Christ, had gone out into the world (2:18,22).

The best defense against such antichristian teachers was to respond to the Lord with faith and love. Believers will cling to the fellowship God has given them with himself (3:24). They will purify themselves as they look forward to the glorious day of Jesus' appearing (3:3). They will joyfully accept the testimony of the apostles, eyewitnesses to Jesus' life (1:3).

Their response of faith will show itself in loving lives. John urges his readers to love one another and cherish the fellowship they have with each other (3:18). They are to resist sin in their lives, confessing their sins to God and leading others to repentance. Their faith will test their religious teachers and avoid all who speak as antichrist or are infected with the world's viewpoint (4:1,5).

Simple in style and language, John's words speak to the hearts of "dear children" of God. The sermon text picks up John's argument that God's love has made us his children and that we look forward to the day we will be like him.

> v. 1 — *How great is the love the Father has lavished on us, that we should be called children of God! And that is what we are! The reason the world does not know us is that it did not know him.*

John invited his readers to marvel with him at the greatness of God the Father's love. Ποταπήν, introducing an indirect question, emphasizes the greatness, the surprisingly different nature, of the love which the Father has given his believers. The unique nature of that love finds expression in "lavished." Καὶ ἐσμέν is a simple interjection. John emphatically blurts it out, almost in surprise, for he can hardly believe it himself, so great is the Father's love for us.

God's love, ἀγάπην, is his one-sided, unconditional love. John later (4:10) describes this love in action: God "sent his Son as an atoning sacrifice for our sins." Jesus provided a more familiar description in John 3:16. It is a sacrificial, no-holds-barred type of love which will go any distance, pay any price, to reclaim our lost race for God. The Father's love is so amazing because it is so undeserved. The forgiveness Jesus won for us on the cross made us part of God's family. This, too, is a description of God's love. Ἵνα κληθῶμεν is not a purpose clause. Rather, it explains ἀγάπην. A similar construction occurs with ἀγάπη in 5:3, where it defines love *for* God.

The world does not really understand believers. In John's vocabulary γινώσκω means more than knowledge by experience. It is a loving and living association with what is known. Believers "know" God, enjoy fellowship with him, trust in him, and live in him. It is the knowledge of faith, love, and fellowship.

The world is a stranger to God's gospel love. That's the reason (διὰ τοῦτο points ahead to the ὅτι clause) the world does not really understand believers. It does not accept Jesus as Lord nor does it listen to God's voice expressed through the apostolic testimony. Since the world, under the control of sin and the devil, destined only for hell, has no room for God, it also has no room for believers. The life of faith is a mystery and threat to the world which fills itself with the lie. The lives of believers condemn everything which the world brags of and boasts about. Ὅτι is causal, "because." No wonder there is hostility toward believers. No wonder there is apostasy in the church. God's views and the world's views cannot coexist.

v. 2 — *Dear friends, now we are children of God, and what we will be has not yet been made known. But we know that when he appears, we shall be like him, for we shall see him as he is.*

"Dear friends" weakly renders ἀγαπητοί in this case. John is addressing those who are the objects of God's love. They are the children dearly, wonderfully loved by God.

John takes the status believers enjoy, that of children of God, and uses that status to instill an eager expectation for the future glory

152

that will be ours. This eager expectation, in turn, will empower Christians to purify themselves in this life, confessing sin, walking in the light, living a life of love for the one who loved us so well. There is a switch in focus, from the love of God the Father to the return of God the Son.

Νῦν sets up the temporal comparison. Now we have all these blessings. Where will it end? What's the limit of what God will do for us? Οὔπω concludes the comparison. We just don't know. God's love outruns our wildest imaginations. "No eye has seen, no ear has heard" what God has prepared for those who love him. Only when God reveals it to us on the Last Day will we know for sure what we will be, what that life in heaven will hold for us.

We do, however, firmly know and hold dear—οἴδαμεν is emphatic by position—one of the realities that will be ours for all eternity. Whenever Jesus is revealed from heaven, ἐαν φανερωθῇ, we absolutely, positively will be like him.

John quickly explains why believers will be like Jesus. "Because (ὅτι) we will see him as he is." On the Last Day Jesus will return in glory. Other passages of Scripture describe his appearance in this exalted state. Old Testament believers feared to come face-to-face with God when he appeared in their world (Moses at the burning bush, Isaiah in the temple). After the first miraculous catch of fish Peter expressed this same fear when he told Jesus to depart from him, for he was a sinful man. Sin causes human beings to cringe before God. His holiness threatens to consume unholy people.

The concept of fear, however, is totally absent from John's words. We will not fear to gaze upon Jesus in his heavenly glory on the Last Day because we ourselves will be changed. The sinful human nature, that root of evils and sins, will be destroyed. This is the essence of our life in heaven, one of perfect righteousness and innocence and blessedness. Just as Jesus is holy and perfectly sinless, so will we be in heaven. How that promise thrills us!

There is a hint of progression in John's words. Children grow up. They mature. They gain wisdom and stature. They acquire abilities. So it is with Christians. On the Last Day we will reach the maturity to which God called us when he created faith in us. Unlike a child who in and of himself has the potential for physical and mental maturation, our spiritual maturation is due solely to God's amazing love for us.

Homiletical Suggestions

The Easter season emphasizes the certainty of our Lord's resurrection from the dead and the certainty of our own resurrection. It is a time of joy. Easter also compels us to proclaim and witness Jesus' resurrection in our lives and in our world. It is a time of purpose. Joy and purpose are both evident on Good Shepherd Sunday, the Fourth Sunday of Easter.

The First Lesson shows the hostility of the world and the weakness of Christians who are trying to proclaim the risen Christ in that world. But it also shows the power of the risen and living Christ who protects his believers from the world and inspires them to continue to "speak the Word of God boldly."

In the Gospel readings Jesus tells his flock that he came to carry out the Father's will in spite of opposition from thieves and robbers. He came to lay down his life on the cross and to take it up again so that others may know and benefit from his loving care as their Good Shepherd. The Epistle reading provides the link between the words of Jesus and the actions of the early Christians. John's message provides encouragement and motivation for spreading the news of our Good Shepherd.

The mission emphasis explicit in the First Lesson and implicit in the Epistle (the sermon text) might suggest this treatment:

Let Them Know the Father's Love

1. He calls us his children (v. 1)
2. He will crown us with glory (v. 2)

To emphasize the Easter resurrection theme, the following treatment may be in order:

Gifts of God's Lavish Love

1. A new life as God's children (v. 1)
2. An unimaginable life as God's heirs (v. 2)

Since we have traditionally used Good Shepherd Sunday as a day for emphasis on worker training, the following treatment of the text may be appropriate:

Shepherd the Flock of Jesus

1. Remind us of our Father's love (v. 1)
2. Reveal our God to the world (v. 1b)
3. Inspire us with the glory to come (v. 2)

FIFTH SUNDAY OF EASTER

The Scriptures

> First Lesson — *Acts 8:26-40*
> Epistle — *1 John 3:18-24*
> Gospel — *John 15:1-8*

The Text — 1 John 3:16-24

The simple, yet profound, language of the Apostle John's first letter proclaims the message of God's love in Christ. Various noun and verb forms of ἀγάπη appear over 40 times in this short epistle to drive home this main point.

The recipients of the letter, probably the Christians in Ephesus and the Roman province of Asia, needed this reminder of God's love to give them absolute assurance of salvation and to promote true Christian love in their congregations.

They also needed to combat the false teaching of the gnostic heretics of the late 1st century. Cerinthus, a gnostic teacher active in Ephesus, cast doubt on God's love in Christ by denying that Jesus is God incarnate. In his letter John establishes with eyewitness testimony that Jesus is true man and true God in all his work, so that "the blood of Jesus, his Son, purifies us from all sin" (1:7).

Furthermore, John attacks the gnostic tendency toward licentiousness by preaching true Christian love. This love, motivated by God's love in Christ, leads to righteousness, obedience, obedience to God's commands, and genuine brotherly love.

The sermon text comes from a section which teaches that God's children show they belong to him by their love. Very simply, the apostle has stated: "We should love one another" (3:11b). Or, as a familiar folk hymn states, "They'll know we are Christians by our love."

We have expanded the pericope to include verses 16 and 17.

v. 16 — *This is how we know what love is: Jesus Christ laid down his life for us. And we ought to lay down our lives for our brothers.*

In contrast to hatred which manifests itself in murder (vv. 12-15), love manifests itself "in this" (ἐν τούτῳ)—giving one's life for others. John writes, "*We* know" what love is. Knowing what love entails is a corporate experience, enjoyed together with other believers. "To know" here is the knowledge of personal experience (ἐγνώκαμεν), since

Christ's love is personally experienced by the believer and becomes the foundation for showing love to others. The verb is perfect active indicative. The action is completed, but the results continue. Christ's love in action is a demonstrated fact, and believers know, experience, and share it.

This is not love as an emotion, but as a choice. Christ chose to love sinners who did not deserve his love. He demonstrated his love for the world by his death on the cross. "Greater love has no one than this, that he lay down his life for his friends" (Jn 15:13). Life is the most precious gift because it has no price and cannot be replaced. If that's how Jesus loved us, then "we ought to lay down our lives for our brothers."

The believer mirrors his Savior's love in his own life. Again there is emphasis on the corporate nature of love: *"We"* ought . . ." and the address to "brothers." Believers have a family obligation to give of themselves to others, even to the point of death. "We ought," says Paul, but this love is not forced or given grudgingly. The obligation is not carried out by force of the law, but is motivated and made possible by the message of Christ's love, the gospel.

v. 17 — *If anyone has material possessions and sees his brother in need but has not pity on him, how can the love of God be in him?*

The believer who is willing to give the irreplaceable gift of his own life will not hesitate to share the replaceable. First, the believer is willing to give up the ψυχή (v. 16)—the breath of life. Then he is also willing to give βίος—the things of life, the means of subsistence. The Christian has the unique perspective of seeing his possessions as gifts from God to be used, among other things, to provide for the needs of his brothers in Christ. The believer understands that possessions are only for this world, so he uses them to benefit others in this world.

When the love of God dwells in a person's heart, he is moved deeply by the needs of others, moved to help. It is the person who does not have the love of God in him who has no pity on his brother in need.

v. 18 — *Dear children, let us not love with words or tongue but with actions and in truth.*

The child of God is no hypocrite. He doesn't pretend to love.

John speaks in terms of endearment to his readers—dear children, literally "little children" (τεκνία). Jesus addressed his disciples in the same loving manner. The apostle himself is sincere in love as he urges sincere love on his readers.

Christian love is not all talk and no action. John emphatically declares, "Let us *not* love with words or tongue" alone. He uses the stronger negative μή, which denies even the thought of something, placing it at the beginning of the phrase for emphasis. Words are appropriate for making promises and commitments of love. If we never do what we say, however, the words are meaningless.

Christian love differs completely from the empty promises of love some make. 'Αλλά is the strong adversative—something totally other. "With actions and in truth" means that Christians will be known more by what is done than by what is said. Good intentions result in a mission accomplished. Actually carrying out the acts of love is the proof that love really dwells in the believer's heart and influences him (cf. Jas 2:15-17).

To be sure, our love will always be imperfect, stained by sin, even when love is sincere and motivated by Christ's love. We have this assurance:

vv. 19,20 — *This then is how we know that we belong to the truth, and how we set our hearts at rest in his presence whenever our hearts condemn us. For God is greater than our hearts, and he knows everything.*

Those who "belong to the truth" are believers in the Truth, Jesus Christ (Jn 14:6). They do not deceive themselves into thinking they have no sin as do those who deny the truth. Neither do they "crucify" themselves for their sins, since they know the truth that Jesus paid for the world's guilt on the cross. Those who deny the truth must try to still their guilty consciences with some kind of work-righteousness. We look to the spiritual rest God brings us in love through Christ.

"This . . . is how we set our hearts at rest in his presence whenever our hearts condemn us." Our hearts condemn us every day. The child of God knows he has failed many times to love as God desires him to love. That's enough of a burden, but God, who "is greater than our hearts and knows everything," even sees sins we are not aware of (Ps 19:12).

At the same time God's knowing everything includes this, that he chose us to be his children through faith in Christ. The restless conscience is given rest through the forgiveness Christ won for the world (Mt 11:28).

vv. 21,22 — *Dear friends, if our hearts do not condemn us, we have confidence before God and receive from him anything we ask, because we obey his commands and do what pleases him.*

John again addresses his readers with affection, this time using the term ἀγαπητοί—beloved. In this setting they are those who have received Christ's ἀγάπη. Because of Christ's love "our hearts do not condemn us." The stronger negative μή is used here, as in verse 18, so that we might translate, "Our hearts do no even think of condemning us."

There is no condemnation for those who belong to Jesus (Ro 8:1), so that "we have confidence before God." The child of God does not hesitate to speak freely and confidently with the One who loves him. When the believer talks to God, it is like talking to a best friend. There is no subject matter off limits. For he is our greatest friend.

We "receive from him anything we ask." We can ask anything of someone who loves us, knowing he will do what is best for us. Jesus made this same promise on several occasions (Jn 14:13,14; 15:7; 16:23,24). We understand that certain limitations go with the promise. The child of God, according to his new man, does not ask for anything that is not good for him. Also, God does not give us anything that is not good for us.

The main point is that we remain in such a state of love that we may approach God "with freedom and confidence." (Eph 3:12). As we remain in his love, we show our love for him "because we obey his commands and do what pleases him." Obedience is not the cause of God's love, but the result of it. The grateful person whose life has been saved by another says, "Your wish is my command." Τηροῦμεν, present active, indicates that we continually obey, keep and carefully attend to, God's commands. We say along with Jesus, "I always do what pleases him" (Jn 8:29).

v. 23 — *And this is his command: to believe in the name of his Son, Jesus Christ, and to love one another as he commanded us.*

There is no burden in obeying the command to believe in Jesus. If the burden were on us to decide to believe, we could never be certain if we had done it right. This is, however, a gospel command. The words themselves have the power to bring us to faith even as they ask us to come to faith. God's command to believe is the invitation and offer of his grace.

God so loves us that he commands or wills that we believe "in the name of his Son, Jesus Christ." Jesus' name stands for everything he is or has done. By calling on this name, we are saved (Ro 10:13; Ac 4:12). Three names are given here: 1) Son = God's Son, fully divine and thus able to pay for the world's sin; 2) Jesus = Savior, whom God sent to bear the world's sin; 3) Christ = Anointed One, set apart by God to serve as Prophet, Priest, and King.

Those who believe in Jesus' name are to "love one another as he commanded us." Ἀγαπῶμεν is subjunctive, according with πιστεύσωμεν and still part of the ἵνα clause. Note that John does not say, "We should, must, or ought to love one another." Rather, he states a simple fact. One who believes in Jesus Christ is to love others, just as Christ himself (the subject of ἔδωκεν) gave command (Jn 13:34).

v. 24 — *Those who obey his commands live in him, and he in them. And this is how we know that he lives in us: We know it by the Spirit he gave us.*

He who continues to obey (ὁ τηρῶν) continues to live (μένει) in him. The mindset of the Christian is continual obedience and love because Christ lives in him (καὶ αὐτὸς ἐν αὐτῷ). Since Christ lives in us, we are able to do what we would never be able to do without him—to truly love others.

God loves us and dwells in us by the Holy Spirit. This cannot be seen or proven. It is an invisible dwelling. Yet there are visible tangible evidences of it. Our works of love are the fruit of the Spirit. They show on the outside what exists on the inside. "By this all men will know that you are my disciples, if you love one another" (Jn 13:35).

Homiletical Suggestions

In the Easter Season we celebrate the joy of our Savior's victory. His resurrection guarantees our justification. It also motivates and effects our sanctification as we are raised from our dead sinful nature to serve God with the new life we have received. John's words encourage the sanctified life of Christian love.

We all understand that every person needs love. There is a universal need to feel accepted and worthwhile. A person needs a sense of life's purpose and the security of being loved. The text shows how God provides our security and significance in the love of Christ.

Specific law application: We have a personal responsibility to love others. Here it is sad and unfortunate that we are by nature cold and loveless. Our "love" is limited to those closest to us or to those from whom we receive benefit. Instead of a gift, our love may be a tool, withheld or given to control others. It is not love that causes a spouse to berate his partner, harshly criticizing every little fault. It is not love that withdraws affection from a child until he behaves. It is not love that shirks our responsibility to rebuke the sinner, to correct or discipline children.

Why are there unwanted children, so unloved that they are killed in the womb? Why are there people who are so lonely that they commit suicide? Why are there teenagers so desperate for love that they grasp for the physical "love" of promiscuous sex? Why are there elderly people in their own homes or in nursing homes with broken hearts, just waiting to die? Why are there prisoners who have sat in a cell for years without receiving any visitors? We must confess, our love has been inadequate.

Specific gospel illustration: Perhaps you remember the true story of what took place in the nursery of an orphanage. Physically healthy babies were mysteriously dying. The mystery was not solved until a connection was noticed between personal loving attention and physical health. "Professional mothers" were hired to cuddle the babies, holding them close and warm, gently caressing them. The babies lived.

God's love in Christ is like God picking us up in the orphanage. We were outcasts from his family because of sin. Yet, for the sake of Jesus he picks us up and makes us secure, significant, and worthwhile. Though we often fail to demonstrate that we are his children, though our conduct is often more infantile than mature, he is there to love us still, unchanging and constant, the perfect Father.

Here are two outlines, each utilizing a part of the text:

Love Has No Limit

1. Love is unlimited in giving (vv. 16,17)
2. Love is unlimited in acting (v. 18)
3. Love is unlimited in comforting (vv. 19,20)

Live in Jesus' Love

1. Trust it (vv. 21-23a)
2. Reflect it (vv. 23b,24)

SIXTH SUNDAY OF EASTER

The Scriptures

> First Lesson — *Acts 11:19-30*
> Epistle — *1 John 4:1-11*
> Gospel — *John 15:9-17*

The Text — 1 John 4:1-11

True children of God believe the truth and love one another (3:11-24). Now, John exhorts his beloved readers to test all spiritual teachers and believe only those who are found to be from God. They are to see that they go on loving one another, which is the characteristic of people who are from God. The text is most easily divided into two main parts, verses 1-6 and verses 7-11.

> v. 1 — *Dear friends, do not believe every spirit, but test the spirits to see whether they are from God, because many false prophets have gone out into the world.*

Believing everybody can be just as dangerous as believing nobody. Because many pseudo-prophets have gone out into the world, proclaiming their various messages and claiming to be God's inspired spokesmen, Christians dare not accept uncritically any and all "spirits." There is an on-going need for critical assessment of all who claim to speak for God.

A gullible person can be too easily impressed by purported signs and wonders performed by this or that "prophet." Or one might fall for the charisma, the personal magnetism, of a preacher. Some might be attracted by outward show or success or power. Others might be induced by the appearance of great scholarship or intellect. There are indeed many pseudo-prophets in the world, and people who want to listen to God's message must be on guard, must carefully test, must critically examine all such teachers to see "whether they are from God"—or not.

> vv. 2,3 — *This is how you can recognize the Spirit of God. Every spirit that acknowledges that Jesus Christ has come in the flesh is from God, but every spirit that does not acknowledge Jesus is not from God. This is the spirit of the antichrist, which you have heard is coming and even now is already in the world.*

There is no way we can test the teachers' hearts to see if they are genuine or not, but we don't need to. All we need to test is their confession, and this is a decisive test. John tells us that we can know, we can recognize, the Spirit of God at work in a teacher by applying this test. Does he confess openly and boldly that Jesus, the man, is the Christ, the Son of God come into the flesh? Does the so-called prophet acknowledge Jesus as the incarnate Son of the Father? Does he profess Jesus Christ as God and man, human and divine?

We understand, of course, that John is not limiting the test to one or two doctrines about the person of Christ. The truth about Jesus certainly includes and involves the entire gospel.

Anyone who does not confess the full truth about Jesus Christ is, or has the spirit of, the antichrist. That prophet or preacher or teacher cannot be from God, since his message clearly is not from God. Those who deny the Son in any way do not have the Father (2:23), nor do they possess the Spirit. Their doctrine has another source.

v. 4 — *You, dear children, are from God and have overcome them, because the one who is in you is greater than the one who is in the world.*

John's readers, his "dear children," are from God. They are God's true children and have overcome the false teachers by not falling for their falsehoods. This was not due to any special quality of their own but simply because the Spirit of truth was at work in them. Indeed, the one in them (God) is greater than the one who is in the world (the devil). The Spirit of truth has defeated the father of lies again and again. What a world of comfort for weary sinners, worn by their weaknesses and by warring against Satan, lies in these words. The Spirit, who speaks in the Word, by that same Word dwells in us, and thus we, too, are greater than the world.

vv. 5,6 — *They are from the world and therefore speak from the viewpoint of the world, and the world listens to them. We are from God, and whoever knows God listens to us; but whoever is not from God does not listen to us. This is how we recognize the Spirit of truth and the spirit of falsehood.*

Another way to test teachers is by considering their audience. False teachers have no trouble gathering a following in this world because they speak the world's language; they tell the world what it likes to hear, they scratch itching ears. In contrast, John says, we (the apostles and those who teach the apostolic word) *are from God*, as our message demonstrates. And God's real people are glad to listen to that message from the real messengers. The sheep listen to the Shepherd's voice. All on the side of truth listen to Jesus and his spokesmen (cp. Jn 8:47; 10:16; 18:37). Those, however, who are not from God don't want to listen to messengers who are from God.

This, then, is how we can without a doubt recognize the Spirit of truth and the spirit of falsehood and determine which is at work in any particular preacher or teacher. We examine the message to see if it is the full truth about Jesus Christ, and we consider the audience to see if it is people of the world or people of God.

vv. 7,8 — *Dear friends, let us love one another, for love comes from God. Everyone who loves has been born of God and knows God. Whoever does not love does not know God, because God is love.*

John moves on to another mark of God's true children, love. The Greek play on words is lost in the English, especially in the NIV. "Beloved, let us love," the apostle writes. Believers who are bound together in the confession of the truth about Jesus Christ will demonstrate their unity and their "family ties" by loving one another with the love of God. This love (*agape*) comes from God and can't be known, experienced, or shown apart from God. Those who have it in their lives thus have evidence that they are God's children and that they really do know him.

Those, on the other hand, who claim to be God's children but do not love are wrong in their claim. They aren't related to God; they don't know him. Since God's very nature is love, the child of God will reflect that nature, will resemble the Father in that respect. Where there is no resemblance, there is no relationship. The true children of God manifest the nature of the Father, at least to some degree. They love, though never perfectly, always imperfectly, haltingly, and sometimes weakly. Yet *agape* is there!

vv. 9,10 — *This is how God showed his love among us: He sent his one and only Son into the world that we might live through him. This is love: not that we loved God, but that he loved us and sent his Son as an atoning sacrifice for our sins.*

God is love—that's one basis for God's children to love one another. Here's another: because God demonstrated his love for us in the most marvelous way! Though this world was as unlovable as it could possibly be, God loved it, loved us, loved sinners so much that he sent his Son. God gave his one and only, sent him into the world so that we might live through him.

God's love manifested itself in loving action, the ultimate loving action in the ultimate self-sacrifice, for that's what love is. Love is doing what is good for the other person, regardless of the cost or consequences for self. God gave the best. The Father commissioned his Son to save the world, and no greater demonstration of love was possible.

That Son came in the flesh to be the "atoning sacrifice" for our sins. Jesus the Lamb, Jesus the Victim, Jesus the Substitute for sinners—that's the heart of the gospel of our salvation. Jesus is the God-given propitiation, the covering for all the sins of all sinners (2:2). By his holy blood and by his vicarious death sinners have been redeemed, not because we were lovable but because God is love and because God so loved.

v. 11 — *Dear friends, since God so loved us, we also ought to love one another.*

This is the obvious deduction. No one who has been to the cross of Christ and experienced God's saving love can return to a life of self-love. The love of Christ frees, motivates, empowers—and we love. Yes, we love God (vv. 19,20), but the real visible proof is in our love for one another. Children who are born of God do reflect the nature of God. Sinners who have been forgiven through Christ do imitate the *agape* of their Savior-God (cp. 3:16-18; Jn 13:35; 15:12; 1 Pe 1:22).

Homiletical Suggestions

While the particular Sunday of the Church Year doesn't offer too much specific guidance for the preacher, the Scripture readings do coordinate with the sermon text rather well. The first lesson describes the Antioch church, blessed with spirit-filled preachers, teachers, and prophets—all of whom spoke the truth about Jesus Christ. In the Gospel Jesus emphasizes his will for his followers: "Love each other as I have loved you."

Here are two possible ways to approach this text—the first treats verses 1-6 and the second treats the entire text.

Test Before You Trust

1. Examine the message (vv. 1-3)
2. Consider the source (vv. 5,6)

Blest Be the Tie That Binds

1. The truth of God unites those who confess it (vv. 1-6)
2. The love of God binds those who manifest it (vv. 7-11)

ASCENSION OF OUR LORD

The Scriptures

First Lesson — *Acts 1:1-11*
Epistle — *Ephesians 1:16-25*
Gospel — *Luke 24:44-53*

The Text — Ephesians 1:16-23

It is generally agreed that Paul wrote this letter around 60 A.D., from Rome, during his first imprisonment there (Ac 28). Paul had spent two years and three months in Ephesus, on his third missionary journey (Ac 19). It was his longest stint in one city. Ephesus had served as the base from which the gospel had spread throughout the province of Asia (Ac 19:26). The Ephesian Christians were close to his heart, as shown by his tearful farewell to the elders (Ac 20:17-38).

Now, in prison, Paul hears that they are still fighting the good fight (1:15). It seems from this letter that the Ephesians were well grounded in their faith. Paul does not correct any doctrinal errors as he does in most of his letters. He writes to instruct and encourage these good Christians further. The first verses of this letter contain words of greeting (1,2) and praise to God for the spiritual blessings he has lavished on the Ephesian believers (3-14).

v. 16 — *I have not stopped giving thanks for you, remembering you in my prayers.*

Paul, like Jesus, was a model of prayer. He prayed often, and he prayed thankfully. When he prayed for the Ephesians, he first gave thanks to God for the faith they had and the love they showed (v. 15).

v. 17 — *I keep asking that the God of our Lord Jesus Christ, the glorious Father, may give you the Spirit of wisdom and revelation, so that you may know him better.*

Why does Paul use this striking name for God the Father: "the God of our Lord Jesus Christ"? Keep in mind that Paul uses this name for God in the context of prayer. We are reminded that when Jesus himself was on earth he prayed to the Father as his God. As God the Father always answered God the Son, so also Paul is confident of being heard. So also we can confidently pray to the God of our Lord Jesus Christ.

Paul first requests God to give his Ephesian friends "the Spirit of wisdom and revelation, so that [they] may know [God] better." What does this mean? Although Paul mentions "revelation" second, let's consider it first. Paul is not talking about revelation in the sense of imparting something nobody else knows or can know. "I experienced a revelation" might mean, "In a special and miraculous way God revealed something to me and to nobody else." God did do that for the Bible-writing prophets and apostles by giving them special revelations of his will.

Paul, however, is praying God to give them the Spirit so that they will hunger and thirst to dig deeper into the Spirit-produced revelation, the gospel. The Ephesians have the Old Testament Scriptures. They have this Spirit-inspired letter from Paul. Perhaps they already are familiar with or possess copies of other New Testament writings. Paul prays that God will give them the desire to be taught by the revealed Word.

Then they would also have true wisdom. When Paul asks God to give them the Spirit of wisdom he is asking God to give them what comes from knowing his Word and his will. This wisdom can come only from studying God's ἀποκάλυψις, the Scriptures.

As they do this they will "know him better." Adam and Eve had intimate knowledge of God before the Fall. They walked and talked with him. They knew him as we know our best friends, even better. That intimate knowledge is lost to unregenerate sinners. But as reborn children of God we regain that knowledge. As we grow in faith through the hearing and study of God's Word (gain wisdom through the study of God's revelation), we get to know our Savior God better and better. That's what Paul prays will happen for his readers. What a wonderful prayer to pray on behalf of our fellow Christians!

v. 18 — *I pray also that the eyes of your heart may be enlightened in order that you may know the hope to which he has called you, the riches of his glorious inheritance in the saints,*

The next gift which Paul asks God to give the Ephesians is "enlightened eyes of the heart." The ancients considered the heart to be the seat of not only the emotions but also of the intellect. To pray that the eyes of someone's heart be enlightened means to pray that they know something.

This is what Paul prays the Ephesians will know: "the hope to which he has called you." Hope is a forward-looking joyful feeling. On earth, hope is often shaky. "I hope my car makes it" indicates considerable doubt that it will. Overly hopeful people can be too gullible and then be crushed when their high hopes prove to be in vain.

Paul, however, is talking about the hope of God's calling. This is the hope that is connected to the call of God when he called us to faith. This hope is certain, not shaky. It is not gullible hopefulness but confidence based on the promises of God. It is the sure knowledge that one day we will be in full possession of something we do not yet completely have but which God has promised us: heaven. That's what God has called us to.

Paul also prays that the eyes of their hearts will be enlightened to know "the riches of his glorious inheritance in the saints." Some commentators interpret κληρονομίας αὐτοῦ to mean God's inheritance, the harvest of souls which God will receive on the last day. In this view Paul is praying that the Ephesians will know that they are part of that inheritance.

More likely Paul is praying that the Ephesians will have better knowledge of the inheritance which *they* will be receiving. "His inheritance" then means the inheritance which God gives. Ἐν can be translated "among." Αὐτοῦ can also be understood as genitive of source. The expression can then be understood: "the inheritance among the saints, which has its source in God."

v. 19 — *and his incomparably great power for us who believe. That power is like the working of his mighty strength,*

God, of course, has power. He made the universe. He holds it together. The final part of Paul's prayer is that the Ephesians might know God's power "for us who believe." He wants them to know and feel how God imparts his power to the hearts and lives of his believers.

They had already experienced God's power when the Holy Spirit smashed their stony hearts and brought them to repentance and faith. Paul wants them to grow in their knowledge of how God can bring that power to bear in our lives. God unleashes that power into the lives of believers in many ways. He does it when he strengthens our faith through the means of grace. He does it when we grow in understanding of his will through the study of his Word. He does it when he helps us to do his will, difficult as that can be. He does it when he strengthens us in time of temptation. He does it when he gives us courage to bear up under persecution. He does it when he emboldens us to share the gospel. He does it when he gives us strength to bear crushing physical and emotional burdens.

v. 20 — *which he exerted in Christ when he raised him from the dead and seated him at his right hand in the heavenly realms,*

Paul's mention of the mighty strength which God can exert in our lives leads to a new thought. God also exerted that mighty strength in the life of Jesus. How he does so has meaning and comfort for us. God exerted his mighty strength in Christ when he raised him from the dead. On Easter morning God made the dead body of Jesus alive. Such is the mighty strength of God, which he exerted in Christ.

He did more. He seated Christ at his right hand in the heavenly realms. Thus Paul affirms Jesus' ascension, the event which we celebrate today. In Acts 1, Luke describes the ascension from the viewpoint of the disciples who were beneath the cloud which received Jesus. In the Gospel Mark describes Jesus' ascension as though he were above the cloud: ". . . He sat at the right hand of God" (Mk 16:19). We know, of course, that "the right hand of God" is an expression for the position of power and authority. Ascension Day reminds us that Jesus now occupies that place of power and authority.

v. 21 — *far above all rule and authority, power, and dominion, and every title that can be given, not only in the present age but also in the one to come.*

An immature mind could ask some pointless questions about this verse. What kind of rules, authorities, powers, dominions, and titles does Paul have in mind? What kind of rules, authorities, etc., will there be in the next life, other than God and the angels? It is fruitless to be distracted by such questions. Paul is making a simple comforting point here. Let us simply be comforted by it. His point is that at the right hand of God Jesus now and forever occupies the place of authority above any power or authority—benevolent or hostile—that could ever exist in any way.

We know there are different kinds of authority here on earth, leaders in government, etc. There is a spiritual power which is evil and hostile, the devil and his minions. There is the friendly power of the angels. Jesus is above them all.

v. 22 — *And God placed all things under his feet and appointed him to be head over everything for the church,*

The first clause restates verse 21. The new and striking thought in this verse is that Jesus is the head over everything for the church. Jesus does not bask in all that power and authority. He uses it on behalf of his church. He protects his believers from their enemies. He adds to the numbers of his church by causing the gospel to be shared all over the globe and by sending his Holy Spirit to bring souls to faith through that gospel.

v. 23 — *which is his body, the fullness of him who fills every-thing in every way.*

The church as the body of Christ is a familiar Pauline expression. In this verse he says that the church as Christ's body is "the fullness of him who fills everything in every way." The church complements and completes Christ. It is his manifestation in the world. This is pure grace. It is not out of necessity, as though he needed a body. Rather, we are his body because in his love he chose us to be so. We do not deserve such honor.

Paul employs a neat play on words which also reminds us that the church is not Christ's body in a physical sense. The church is the full-ness of Christ, but Christ is the one "who fills everything in every way." The church fills out Christ, but Christ fills everything.

What does it mean that Christ "fills everything in every way"? The sense seems to be that of Romans 11:36: ". . . from him and through him and to him are all things"; and Acts 17:28, ". . . in whom we live and move and have our being." Christ sustains everything. Without him nothing could exist.

Homiletical Suggestions

This text has an obvious two-part division. Verses 16-19 are Paul's prayer for the Ephesians. Verses 20-23 provide encouraging informa-tion for the church as a whole: Jesus our Head is controlling every-thing on our behalf.

This text is for a specific festival, the Ascension of our Lord. Aspects of the other readings can be incorporated into the sermon. The reading from Acts recounts Jesus' ascension and the angels' promise that he will return. It also shows the disciples' lack of understanding (Ac 1:7). They needed the "Spirit of revelation and wisdom," so that they could grow in their understanding of God's purposes. The Gospel reading tells us how Jesus' pre-ascension instructions led them to wait joyfully for the gift of the Holy Spirit. That same Lord of the Church still in-structs us through the Word which he gave us through them.

It is natural to follow the two-part division of the text. The outline should do justice to the occasion of the Ascension.

Our Ascended Lord Blesses Us

1. He helps us grow in faith (vv. 16-19)
2. He shepherds his church (vv. 20-23)

The sermon could focus on what is happening since Jesus disap-peared behind the cloud:

The Rest of the Ascension Story

1. Our ascended Lord helps his believers grow in faith (vv. 16-19)
2. Our ascended Lord uses his power on behalf of his church (vv. 20-25)

The theme may be put in the form of a prayer, in keeping with the tone of verses 16-19.

May Our Ascended Lord Bless Us

1. As individual believers (vv. 16-19)
2. As his body the church (vv. 20-25)

Utilizing only verses 20-23:

Jesus Reigns to Eternity

1. Trust him wholeheartedly (vv. 20-22a)
2. Serve him humbly (vv. 22a,23)
3. Proclaim him confidently (v. 22)

SEVENTH SUNDAY OF EASTER

The Scriptures

First Reading — *Acts 1:15-26*
Epistle — *1 John 4:13-21*
Gospel — *John 17:11b-19*

The Text — 1 John 4:13-21

The primary problem which John addresses in his first epistle is an early form of gnosticism. Gnosticism's basic tenet was that the spiritual is good while the physical is bad. Some gnostics concluded that as long as you sang the "Hallelujahs" and "Amens" on your spiritual side on Sunday morning, it didn't matter what you did with your body on Saturday night or in your life during the rest of the week. One of John's emphases in this letter is to stress that God has redeemed us body and soul. If God's love has sanctified our hearts, that love will radiate into our lives as well. If he has graciously led us to faith and a change of heart, our outward lives will also be changed, and good works will naturally follow and showcase that love.

This brings us to a key concept in our text, love. The word "love" is used *fourteen* times in our text. It is also used thirteen times in the previous six verses and five times in the following three verses. It is critical that our congregation understand love before an in-depth study of the text can commence.

In English, unfortunately, we are stuck with one word which covers three distinctly different Greek words: ἀγάπη, φιλία, and ἔρως. The word used exclusively in our text is ἀγάπη. This is divine love. This is self-sacrificing love. This is love which compels me to do what is best for you, even though it is inconvenient or painful for me.

An example might make it more concrete for our hearers. You are walking along the shore. Suddenly you see a gaunt, sickly man stagger out of the water and collapse on the beach. He isn't breathing. You realize that mouth-to-mouth resuscitation may be his only chance. The thought occurs, "What if he has AIDS? I don't even know him." Self-sacrificing love, ἀγάπη, compels you to help, in spite of possible danger to yourself. The best and best-known example of such love is that summarized in John 3:16. God didn't have to love in that way, but he did! That is the love of which John speaks in our text.

vv. 13,14 — *We know that we live in him and he in us, because he has given us his Spirit. And we have seen and testify that the Father has sent his Son to be the Savior of the world.*

The opening two verses serve as a bridge between Ascension and Pentecost. Jesus promised that the Spirit would come, and he did. Jesus assured the disciples that the Counselor would open their eyes and teach them all things. Those 'things' were the real meaning, purpose, and result of Jesus' life and death. He is the Savior of the world. It was only after Pentecost that they fully realized why Jesus had to leave them at his ascension.

The verbs in this section which tell what God did are all in the perfect tense. God did it; it's done; the benefits of his doing go on. What did he do? He carried out his salvation plan for us. It was *he* who gave his Spirit and he who sent his Son.

Our living in him and his living in us is not the result of a mutual contract. It is the result of his loving plan to save us, and he alone is responsible for this relationship. The word translated "live" is μένω. The English "remain" carries more weight than "live." It describes an ongoing relationship. He sent, he established, he gave our eternal relationship. He is the Source of all that is called love in the following verses.

vv. 15,16 — *If anyone acknowledges that Jesus is the Son of God, God lives in him and he in God. And so we know and rely on the love God has for us. God is love. Whoever lives in love lives in God, and God in him.*

Acknowledgment (confession, ὁμολογήσῃ) is one of the outward signs that God's love is alive and well in the heart. It is a fruit of his redemptive work in us. Again, that mutual "energy" between God and his children is referred to. He lives in us and we in him.

Verse 16 describes the inner workings which led to that confession, "And so we know and rely. . . ." "Rely" (πεπιστεύκαμεν) might better be rendered as "believed." Lenski captures the force of the perfects when he translates in this way: "We have known and still know; we have believed and still believe." The object of the verbs is the love which "God has for us."

"God is love": He is for us, acts in our behalf, not selfishly.

The relationship of remaining in him and his remaining in us is reaffirmed. This cyclical concept of remaining in each other could be compared to an electrical circuit. As long as we are plugged into the Source of love and power, we have love and power. We're like wires. Wires are cold, dead, lifeless objects. By themselves, they won't run your microwave or heat the oven or light the lamp. But when you hook a wire up to a power source, it becomes alive. It glows. It gives warmth. You can run your appliances off it because it has the power and energy of the source flowing through it. It is a modern version of the Vine and the branches.

vv. 17,18 — *In this way, love is made complete among us so that we will have confidence on the day of judgment, because in this world we are like him. There is no fear in love. But perfect love drives out fear, because fear has to do with punishment. The man who fears is not made perfect in love.*

'Αγάπη has the article. The English comes off as quite generic and may leave the reader grasping for what love is spoken of. Is it our love for God, our love for our brother, or both? The answer is "none of the above." The Greek article here functions as a demonstrative, "that." It specifies the love which has been spoken of. It is the overriding love which comes from the Source, God's self-sacrificing love for us.

Our love would be a poor basis for any confidence, come Judgment Day. It is tainted by sin and imperfect this side of eternity. If the basis were our love, we would be left like the Olympic athlete who has finished his event and now must wait with trepidation to see whether he has scored high enough to win. Only God's love could give such confidence that every trace of fear is driven out.

It is in this section that love is repeatedly modified by forms of τελειόω. Perhaps "perfected love" would be clearer than "perfect love." The idea of completed love or love which has attained the goal which God has in mind must not be overlooked. There is no punishment for those who live in love. God has made the payment in Christ's loving sacrifice.

v. 19 — *We love because he first loved us.*

This is one of the best known passages in Scripture. It sums up the text. It clearly defines how and why we are in our relationship with God. The KJV renders the variant, "We love *him*." Including the object narrows the scope. The NIV allows for a broader scope of objects, such as love for the brother, which follows. Either reading states the truth.

vv. 20,21 — *If anyone says, "I love God," yet hates his brother, he is a liar. For anyone who does not love his brother, whom he has seen, cannot love God, whom he has not seen. And he has given us this command: Whoever loves God must also love his brother.*

Powerful language! A person who says he can love God and simultaneously hate his brother is worshiping his own fictitious god. The energy of God's love, which is constantly flowing through us directly from the Source, will bear positive fruit whenever it touches another person. If our brother comes into contact with us and feels no warmth or light, he knows that something is dead somewhere along the line. We have never seen the Source with our own eyes, but we can see the objects of the Source's love, our fellowman. If his love flows out to them, and our love is his love, then we must love too. It is a command from him. Perhaps John had in mind the words of our Savior recorded in his Gospel: "Love one another" (Jn 13:34).

Homiletical Suggestions

Most suggestions have been offered at the appropriate verses. The timing of the Sunday, between Ascension and Pentecost, allows the preacher to look back and ahead. It allows one to overview God's loving plan for salvation and all of the intricate details of the plan. All three persons of the Trinity are at work in the plan and can be drawn on without ever leaving the text.

Specific gospel can be drawn from virtually any place where the word ἀγάπη shows up. Appropriation and application can be honed to speak of our confidence to the end, the never-ending power Source from which love flows freely to us all, and how that love affects our relationships here on earth.

The first suggested outline focuses on love. A possible introduction to such a sermon could comment on the number of the Beatles' hit songs which had the word "love" in their titles:

All You Need Is Love

1. The source of that love (vv. 13-16)
2. The duration of that love (vv. 17-19)
3. The impact of that love (vv. 20,21)

Another approach might be to focus on τελειόω and view the text from a goal-oriented division of love:

God Loves Us with Goals in Mind

1. That we remain in him (vv. 13-16)
2. That our fears are cast out (vv. 17-19)
3. That our love touches others (vv. 20,21)

For the more flamboyant preacher in search of a three-part outline the following approach might work:

The Electricity of God's Love

1. It is grounded in the power Source (vv. 13-16)
2. It provides the energy to touch our own lives (vv. 17,18)
3. It provides the energy to touch the lives of others (vv. 19-21)

PENTECOST

The Scriptures

> Old Testament — *Ezekiel 37:1-14*
> Epistle — *Acts 2:22-36*
> Gospel — *John 7:37-39a*

The Text — Acts 2:22-36

Our text is the second part of Peter's Pentecost sermon. For a thorough understanding of part two, we must remember the groundwork that Peter laid in part one (2:14-21). He spoke up to explain the unusual events to the crowd. The Lord Jesus had kept his promise to his disciples, sending the Holy Spirit. The gift came on a day when many Jews from throughout the world were gathered to celebrate the feast. The crowd could not understand how these unlearned men were suddenly able to speak in foreign languages about the wonderful works of God. A mistaken human explanation was that these disciples were drunk.

Peter arose to defend Christ's followers. He used part one of his sermon to relate the day's events to Old Testament prophecy. Joel had predicted this outpouring of the Holy Spirit. Peter answered the disciples' critics while explaining for the crowd what had happened. His goal, however, was more than a simple explanation. Through the guidance of God the Holy Spirit, Peter preached law and gospel.

One final note. On Pentecost we focus on the work of the Holy Spirit. Like Peter, however, we should proclaim the central message of the gospel concerning the person and work of the Messiah. On Pentecost, as on any other day, we point to our Savior Jesus Christ. That is what the promised Spirit does; that is what he did on Pentecost.

> v. 22 — *"Men of Israel, listen to this: Jesus of Nazareth was a man accredited by God to you by miracles, wonders and signs, which God did among you through him, as you yourselves know."*

Peter was speaking to the Jews who had gathered in Jerusalem. They would know the Old Testament prophecies of the coming Savior. They would also be aware of the reports of Jesus of Nazareth. Because of his audience's background Peter didn't have to spend time introducing God's plan of salvation or Jesus. He could simply point to

Christ's well-known actions. Peter used that familiarity to show the significance of Jesus' actions.

The miracles, wonders, and signs were God's accreditation of Jesus' person and work. Many times the people had asked for a sign and just as often they failed to see the significance of the wonders taking place before them. Those miracles were signs pointing to the fulfillment of God's promises in Jesus.

> vv. 23,24 — *"This man was handed over to you by God's set purpose and foreknowledge; and you, with the help of wicked men, put him to death by nailing him to the cross. But God raised him from the dead, freeing him from the agony of death, because it was impossible for death to keep its hold on him."*

God's Son had come to earth to save sinners, but the Jews had rejected him and opposed God's plan. To be sure, Peter was not addressing only the Jewish leaders who were directly responsible for Christ's death. These leaders, however, had acted as the representatives of the people. Through the agency of the Romans they were responsible for the death of God's Son and the responsibility was shared by all. It happened according to "God's set purpose and foreknowledge," but they were responsible for what they did.

The crowd shared in the guilt of opposing God. But there was also good news. God had not allowed their opposition to frustrate or prevent his saving purpose. They had played a negative role in God's plan, but now the Holy Spirit was working to convict these sinners of their guilt and to direct them to the Savior from sin.

The resurrection was evidence that they had been wrong to oppose God in rejecting Jesus (law). But it is also the sure sign that he has accomplished the salvation of sinners (gospel).

Now Peter turned to Psalm 16:8-11 as further proof of what God had accomplished:

> vv. 25-28 — *"David said about him: 'I saw the Lord always before me. Because he is at my right hand, I will not be shaken. Therefore my heart is glad and my tongue rejoices; my body also will live in hope, because you will not abandon me to the grave, nor will you let your Holy One see decay. You have made known to me the paths of life; you will fill me with joy in your presence.'"*

David was one of Israel's greatest heroes. As their king, he had been anointed by God. The Anointed One was to be his descendant and heir. David found his joy, comfort, and assurance in God's promise of this Savior. Rather than oppose God's plan and foolishly refuse to believe, David rejoiced to see the Lord's day through the eyes of faith. That joy was based on two important facts. First, the Lord was always present as David's strength (note the imperfect of προοράω). Second, David saw prophetically that God would bring about his eternal salvation through the resurrection of the Lord's Anointed.

Peter was appealing to his people's knowledge of their history. They would be familiar with this Messianic prophecy. They would understand David's reference and realize that what happened to Jesus was the fulfillment of God's promises of old. David's knowledge of the way of life was the result of the Holy Spirit's work. The same Holy Spirit was at work in Peter's preaching to bring the crowd to the same knowledge.

> vv. 29-32 — *"Brothers, I can tell you confidently that the patriarch David died and was buried, and his tomb is here to this day. But he was a prophet and knew that God had promised him on oath that he would place one of his descendants on his throne. Seeing what was ahead, he spoke of the resurrection of the Christ, that he was not abandoned to the grave, nor did his body see decay. God has raised Jesus to life, and we are all witnesses of the fact."*

Peter interpreted the text: David died and therefore must not have been speaking of himself. As a prophet he was "speaking ahead" to a later time. He knew God's promise of a coming descendant who would sit on his throne forever (2 Sa 7:12,13; Ps 132:11), who would be the promised Messiah. David not only foresaw his Savior; he also looked forward to his resurrection.

None of Peter's hearers could disagree with this interpretation. Now he "set the hook." He identified Jesus of Nazareth as the one of whom David sang. Peter and his fellow disciples were witnesses of the fact that God raised Jesus from the dead. Jesus fit the criteria of David's description and God's promise.

> v. 33 — *"Exalted to the right hand of God, he has received from the Father the promised Holy Spirit and has poured out what you now see and hear."*

Peter had concentrated on the Savior's death and resurrection; now his exaltation! Ὑψωθείς is an aorist passive participle. It emphasizes that God the Father did exalt his Son. The exaltation is a fitting climax to the struggle that had taken place. People had opposed Jesus and put him to death. God raised him and exalted him to his right hand. Jesus has resumed his place in heaven. Now, also according to his human nature, he makes full use of his divine authority—and rules the world for the benefit of his church.

It is the exalted Savior who kept his promise to pour out the Holy Spirit. The crowd did not understand the events of that Pentecost day. Here is Peter's simple explanation: It is the fulfillment of the Savior's promise to his disciples (Jn 15:26,27; Ac 1:4-8). Again, Peter pointed to Jesus as the Messiah. The disciples were obviously Jesus' disciples. He had promised them the Holy Spirit. Now the ascended Lord had sent that Spirit. It was further proof of who Jesus of Nazareth really is, the promised Messiah.

vv. 34,35 — *"For David did not ascend to heaven, and yet he said, 'The Lord said to my Lord: "Sit at my right hand until I make your enemies a footstool for your feet."'"*

Peter again quotes David (Ps 110:1). As before, the Psalmist was not speaking about himself. Again Peter reminded his listeners that David was speaking of the Messiah, the one who would ascend to heaven. There the Anointed One received the rewards of his victory over sin, death, and the devil.

v. 36 — *"Therefore let all Israel be assured of this: God has made this Jesus, whom you crucified, both Lord and Christ."*

The Jewish leaders had shouted, "Take him away! Take him away! Crucify him!" (Jn 19:15). The chosen people had rejected the promised Savior. That did not stop God's plan. The people could know that Jesus of Nazareth was the Messiah from his works, from Old Testament prophecy, from the resurrection, and from the outpouring of the Holy Spirit which they themselves had witnessed. Above all, they could know from his exaltation that he is the one of whom his ancestor sang.

God had turned their evil purposes to good. He brought salvation to sinners. There could be no doubt: ἀσφαλῶς connotes a certainty concerning which there can be no doubt.

As much as the people had sinned, there was still hope. Peter was not only certain about who Jesus is but also about God's forgiveness for sinners. In fact, Peter knew his Savior's forgiveness firsthand. Just as there had been restoration for Peter, there could be reconciliation for those who had failed to recognize the promised Redeemer. In a single bold sentence Peter captured the essence of law and gospel.

Homiletical Suggestions

The festival of Pentecost usually focuses on the Holy Spirit's work. Our text reminds us of that work, but it clearly focuses on the Savior. The Holy Spirit's goal on this day is no different from what it was on that day: the conversion of sinners and the strengthening of believers. That can only be done through the gospel in word and sacraments. In a day when many emphasize the Holy Spirit to the exclusion of Christ, our text is a fitting reminder that even on Pentecost Jesus is the focus of our message.

For the most part the Jewish people had failed to recognize the promised Savior. As a remedy Peter did not preach the Holy Spirit; he preached Christ crucified and risen. A sermon on Pentecost must do the same. Through a Christ-centered sermon the Holy Spirit will work in the hearts of our listeners as he did on the first Pentecost.

God Has Brought Us Salvation

1. In spite of man's opposition (vv. 22-24)
2. As promised through David (vv. 25-31)
3. As certified by the outpouring of the Holy Spirit (vv. 32-36)

If the preacher prefers to emphasize the day of Pentecost, he can use the following outline, which still emphasizes the Savior's role:

On Pentecost We See Jesus

1. The Holy Spirit tells us who Jesus is (vv. 22-24)
2. The Holy Spirit tells us what Jesus has done (vv. 25-32)
3. The Holy Spirit tells us how Jesus blesses us (vv. 32-36)

A final suggestion for a sermon on verses 32-36:

Jesus Pours Out the Holy Spirit

1. This is his right (vv. 32-35)
2. This is his gift (v. 36)

180

HOLY TRINITY—
FIRST SUNDAY AFTER PENTECOST

The Scriptures

Old Testament — *Deuteronomy 6:4-9*
Epistle — *Romans 8:14-17*
Gospel — *John 3:1-17*

The Text — Romans 8:14-17

After demonstrating that God has justified all people by grace and that justification is received through faith alone (chapters 1-5), Paul continues in chapters 6-8 to show how that justification issues in a life of sanctification.

Building on the twin freedoms we enjoy (from sin and the law), Paul points us in chapter 8 to the consolation of Christ as the power we draw on to lead a sanctified life. Verses 1-11 contrast the mind controlled by the flesh, which is death, to the mind controlled by the Spirit, which is life. Verses 12 and 13 draw the conclusion from those verses that we should live according to the Spirit and, thus, really live.

Verses 14-17 introduce the relationship of the Father and his children. The thought is not, as in verses 12 and 13, one of encouragement to sanctification. Rather, Paul directs us to the power for sanctification, the fact that we are the children of God.

v. 14 — *Those who are led by the Spirit of God are the sons of God.*

Being led by the Spirit is sanctification. Those who are led by the Spirit, who "put to death the misdeeds of the body" (v. 12), are sons of God. They will live.

῞Οσοι is descriptive, not etiological. They are not the sons of God because they are led by the Spirit in a life of sanctification. Rather, all who are led by the Spirit in a life of sanctification are the sons of God. Paul uses υἱοί: children who have legal status in the family and are recognized as heirs.

v. 15 — *For you did not receive a spirit that makes you slaves again to fear, but you received the Spirit of sonship, and by him we cry, "Abba, Father."*

In this verse Paul appeals to the experience of the Roman Christians. The Holy Spirit who led them to faith and sanctification did not inculcate in them a spirit of servile fear. Rather, when they looked back to their conversion and considered the Spirit's leading, they could clearly see that the Spirit imparted sonship and the confidence that they were legitimate sons.

This sonship is more than a formal arrangement. They are freed from the slave mentality to the extent that they can cry out, "Abba, Father." This phrase is most likely based on Jesus' prayer in the Garden of Gethsemane (Mark 14:36), which was taken over into the prayer life of the early Christians. It is used to express an intimate child-parent relationship of trust and devotion.

Paul, in effect, is using the work of the Holy Spirit which these people experienced in their lives as a line of defense against doubts which might arise concerning their salvation. This introspection for assurance is valid. It is not the only way in which believers can be assured. Nor is it the most effective and long-reaching solution to the problem of doubt. But it can be used both personally and in pastoral counseling.

v. 16 — *The Spirit himself testifies with our spirit that we are the children of God.*

A new note of assurance is now added, αὐτὸ τὸ πνεῦμα συμμαρτυρεῖ. The Spirit himself testifies, gives confidence in sonship. A believer's heart already testifies to his adoption, but that testimony can easily be dimmed by the devil, world, and flesh. The Holy Spirit's testimony makes an individual's adoption sure.

The question is, what is this testimony of the Holy Spirit and how does a believer receive it? There are three possibilities: 1) an immediate revelation of the Holy Spirit, 2) the testimony of the Scriptures through which the Holy Spirit works to give assurance, and 3) the testimony in a life of sanctification guided and inspired by the Holy Spirit.

The first can be ruled out. It is enthusiasm, the notion that the Holy Spirit works without means.

The third has a great deal of merit, considering the context. "If the Holy Spirit proves himself living and effective in us [in the drowning of the old Adam], then it is sure proof that we are the sons of God" (Stoeckhardt). The second is the most objective: understanding the Holy Spirit's testimony as the Bible removes it from the realm of subjectivity. An objective witness will rule out any self-delusion and thus bring greater assurance.

v. 17 — *If we are children, then we are also heirs—heirs of God and co-heirs with Christ, if indeed we share in his sufferings in order that we may also share in his glory.*

The last phrase of this verse, εἴπερ συμπάσχομεν ἵνα καὶ συνδοξασθῶμεν, is subject to various interpretations. The main point of contention is the syntax of ἵνα. A ἵνα denoting purpose lays greater weight on man's sufferings with Christ. A ἵνα denoting result simply describes the destiny of those who suffer with Christ without any implications as to their merit. The ἵνα denoting result is not as common, but it is an accepted usage in koine Greek (B-D 391 [5]).

It is theologically possible to argue for a ἵνα denoting purpose here. The idea of *Christ's* substitutionary work is foreign to the context, but believers suffer because of and as a test of their faith, to refine it (1 Pe 1:6,7). But it is incorrect to speak of man's suffering with Christ as a cause of glorification with him.

A believer's glorification *does,* in a certain sense, result from joint suffering. All believers suffer with Christ. All believers will be glorified with him. Thus, as joint-sufferers they can expect joint glorification. The εἴπερ is syllogistic, not etiological. Since we are God's dear children (τέκνα) our sufferings with Christ will result in our sharing his glory.

Paul now completes the thought which he began in verse 12. He draws the ultimate conclusion from the fact that believers live in the Spirit. They will have eternal glory. Reception of the Spirit means sonship, a sonship which is sure. The adoption leads to a final inheritance.

Believers are heirs of God. They receive their inheritance from God. The inheritance they receive is the same inheritance their joint-heir, Christ, has received: glory in heaven. While life on this earth meant suffering for Jesus and still means suffering for believers, the result will be eternal blessedness.

Homiletical Suggestions

Trinity Sunday celebrates the majesty and wonder of the one God who is three Persons. Sermons for this day must not be dogmatic dissertations. Texts such as this Epistle lesson do, however, provide the opportunity to recapitulate what we confess in the creeds—not abstractly but in terms of the triune God's *activity.*

A key thought in these four verses is assurance. In this world of doubt, that is a very important word. Assurance is exactly what every believer can have because of the work of Father, Son, and Holy Spirit.

When doubt about salvation arises, the Holy Spirit can bring confidence through introspection, an evaluation of one's sanctification. If a person is led by the Spirit, he is a true child of the Father. Because he belongs to the Father, his inheritance of eternal life is certain.

The Spirit gives more objective testimony in the Word. Even though a believer's sanctification is not perfect, Jesus was and is perfect in our stead. He fulfilled the law. He suffered the punishment for sin. Salvation is assured to us through him, no matter what we suffer. Working through the means of grace, the Holy Spirit testifies to each believer that he is a member of God's family.

The following outlines are all divided into three parts. The content of the verses supports this arrangement and the fact that it is Trinity Sunday suggests it.

I Believe in One God

1. I believe in the Spirit, who has made me God's child (vv. (14,15a,16)
2. I believe in the Father, who opens his heart to me (v. 15b)
3. I believe in the Son, who shares his inheritance with me (v. 17)

You Are Part of God's Family

1. You have the Spirit's testimony (vv. 14,15a,16)
2. You have the Father's ear (v. 15b)
3. You have the Son's inheritance (v. 17)

How Can I Be Sure?

1. Because the Spirit leads you (vv. 14,15a,16)
2. Because the Father adopts you (v. 15b)
3. Because the Son suffered for you (v. 17)

You Belong to the Triune God

1. The Spirit is your guide (vv. 14,15b,16)
2. In the Father you can confide (v. 15b)
3. The Son for you has died (v. 17)

SECOND SUNDAY AFTER PENTECOST

The Scriptures

> Old Testament — *Deuteronomy 5:12-15*
> Epistle — *2 Corinthians 4:5-12*
> Gospel — *Mark 2:23-28*

The Text — 2 Corinthians 4:5-12

The main purpose of 2 Corinthians is to defend the ministry of the gospel. Certain men in Corinth were attacking this ministry. They set themselves up as "super-apostles" (11:5) and criticized Paul and his ministry because of Paul's poor speaking ability and his lowliness (11:6,7). They led the people to believe that true apostles, true servants of God, are powerful and great in worldly ways: in worldly wisdom, influence, and possessions. They promoted ideas of the ministry that were man-centered (11:17-19).

It may well have been these men who had confused the Corinthians about the resurrection and about adiaphorous matters. Paul had to deal with those misunderstandings in his first letter (1 Co 15:12 and chapters 4-14). But the "super-apostles" kept undermining Paul's ministry and kept trying to thwart the work of Paul's first letter (2 Co 10:7-11; 12:19—13:10). Paul had to destroy their influence by teaching the people once again what the ministry is all about.

When this series last focused on 2 Corinthians (Transfiguration Sunday), Paul was showing the church how the ministry of the gospel has nothing to hide, and nothing of which to be ashamed. It commends itself and its servants so that they don't have to use "secret and shameful ways" or "deceptions" to convince people of the truth. This text grows out of that discussion. Paul reveals how God shows the true value of the gospel through the lives of Paul and all of God's called workers. The texts that follow in the next five weeks build on that. The pastor who is preaching week-by-week on the Epistles will on this Sunday be setting a foundation for reference in the weeks to come.

This section begins with a statement that grows out of the previous verses and helps summarize what follows:

> v. 5 — *For we do not preach ourselves, but Jesus Christ as Lord, and ourselves as your servants for Jesus' sake.*

In the previous verses Paul said that he commended himself to every man's conscience in the sight of God. He also knew that if his preaching did not bring people to faith, it wasn't so much his fault. It was the god of this age who blinded the minds of unbelievers. Here, with the transitional γάρ, Paul explains why he can say that. When he stood before people to speak, it had nothing to do with him personally. He did nothing to draw attention to himself (cp. 1 Co 2:1,2).

Paul preached Jesus Christ as Lord. The Greek κύριος may have called to Paul's Hebrew mind what the LORD says of himself in Exodus 34:6,7. Perhaps he thought of how Jesus said, "Before Abraham was, I AM!" (Jn 8:58)—revealing himself as the LORD God of love and justice, who hated sin so much that he came to save mankind from it. This was the Jesus Paul preached, who revealed to Paul that Paul's righteousness was nothing.

He preached himself as the Corinthians' servant for Jesus' sake. The use of δοῦλος is not insignificant. God chose Paul especially to be his slave for the sake of the gospel, as the Lord said to Ananias in Antioch, "Go! This man is my chosen instrument to carry my name before the Gentiles and their kings and before the people of Israel" (Ac 9:15). Paul made it a point to tell his congregations this so that they would realize, not how great he was, but how merciful and loving God was to make sure his gospel reached them (Ro 1:5; 15:14ff.; Eph 3). Paul did all he could to stay out of the way of the gospel so that people could see Christ, and not Paul. In this way he was their slave, but only for Jesus' sake, where the gospel was concerned.

v. 6 — *For God, who said, "Let light shine out of darkness," made his light shine in our hearts to give us the light of the knowledge of the glory of God in the face of Christ.*

Verse 6 begins with the causal ὅτι. Paul explains here why he is proclaiming Jesus and not himself, why he is their slave and not seeking to be their master. It is because Paul had nothing to do with creating this salvation. God the Creator, who made light out of nothing, in the midst of blackest darkness, did it. He proved his lordship even in our conversion. He placed his light (Jn 1) in the heart of a man who once lived in darkness (Eph 2:1-5; 4:17-24). The ministry of the gospel is based on a justification and a conversion which are entirely the decision and work of God. Paul has nothing to say about a contribution on his part. God did it all. This is why he preaches only Christ.

God made light shine in Paul πρὸς φωτισμόν, with the goal or conscious purpose of revealing the γνώσεως τῆς δόξης τοῦ θεοῦ ἐν

προσώπῳ Χριστοῦ. God's will is that people see his glory and be saved,
His glory is seen nowhere more clearly than in Jesus, his person and
his work. With faith the light, the Holy Spirit gave Paul a drive to reveal Christ, God's embodied glory. In the end it was God who
preached Christ in and through Paul.

v. 7 — *But we have this treasure in jars of clay to show that this
all-surpassing power is from God and not from us.*

This light of God is a great treasure and an all-surpassing power.
It changes people, as it changed Paul. It causes them to preach
Christ, too. It leads others to ask them for the reason for the hope
that lives in them.

But human beings would not naturally assume this was from
God. Every Christian is a saint and a sinner. The sinner in all
Christians, with its *opinio legis,* will always try to take some credit
for what God has done. And people listening to a preacher may try
to give humanity the credit for what they hear: "It was his educa-
tion, his family background, his parents. The people he preaches to
must be wonderful people." God made sure that anyone looking at
Paul would not be inclined to give mankind the credit for Paul's
faith and accomplishments. God did that by using such a fragile,
homely, clay jar as Paul.

vv. 8,9 — *We are hard pressed on every side, but not crushed;
perplexed, but not in despair; persecuted, but not abandoned;
struck down, but not destroyed.*

People could see that Paul's life was in danger of breaking. The
NIV translates ἐν παντί as "on every side," but we can interpret this
as "in every aspect of life." No part of Paul's life—mental, physical,
emotional, public, private—was unaffected by the contrast between
Paul's helplessness and God's power.

The series of present passive participles displays Paul's powerless-
ness. All the problems were constant barrages from the outside:
things that might have crushed him, caused him to despair, left him
abandoned, destroyed him. In every case another force from the outside unfailingly prevented those disasters.

The lists of Paul's hardships in 6:3-10 and 11:23-29 indicate some
of what Paul was talking about. He was plagued by Satan, sinful people, a sin-riddled world, and his own sinful self with its doubts and
anxieties. Other things made life difficult for him (Ac 16:6; 2 Co
1:23,24; Ro 1:11-13). But he never became hopelessly pessimistic. The
light of the gospel kept that from happening.

vv. 10,11 — *We always carry around in our body the death of Jesus, so that the life of Jesus may also be revealed in our body. For we who are alive are always being given over to death for Jesus' sake, so that his life may be revealed in our mortal body.*

God had a purpose in letting Paul endure these things, and in defending Paul at that time. It is the νέκρωσιν τοῦ Ἰησοῦ, "the putting to death of Jesus," that Paul is carrying around in his body. Satan and his minions hated Jesus and moved men to kill him. Now the result is his victory instead of theirs. They still seek to kill Jesus by destroying his church and the faith. See Jesus' warnings in John 15:18,19 and see also Luke 6:22, Mark 13:13, Matthew 10:22-24; 24:9.

God saw fit to hand Paul over to God's enemies, just as he handed Jesus over, not because he was cruel but because he wanted to bring life to others. The life of Jesus already existed in Paul, with the light of the gospel. God wants that light to be seen. His Spirit works through the Word and causes people to see in the proclaimer's life how valuable the gospel is.

Paul was so intent that his readers understand this that he twice told them the reason for his suffering. With the ἵνα of verse 10 he shows us the reason: so that God would reveal the life of Jesus in his body. In verse 11, with the γάρ he reminds us why he can say this: God is so concerned about revealing the life of Jesus that he hands his living disciples over to death so that eternal life through Jesus may be seen in their mortal bodies.

v. 12 — *So then, death is at work in us, but life is at work in you.*

Paul drives home his lesson on the ministry of the gospel. He becomes very personal with his readers. If God had not let this happen to Paul, they might not have realized what Jesus had done for them. Paul speaks in very matter-of-fact language: "This is the way it is. God wants to save people. So he proclaims Jesus in and through us, even with suffering."

Homiletical Suggestions

A first look at this text might lead a pastor to think that application will be easy. But the difficulty of this text is not finding applications. Rather, it is living this text while you preach the applications. A major point here is that we don't preach ourselves, but Christ. And yet Paul speaks a great deal about himself here. How can a pastor preach Christ while talking about himself? If our goal is to reveal

Christ as Lord, and not get in the way of the message, can we talk about ourselves at all?

Pastors who are uncomfortable talking about their own personal and vocational agonies—and how these reveal the life of Christ—might be inclined to apply this text to members instead. Talk about how the congregation's personal agonies make them missionaries of Christ's life. But this, too, might distract people's attention from the message if the applications are too personal.

A more objective approach might be to show specifics from the Scriptures and make more general applications to pastors and to Christians in general. Talk about how conversion (God making his light shine in us) proves that Christ is Lord, and not we. Talk about how God preserves people in the faith. Still, if you know your hearers and yourself well—as Paul did—a more personal approach may display Christ in your life and in your people's lives and show how much the life of Christ lives in the "deaths" of his people.

The text, however, is really for appropriation. Paul is not speaking of how he proclaims Christ as much as how God proclaims Christ in him. This is a great comfort to Christians who look at all those thriving worldly-minded ministries and wonder whether they are in the right church. A theme for this text, derived from verse 5, can say:

God Proves the Truth of His Ministry in Us

1. By showing that Jesus Christ is Lord (vv. 6,7)
2. By showing that we are his servants (vv. 7-12)

Another theme may simply imply the words of verse 5 without stating them, or use them in the introduction. Let the parts utilize the color of verses 6-12:

God Proclaims His Gospel Through Us

1. As he makes light shine in darkness (v. 6)
2. As he delivers power in clay pots (vv. 7-9)
3. As he brings life from death (vv. 10-12)

Or:

God Makes His Treasure Known

1. By making light shine from darkness (v. 6)
2. By making life grow from death (vv. 7-12)

This color might be drawn into the theme itself:

God Works with Jars like Us

1. To make his light shine (vv. 6,7)
2. To make his life spread (vv. 7-12)

The last three outlines focus on God's work in us. They do not contrast the truth of God's ministry with the falsity of worldly-minded ministries, as the first outline might. Sometimes people aren't troubled about the truthfulness of God's ministry, but they are worried about its effectiveness in their own lives—in themselves, their children, their friends. God speaks to both concerns in these outlines.

THIRD SUNDAY AFTER PENTECOST

The Scriptures

> Old Testament — *Genesis 3:9-15*
> Epistle — *2 Corinthians 4:13-18*
> Gospel — *Mark 3:20-35*

The Text — 2 Corinthians 4:13-18

The Scriptures for the day seem to connect in regard to the Spirit's work in this way: The Old Testament selection tells how direly we are in need of spiritual help, as fallen sinful beings. The Epistle demonstrates that the Spirit gives us faith and great hope through God's promises (both those already fulfilled and those whose fulfillment is forthcoming). The Gospel warns against the one sin that will still keep us out of the heavenly garden—spurning the Spirit in unbelief.

The apostle's subject in 2 Corinthians 4 carries over from chapters 2 and 3. As stated in verse 1, we are talking about "this ministry." It is a ministry we all have as Christians, a glorious ministry "that brings righteousness" (3:9), proclaiming the "new covenant" which is "of the Spirit" (3:6). Among Christians and for Christ, this ministry is also entrusted to certain spokesmen, "like men sent from God" (2:17), who have a special calling to spread everywhere "the fragrance of the knowledge of him" (2:14). Such was the calling of Paul as an apostle and of his cohorts in ministry. Such is also the calling of God's servants in public ministry today. The text for this day's consideration speaks of the convictions we cling to in carrying out this ministry, as well as the comfort we have from God in his promises to us as Christians and as ministers.

> vv. 13,14 — *It is written: "I believed; therefore I have spoken." With that same spirit of faith we also believe and therefore speak, because we know that the one who raised the Lord Jesus from the dead will also raise us with Jesus and present us with you in his presence.*

The quotation from Psalm 116:10 follows the Septuagint. In the Psalm the thoughts of believing and speaking are set in the context of much suffering, but also of great confidence in the Lord's salvation and resurrection. The setting is similar in Paul's use. Suffering for the sake of the ministry is viewed from the eternal perspective of resurrection and glory. Thus, any and all hardships appear minimal and surmountable, as is truly the case.

The NIV has altered the word order and sentence structure of the Greek to make for easier understanding of verse 13. It may, however, be helpful in preaching to recognize and make use of the original phrasing: "But since we have the same spirit of faith which is in accord with (κατά) the Scripture (τὸ γεγραμμένον), 'I believed, therefore I spoke,' we also believe and therefore speak." Word order emphasis is placed on the heritage of faith that we share with our ancient fathers, a solid belief that life and resurrection are our possession through the grace of God in the person of his appointed Savior. We share this spiritual conviction with those who have already gone to be with their Lord, and look to share it with others before they go to be with him.

The expression "spirit of faith" is usually construed as a descriptive genitive: a spirit characterized by faith. We could also, however, take the genitive as objective—a reference to the Spirit who gives faith. Combining these ideas, we could say that by the one Spirit who gives faith we have the same spirit of faith with one another.

Λαλέω has the lexicon meanings "speak, talk, say, preach, proclaim, converse." In the case of our Christian convictions and ministry, all of the above are involved. We believe, and so we tell it, preach it, proclaim it, converse about it! The gospel is and should be constantly the content of our communication.

Εἰδότες (v. 14) specifies knowledge of something we've not yet experienced but nonetheless know in our hearts and minds to be true. We've not yet been raised or seen anyone raised, but we know God will do it. He will raise us with Jesus and present us to him like a bride to her bridegroom.

v. 15 — *All this is for your benefit, so that the grace that is reaching more and more people may cause thanksgiving to overflow to the glory of God.*

Everything a minister of the gospel does—or suffers—is undertaken for the sake of the souls in his care. So it was with Paul and the Corinthian people. So it is for workers called to convey their convictions of faith to congregations and communities today.

The goal of our ministry of the gospel is twofold: that more and more people may be reached with redeeming grace, and that thus the ultimate end be achieved—greater glory for God, as more and more voices are raised to praise him. God's grace and glory, though infinite in themselves, are described as on the increase as the number of souls touched by the gospel grows.

vv. 16,17 — *Therefore we do not lose heart. Though outwardly we are wasting away, yet inwardly we are being renewed day by day. For our light and momentary troubles are achieving for us an eternal glory that far outweighs them all.*

Most who read and use this volume are parish pastors. Most also will admit that there are times we do "lose heart." We've become tired, faint, discouraged by the pressures and apparent failures in our ministries. How we need these words of God! How surely our parishioners need them also, for discouragement and wavering faith can afflict the lay person's personal service just as readily as the pastor's public ministry.

The apostle drew his strength and courage directly from God's gospel promises. He believed that, in contrast to our present troubles, there is "an eternal glory" that awaits us and outweighs everything we may suffer.

To be sure, "outwardly we are wasting away." The present tense of the Greek verb indicates the continued, ongoing nature of our human suffering, struggle, and decay. But at the very same time, inwardly, through the Spirit working in our spirits, we are continually being renewed (also present tense). The gospel's power in Word and sacrament keeps us alive, surviving and thriving, keeps us from becoming empty human shells. Thus it is vital to be in contact with these means of God's grace daily, the means by which God will renew us "day by day."

Paul boldly describes the contrasts between trouble and glory. Our troubles are "light and momentary," not heavy at all and not lasting more than an instant. To the person in the midst of a burdensome, lingering trial, these words may sound like a pipedream. But when considered in view of eternity, this truth can be seen. The splendid words which follow expand upon this theme: καθ᾽ ὑπερβολὴν εἰς ὑπερβολὴν αἰώνιον βάρος δόξης κατεργάζεται ἡμῖν. "In excess of excess, an eternal weight of glory (these troubles) are bringing about for us." The best part is that this future glory is no exaggeration; it is real! In almost untranslatable but wonderful fashion Paul has expressed the immeasurableness of what God has in store for us.

What a wonderful and reassuring truth! Troubles in ministry and life are but momentary and light, while the glory God grants us is endless and immense.

v. 18 — *So we fix our eyes not on what is seen, but on what is unseen. For what is seen is temporary, but what is unseen is eternal.*

Because, through the Spirit of faith, we see the eternal spectrum of things, we don't stare at things which eyes can see. We rivet our attention not on what our eyes may view but on what our spirits perceive. Again the contrast is spotlighted, between the temporary nature of this world and its troubles versus the unending quality of the unseen world. Our lives and our ministries must have an eye on eternity if we are to maintain a godly and proper perspective.

Homiletical Suggestions

This text is rich in value for preaching at installations or conferences of called workers, since the public ministry is highlighted. At the same time, these words of God are profitable for teaching all the saints, training them in righteousness, equipping them for personal ministry.

A theme and outline with each Christian's personal ministry in mind is:

We Tell What We Believe

1. We believe in the resurrection to eternal life (vv. 14,16-18)
2. We tell because we want many more to share faith's blessings (vv. 13,15)

Another useful division for congregational preaching focuses on the contrasts seen in the text, with the Scripture quotation in verse 13 serving as the theme:

We Believe and Therefore Speak

1. Death will be changed to life (vv. 14-16)
2. Troubles will be changed to glory (vv. 16,17)
3. Time will be changed to eternity (v. 18)

One other suggestion for the Sunday setting, using only the first part of the text:

We Speak with Conviction

1. Our faith will not keep silent (vv. 13,14)
2. Our speaking will spread grace (v. 15)

If preached for a pastoral conference, ordination, or installation, this outline is a possibility:

God's Spokesmen Preach the Faith

1. Confident of its truth (vv. 13,14)
2. Desiring the church's benefit (v. 15)
3. In spite of trials and afflictions (vv. 16-18)

FOURTH SUNDAY AFTER PENTECOST

The Scriptures

Old Testament — *Ezekiel 17:22-24*
Epistle — *2 Corinthians 5:1-10*
Gospel — *Mark 4:26-34*

The Text — 2 Corinthians 5:1-10

Paul writes this letter to further instruct a troubled congregation. Division and lax attitudes with regard to God's will had already engendered two letters (cf. 2 Co 2:1-4) by means of which the apostle intended to move the offenders to contrition, repentance, and a renewed celebration of the forgiveness which was theirs in Christ Jesus. This second canonical letter seems to have been written to a congregation which was growing in grace and knowledge of its Savior. While it is severe at points (10:1—13:10), there is less mention of specific sins in this letter. This fact, as well as the admonition to forgive a penitent brother (2:5-11), would indicate that the congregation was moving toward spiritual maturity.

The general attitude of the members of the congregation toward Paul's apostolic authority did, however, generate much concern on his part. He spends major portions of this letter explaining his personal and apostolic ministry (1:12—7:16) and defending it from those who would attack his credibility (10:1—13:10). The verses under consideration fall into the section in which Paul is explaining the apostolic ministry along with its hardships and, more importantly, its joys.

v. 1 — *Now we know that if the earthly tent we live in is destroyed, we have a building from God, an eternal house in heaven, not built by human hands.*

The NIV drops the logical connection to the previous section (γάρ). This omission makes it appear that Paul is beginning a new or tangential topic. He is not. Rather, he is developing his confident assertion in the concluding section of chapter 4. He has boldly stated that even though he and those ministering with him are wasting away outwardly and enduring what he describes as "light and momentary troubles," they do not lose heart. He has asserted that they are preparing for an unseen eternal glory which will make the present time of suffering seem insignificant. This verse and the rest of the text give the reason that Paul can speak so confidently about his unseen glory which is to come.

Paul uses a vivid word picture: The "earthly tent" is a picture of impermanence which reminds us that our earthly existence is only for a time. Καταλυϑῇ, when used with reference to a tent, indicates a dismantling process.

Paul's confidence and joy can be found in the fact that, while we now labor in a tent, we already have (present tense) a building of our own from God. Οἰκοοδομήν shows the superiority of what God will give us in the next life. To the Jewish mind, the Old Testament imagery of the Feast of Tabernacles (Lev 23:33-43) would also be in view. During this feast the Israelites commemorated their wilderness sojourn, when they lived in tents. The eternal house not made by human hands is a fit domicile for those who will dwell eternally with their God in heaven.

vv. 2,3 — *Meanwhile we groan, longing to be clothed with our heavenly dwelling, because when we are clothed, we will not be found naked.*

Now Paul returns to the reality of life lived on this plane. The body in which we now live has imperfections and must face struggles which we will not face in the new body which our God has prepared. It bears the marks of sin and all of its consequences. This causes us to groan. In Romans 8:22,23 Paul speaks of the groaning in which believers and creation join as they look forward to the revealing of the sons of God. It is a groaning filled with a certain hope (Ro 8:24), a longing for the consummation of God's promises in the putting on of a permanent dwelling from heaven.

In verse 3 Paul provides the reason for his groaning and longing. A life lived in this world is a life of nakedness before God. When Adam and Eve first fell into sin, they were stripped of the righteousness which was the image of God. Their new spiritual nakedness made them recognize their physical nakedness and feel shame. Since that time all people have been born spiritually naked. The tragedy is compounded by the fact that people by nature do not even recognize their nakedness. In Revelation 3:17 Jesus says to a wandering church: "You say, 'I am rich . . . and do not need a thing.' But you are . . . naked.'" In Revelation 16:15 Jesus explicitly states that this is not a desirable condition; it is the ultimate disaster.

It is no wonder that Paul wishes to be permanently clothed with the heavenly dwelling. This life is one in which our sinful flesh, which is naked, struggles against the new man, which is clothed with

Christ (Eph 4:24; Col 3:10-12). Our spiritual clothing is found in the renewed image of God which we have through faith in Jesus Christ. In Galatians Paul teaches that all who have been baptized into Christ have been clothed with Christ (3:27). His robe of righteousness covers our spiritual nakedness (Isa 61:10). On the last day we will not be found naked, for we are wearing Jesus Christ.

v. 4 — *For while we are in this tent, we groan and are burdened, because we do not wish to be unclothed but to be clothed with our heavenly dwelling, so that what is mortal may be swallowed up by life.*

Paul continues his explanation of a believer's groaning. It is as if he does not want us to miss the reason for the groaning. It is not that we do not have a confident hope. Instead, the reason is found in the fact that our heart's desire and wish is to be clothed with our heavenly dwelling. Our longing is that the mortal will be swallowed up by the life (τῆς ζωῆς) which is eternal life (1 Co 15:53,54). Καταποθῇ conveys the idea of a swallowing which will result in the extinction of the mortal. It will cease to exist as it is replaced by the immortal. When the mortal is swallowed up, the groaning will cease.

v. 5 — *Now it is God who has made us for this very purpose and has given us the Spirit as a deposit, guaranteeing what is to come.*

Paul has been giving us the reasons for his confidence as he faces the struggles of this life in the Lord's service. He has been building his case upon the certain hope which he has in his Savior. He caps his argument by stating that this is all by divine design. It is God who is preparing us for this very purpose. It is God's purpose that we have immortal bodies in which we can dwell in his presence and enjoy him for all eternity. God has made us so that we can have new life with him. Believers are the work of the Lord's hand (Isa 29:23; 60:21). He is working in the lives of his elect so that his will is accomplished (Eph 2:10; Php 2:13), and they are brought safely to his heavenly kingdom (Jude 24).

But how can Paul have such confidence? Because the Lord has given a down payment, a deposit guaranteeing what is to come. That deposit is the Holy Spirit. Paul uses the terminology of the business world to convey a beautiful truth. The ἀρραβών was the pledge or down payment which guaranteed that full payment would be made. The Spirit who called us by the gospel, keeps us in faith, and dwells in us is the guarantee of what is to come.

vv. 6-8 — *Therefore we are always confident and know that as long as we are at home in the body we are away from the Lord. We live by faith, not by sight. We are confident, I say, and would prefer to be away from the body and at home with the Lord.*

Paul has developed a rock-solid foundation for our confidence in the Lord as we walk through this life. Now, based upon everything he has said (οὖν), he applies these solid truths to life. The first application is that we can now walk through this life with confidence, no matter what our situation, no matter what difficulty or hurt we face. We can be confident that our God is good for his promise of life. The practical ramification is that we need not fear death or the things that happen to our body. As long as we are in these bodies, we are away from the Lord. We can take advantage of the time in our bodies to serve our Lord (Php 1:21-26). But the truth is that it is far better for us to be with the Lord. We can walk with confidence, knowing by faith that in spite of appearances, physical hardship only brings us closer to our eternal home.

v. 9 — *So we make it our goal to please him, whether we are at home in the body or away from it.*

Paul's second application dwells upon our life of service to our God. Based upon the confidence our God has given us and based upon his love for us in Christ Jesus, we now make it our goal to please him. We want to please the one who has given us the Holy Spirit as a deposit. We want to please the one who gives us an eternal house in heaven and has clothed us with a robe of righteousness. We want to please the one who has removed the sting of death and has brought life and immortality to light.

v. 10 — *For we must all appear before the judgment seat of Christ, that each one may receive what is due him for the things done while in his body, whether good or bad.*

Paul's final reason for serving God is tied to judgment day, when we will receive our permanent dwelling from God. The seat of judgment is a place where one gives account for his actions. Believers are not exempt from standing before that seat of judgment. Through faith we will stand cleansed of our sins because of the blood of the Lamb (Mt 25:34). We will not be held liable for them. But we will still give an account of our fruits of faith before God (Ro 14:10-12). At that time each will receive his appointed praise from God (Mt 25:14-23; 1 Co 4:5).

The basis for God's judgment will be the deeds of service we have done in the body. If the deeds were good, motivated by love for Christ and for his glory, we will receive praise. If the deeds were useless, motivated by selfish pride or seeking our own glory, we will receive nothing for them (1 Co 3:12-15; 4:5). Our goal now is to do things that he can praise so that we might glorify him with our lives now (Mt 5:16) and in eternity (Eph 1:12).

Homiletical Suggestions

On this Sunday in the Church Year worshipers have already heard Ezekiel's message about the church and how the Lord is the one who plants and nourishes it. They have had that message reinforced in the Gospel, from Mark: The kingdom of God grows without the aid of the man who scatters the seed. The power is in the Word of God which is scattered. In view of this emphasis, the thrust of the sermon ought to focus especially on the good news that God works in us so that his church can be with him throughout eternity. An outline which maintains this emphasis is:

It Is God Who Works in Us

1. With a powerful promise (vv. 1-5)
2. With a precious purpose (vv. 6-10)

Another possibility:

This Is Not Our Permanent Address

1. We have an eternal house in heaven (v. 1)
2. We look forward to living there (vv. 2-4)
3. We can be sure of getting there (vv. 5-8)
4. Meanwhile, we try to please the Owner (vv. 9,10)

FIFTH SUNDAY AFTER PENTECOST

The Scriptures

Old Testament — *Job 38:1-11*
Epistle — *2 Corinthians 5:14-21*
Gospel — *Mark 4:35-41*

The Text — 2 Corinthians 5:14-21

It seems rather amazing to us (and at the same time professionally comforting) that many of the people to whom St. Paul preached thought he was something of a disappointment. In the congregation at Corinth, as we learn in 1 Corinthians, factionalism was splitting the church. One result of this was that many Corinthians downplayed, or even disbelieved, Paul's authority as an apostle.

When he heard of all this, and of the laxity in discipline and teaching which had resulted from it, Paul sent not only a letter but also one of his colleagues to straighten things out. Eventually, as Paul was making his way to the city, the colleague returned with an encouraging report. Some progress had been made, but there still seem to have been those who felt that Paul just didn't measure up as their minister.

The section of 2 Corinthians under consideration as our text contains a fascinating blend of three doctrines. First of all, there is the teaching of universal reconciliation. Following hard upon it is subjective reconciliation. Then comes the doctrine of the ministry. Paul explains how the first two make the third an honorable—an essential—thing, nothing to be sneered at or denigrated.

vv. 14,15 — *For Christ's love compels us, because we are convinced that one died for all, and therefore all died. And he died for all, that those who live should no longer live for themselves but for him who died for them and was raised again.*

Why do Paul and Timothy and Titus, why do any Christian preachers and teachers preach and teach? Paul answers that the love of Christ compels them. Τοῦ χριστοῦ is a subjective genitive. The love Christ has for those for whom he died and rose again is the force that motivates the Christian minister.

Every human being is one for whom Christ died. By that substitutionary death all persons, their sin, and their sinful nature are dead. People who are redeemed by Christ are not to continue in sin or factional infighting, but to live for him who died and rose again for them. It is, therefore, to further the aims of the loving Savior and to prepare his people to love and serve him in return that Paul preaches.

vv. 16,17 — *So from now on we regard no one from a worldly point of view. Though we once regarded Christ in this way, we do so no longer. Therefore, if anyone is in Christ, he is a new creation: the old one has gone, the new has come!*

What were some of the Corinthians saying about Paul which he needed to rebut with these words? Perhaps some accused him of favoritism. Perhaps some rejected his apostolic authority because of his former life as a persecutor of Christians. But here Paul wants to set the record straight. Yes, he once regarded Jesus from a worldly point of view as a heretic and a blasphemer, a danger to Israel. But no more. In the same way, he now regards all people from a heavenly rather than an earthly perspective.

Once they became Christians, they became what Paul became when he was converted: new persons. Something had changed in them, so that the preacher simply could not think of them in an earthly way—according to their social status, wealth or poverty, race, nationality, or the like. What had happened is what Paul speaks of next:

vv. 18,19a — *All this is from God, who reconciled us to himself through Christ and gave us the ministry of reconciliation: that God was reconciling the world to himself in Christ, not counting men's sins against them.*

Here is the change. God has reconciled us to himself through Christ by forgiving us all our sins, by counting them against Christ instead of against us. Note the theological precision with which Paul phrases this. God was not reconciled to us, as if some change took place in him. No, Scripture clearly teaches that the Lord changes not, and once Paul wrote down the word καταλλάσσω God could never be its direct object. God, in fact, is the subject, reconciling us to himself. Taking the Greek word quite literally, we would say that he was making something about us completely "other" from what it was.

And that something is our standing in his sight. In Christ, God does not impute sin to us. Indeed, the whole world (κόσμον), is the named beneficiary of this reconciliation. God now considers *all people* to be different from what they were. Formerly, by birth and nature, they were his enemies to be cast into eternal punishment. Now their status is changed to make them holy and blameless in his sight. This is universal reconciliation.

The preacher looks at the whole world, then, as people whom God has reconciled to himself. All that remains is for someone to tell them about this reconciliation, and that is where the church and its ministry come in. God, who reconciled us, "gave us the ministry of reconciliation." The phrase τὴν διακονίαν τῆς καταλλαγῆς could be translated, "the administering of this reconciliation." Universal reconciliation is administered to each sinner individually by those who proclaim it.

vv. 19b-21 — *And he has committed to us the message of reconciliation. We are therefore Christ's ambassadors, as though God were making his appeal through us. We implore you on Christ's behalf: Be reconciled to God. God made him who had no sin to be sin for us, so that in him we might become the righteousness of God.*

And now Paul connects the doctrine of individual reconciliation with both universal reconciliation and the ministry. Through those who preach and teach the Word, God makes his appeal to those whom he has reconciled to himself: "Be reconciled to God." God and the preacher are of one mind in this. God, says Paul, calls people to his side (παρακαλοῦντες). And the preachers entreat (δεόμεθα) people to accept this gift of reconciliation from God and make this universal reconciliation their own.

Those who receive the reconciliation as their own, who give up trying to reach God by their own good works and take forgiveness and life as the gift it is, they are the ones who are finally and effectively reconciled to God. All others, rejecting Christ, reject this reconciliation.

Thus simply Paul explains the relationship between universal and individual reconciliation. Of course, he doesn't go fully into the doctrine of faith, and of how people can only do what he begs them to do because the Holy Spirit enables them to do so. His purpose here is simply to show the importance of the ministry in God's scheme of things.

The ministry is the link between the universal and the individual. Jesus accomplished the universal, and through the preaching of ministers God brings about, for each believer, the individual. Since this is the case, the ministry truly ought to be held in great honor by all Christians. Many in Corinth were not doing so, and many today follow their lead. Any and all reasons for this pale into insignificance in the light of what Paul says here. Ministers are God's tools to bring about, out of universal reconciliation, the personal reconciliation of the sinner to God.

With verse 21 Paul, in simple and forceful terms, gives the gist of the "message of the reconciliation." Jesus had no sin, being born without it. Yet God made him to be sin, so covered him with the sins of the world that Christ became, as it were, sin personified. When God regarded him, he was affronted by all that sinful nature had become and wrought, the sorry history of humankind, all its wickedness, and the ruin of its goodness.

But it was thus that, in Christ, we are made the righteousness of God. Our sins are stripped from us, and the holiness of Christ becomes ours. It is this which the preacher pleads, on God's behalf, for people to accept.

It is quite a picture Paul paints, of a God holding in his hand the gift of universal forgiveness, and sending preachers to plead for him with sinful mankind to accept the gift. This passage does many things. It explains clearly what reconciliation is all about, universal as well as subjective. It explains how God reconciled the world to himself in Christ. And it sets forth the solemn dignity and importance, in God's plan, of the office of the holy ministry.

Homiletical Suggestions

The danger in preaching such a text lies in the fact that it is a *sedes doctrinae*. The preacher must work hard to avoid letting his sermon become a mere essay on the subject of reconciliation. Paul himself gives the cue with his personal and practical approach, especially when he begs his readers to be reconciled to God.

One thing that will be necessary in preaching this text will be clarity of expression. The entire matter of reconciliation between God and the world is one which doesn't come easily to the human mind. The preacher will do well to try to keep this sermon in terms as concrete as possible, using what illustrations he has acquired in his years of preaching and teaching to make the entire subject readily graspable for his listeners. Especially to be avoided is the trap that Erasmus and the synergists set at Paul's plea, "Be reconciled to God." Preach it rightly, or it may sound like a Billy Graham style altar call.

The Old Testament and Gospel readings for the day seem to deal with another matter entirely, namely, the power and sovereignty of God. Job 38:1-11 contains the first part of God's discourse to Job on his omnipotence, and Mark 5:35-41 is the account of Jesus stilling the storm. A poignant point of contact is the picture of the Almighty begging and pleading with puny sinners to be reconciled with him.

Perhaps the simplest approach to this text is to go straight at the idea of the relationship among the three doctrines. The theme will probably depend on which of the doctrines the preacher will want to emphasize. If it is the role of the ministry, then the theme and parts may be something like this:

God Has a Message to Send

1. He has reconciled the world to himself in Christ (vv. 18,19a, 21)
2. He begs you to believe this (vv. 14-17, 20b)
3. He has sent your minister as his ambassador (vv. 19b,20)

If emphasis on the doctrine of universal reconciliation is preferred, the same parts can be used with a theme like:

God Seeks to Save the Whole World

If the doctrine of subjective reconciliation is to be featured, use the above parts with the theme:

Be Reconciled to God

This text also lends itself well to ordination and installation sermons.

SIXTH SUNDAY AFTER PENTECOST

The Scriptures

> Old Testament — *Lamentations 3:22-33*
> Epistle — *2 Corinthians 8:1-9, 13,14, 21-24a*
> Gospel — *Mark 5:21-24a, 35-43*

The Text — 2 Corinthians 8:1-12

Paul had changed his plans to visit the Corinthians after his first letter to them. False teachers in Corinth saw this as an opportunity to discredit his integrity and authority as an apostle. Paul, therefore, wrote this second epistle to defend his reputation and to remind them of the glorious message of reconciliation through Christ which he had proclaimed while among them.

Chapter 8 brings about a change in emphasis. After "setting the record straight," Paul now speaks of the special offering for the brothers and sisters in Jerusalem who were suffering from the effects of famine. A year earlier the Corinthians had begun plans to give financial assistance, but problems with a matter of church discipline (the incestuous man mentioned in 1 Corinthians 5) and the false teachers caused a very unfortunate stop to their efforts. Paul gives strong encouragement and Christ-centered motivation to pick up where they had left off. In so doing the apostle provides us with thoroughly evangelical principles on the subject of the God-pleasing use of our financial resources.

> vv. 1,2 — *And now, brothers, we want you to know about the grace that God has given the Macedonian churches. Out of the most severe trial, their overflowing joy and their extreme poverty welled up in rich generosity.*

To encourage the Corinthians, Paul mentions the Macedonians. He doesn't do this to prod the Corinthians into action by shaming them. He simply mentions the situation of fellow Christians who had exhibited the gift of Christian charity in responding to a need which had arisen in Jerusalem.

This gift, or grace (χάριν) was something God had given them. Those believers from the congregations in Thessalonica and Philippi had received God's grace in Christ and had reflected that grace by graciously and generously giving financial assistance, even though they themselves were also suffering harsh trials and great poverty (ἡ κατὰ βάθους πτωχεία αὐτῶν, "their poverty down to the deep").

This grace of giving out of appreciation for the grace of God was characterized by a "singleness of purpose" (ἁπλότης), which resulted in generosity. Since they knew how the Father had lavished his love upon them in making them his children, they also knew their one task in life was to give glory to him in everything they did. One way of doing this was by letting their own love and joy overflow in carrying out their mission of mercy for the saints in Jerusalem.

vv. 3,4 — *For I testify that they gave as much as they were able, and even beyond their ability. Entirely on their own, they urgently pleaded with us for the privilege of sharing in this service to the saints.*

When the grace of God fills the heart, there is no need to coerce people into serving their Lord. So with the Macedonians. On their own (αὐθαίρετος, "self-chosen, of their own accord") the Macedonians did even more than it seemed they were capable of doing. They wanted to share in the privilege (χάρις, again) and in the fellowship (κοινωνία) of being part of this service to their brothers and sisters, all holy saints cleansed in the blood of Jesus. Realizing these were co-heirs with them of the hope of eternal life, what else could they do but help in their earthly need?

v. 5 — *And they did not do as we expected, but they gave themselves first to the Lord and then to us in keeping with God's will.*

In keeping with their thoroughly God-pleasing attitude, the Macedonians also went the extra mile in making sure their motivation for helping the Jerusalem saints was above board. Instead of just going ahead with collecting the monies, they first offered their hearts to the Lord. They were not trying to earn extra favor from their Lord; they were reflecting his gracious favor to them. There could be no better "firstfruits" than their very souls.

v. 6 — *So we urged Titus, since he had earlier made a beginning, to bring also to completion this act of grace on your part.*

Titus had brought Paul the encouraging report that the church discipline matter had been taken care of. Titus had also been involved in the Corinthians' original plans to take part in this offering. Now Paul was going to send this respected, tested leader back to Corinth to help them carry out their resolve.

vv. 7,8 — *But just as you excel in everything—in faith, in speech, in knowledge, in complete earnestness and in your love for us—*

206

*see that you also excel in this grace of giving. I am not command-
ing you, but I want to test the sincerity of your love by comparing
it with the earnestness of others.*

In his first letter to them, Paul had given thanks for the abundant
gifts the Corinthians enjoyed by God's grace (1 Co 1:4-6). They openly
confessed their faith in Christ, they were zealous in their desire to
live Christ, and they showed Christlike love to Paul and his partners.
Note that the NIV follows the textual variant rather than the UBS
reading, ὑμῶν ἐν ἡμῖν rather than ἡμῶν ἐν ὑμῖν.

They truly excelled in these spiritual traits. Paul encourages them
to overflow in the special grace of giving too. It's simply the consistent thing for people who have had the love of the Father lavished
upon them in gracious abundance.

Paul then assures them that this comparison with the Macedonians is not done in the spirit of legalistic command: "Since they did
this, you should do that." Rather, the apostle knows that God's people
welcome the opportunity to join fellow Christians in carrying out
work that belongs to us all. We even relish this kind of spiritual exercise which helps us refine our Christian conduct in a way that shows
the genuineness (γνήσιον) of our Christian love. We don't see comparisons, then, as a reason to join in a project. We see them as reasons to
be joyful that someone else has taken the lead in a project in which
we also went to participate.

v. 9 — *For you know the grace of our Lord Jesus Christ, that
though he was rich, yet for your sakes he became poor, so that
you through his poverty might become rich.*

Without question this is the key verse of the text. Only the grace of
God in Christ can give the motivation to be gracious to others in their
physical and spiritual needs. Only the grace of God in Christ can create the desire to share our firstfruits without feelings of compulsion
or personal pride. Only the grace of God in Christ can provide joy in
taking part in such a beautiful task.

The Corinthians knew that grace of God very well. This "problem
child" congregation had been "taken over Paul's knee," so to speak,
because of their abuse of God's abundant spiritual gifts to them and
because of their apathy toward the wayward brother. But God's grace
was a charming sound in the ears of these penitent children of God,
who had learned from Paul about the poverty which the Savior allowed himself to endure during his humble life on earth.

Although Jesus never for a moment stopped being the almighty
God, he temporarily gave up the full use of his divine qualities to be

the kind of Redeemer who could suffer for the suffering and die for the dying. Through this poverty we are truly rich.

vv. 10-12 — *And here is my advice about what is best for you in this matter: Last year you were the first not only to give but also to have the desire to do so. Now finish the work, so that your eager willingness to do it may be matched by your completion of it, according to your means. For if the willingness is there, the gift is acceptable according to what one has, not according to what he does not have.*

Paul concludes by giving some practical advice about what would be most beneficial for them, in view of everything he has just said. He reminds them that their eagerness to give assistance had been there before. Now they simply need to get on with this chapter of their congregational life and bring it to a finish.

What an evangelical comfort that our giving is "from the having." God judges our offerings not by the amount of the gift, but by the attitude of the heart. This is true in the stewardship of all the gifts God has seen fit to give us. We don't lament what we don't have. We praise God for what we do possess in the way we faithfully, generously, and thoughtfully use our blessings in his service.

Homiletical Suggestions

Throughout these verses St. Paul has held up the grace of God as the center of his proclamation. For one thing, the grace of God has moved the Macedonians to respond to the need of their fellow believers in Jerusalem. This was a gracious gift in and of itself. It is only through God's undeserved love that we have any desire to share with others. Otherwise, we would be selfishly taking our possessions to eternal death.

Paul also knew that the grace of God would move the Corinthians to listen to the Macedonian comparison with joy-filled thanks. For they knew from humbling spiritual experience the grace of God in Christ which had led their Savior to humble himself for them.

As we proclaim these words, may we be careful to follow the example and spirit of Paul. He does not badger people into giving financial gifts, nor does he shy away from the subject with a timid voice. Rather, he straightforwardly speaks to people of God as people of God, citizens of the kingdom who will respond according to their means in every area of Christian life.

The following outlines are offered with the hope of letting this text speak for itself.

The Grace of Our Lord Jesus Christ
1. Was shown in his poverty (v. 9)
2. Is reflected in our generosity (vv. 1-8, 10-12)

The Grace of Giving
1. Finds its motivation in the grace of Christ (v. 9)
2. Finds its example in the graciousness of others (vv. 1-5)
3. Finds its expression in the gratefulness of our own hearts (vv. 6-8,10-12)

Excel in the Grace of Giving
1. In thankfulness for the generosity of others (vv. 1-5)
2. In appreciation of the generosity of Christ (v. 9)

The following outline could prove helpful when speaking on a "special occasion" or "special effort" Sunday:

According to What One Has
1. We have a wonderful example: the Macedonians
2. We have a wonderful Savior: Christ Jesus
3. We have a wonderful opportunity: [Whatever the special occasion or effort calls for]

SEVENTH SUNDAY AFTER PENTECOST

The Scriptures

>Old Testament — *Ezekiel 2:1-5*
>Epistle — *2 Corinthians 12:7-10*
>Gospel — *Mark 6:1-6*

The Text — 2 Corinthians 12:7-10

Paul's second letter to the Corinthians is the most autobiographical of his letters, and the latter part of chapter 11 and first part of chapter 12 are perhaps the most personal. Paul's integrity and authority had been challenged by the false teachers, and it is natural that he should respond to such a personal challenge so personally. His detailed description of how he met those challenges, particularly in our text, gives us divinely inspired direction for the challenges we face in our lives of personal and public ministry. The section may be incomprehensible to the unbeliever, but for the believer it is a source of richest comfort and encouragement.

>v. 7 — *To keep me from becoming conceited because of these surpassingly great revelations, there was given me a thorn in my flesh, a messenger of Satan, to torment me.*

There are suggestions that the first phrase in Greek, "because of these surpassingly great revelations," should be included with verse 6 rather than 7. Either way, it is obvious that the Apostle Paul closely connects the revelations with the "thorn" in a cause-and-effect relationship. There was danger that either Paul's boasting might be misunderstood, or Paul might become proud because of the "preferential" treatment he received. So, he explains, "a messenger of Satan" was sent to "buffet" or "harass" or "trouble" him.

The σκόλοψ is a "thorn," "sharply pointed sliver," or "pointed stake." What was Paul's thorn? Scores of possible explanations have been given, with the greatest weight leaning towards some very painful physical condition. Severe headaches, epilepsy, ophthalmia, malaria have all been suggested. Some have suggested that the thorn was a temptation, or even a person. It was obviously not God's intent to reveal the specifics. We should see in it an application for any and all who suffer torment from one of Satan's messengers. Paul's thorn was no accident. It was given to him. What might at first have been considered a cruel ploy of the devil must correctly be seen as the gracious gift of God, as Paul develops more thoroughly in the following verses. Here he states the final result of God's intent, ἵνα μὴ ὑπεραίρ-ωμαι, "to keep me from becoming conceited." The phrase appears twice, most likely for strong emphasis.

v. 8 — *Three times I pleaded with the Lord to take it away from me.*

This verse should not be understood to suggest that Paul prayed only three times about what appears to have been a persistent problem. There were three very special times when the apostle gave special attention to this problem in prayer. Παρεκάλεσα denotes an earnest appeal. Ἵνα expresses the purpose of the appeal, that God would remove the thorn.

v. 9 — *But he said to me, "My grace is sufficient for you, for my power is made perfect in weakness." Therefore I will boast all the more gladly about my weaknesses, so that Christ's power may rest on me.*

There is no warrant for assuming that Paul's petitions were self-serving, and therefore denied. No doubt, Paul's concern was very God-fearing: "Will my thorn stand in the way of effective proclamation of the gospel?" But just as grace saved us, so grace is not dependent on us for its effective proclamation. The perfect εἴρηκεν suggests a definitive answer, still holding true: God knows what he is doing!

God's grace "is sufficient." It not only suffices for the present moment but continues to suffice. His power τελεῖται, is being "perfected," "finished," or "completed" in weakness. God continues to bring Paul close to his spiritual goal and blesses others through Paul's work, despite Paul's weaknesses day by day. We see that it is God's power and not ours most clearly when it works despite our weaknesses. Lenski comments: "As long as we sinners imagine that we still have some power, we are unfit instruments for the Lord's hands."

Paul uses a superlative and a comparative to state his reaction: ἥδιστα οὖν μᾶλλον καυχήσομαι: "Therefore I will boast all the more gladly." In other words, "Rather than pray about this (I've received my answer), I'll boast (God's grace is marvelous)." Paul's purpose in boasting is that the power of Christ might "take up its abode," literally, "tent over" him.

v. 10 — *That is why, for Christ's sake, I delight in weaknesses, in insults, in hardships, in persecutions, in difficulties. For when I am weak, then I am strong.*

Διό expresses a causal relationship; Paul can delight in *anything* if it is "for Christ's sake." The wonderful conclusion is: "When I am weak, then I am strong." The generalizing temporal ὅταν helps to express a certainty. With the indicative it is a simple statement of the beautiful fact that our weakness only illustrates and emphasizes our strength in Christ.

Homiletical Suggestions

All of the Scripture readings for this Sunday highlight the opposition which preachers of the gospel may face. The sermon text is God's dramatic answer to the problem of suffering, an answer that does not remove the suffering but redirects the sufferer to the Solution, Jesus Christ.

The cross of Christ reduces our "thorns" to size, putting our most severe troubles in perspective. The grace of Jesus Christ overwhelms our weaknesses so totally that it can even turn our weaknesses into something positive. This wonderfully encouraging text suggests the theme:

Celebrate God's Grace in Time of Trouble

1. Recognize his power (vv. 7,8)
2. Call on him for strength (v. 8)
3. Trust his answer (vv. 9,10)

Remembering that the "thorn" is a "pointed stake" and that God's grace evokes the cross, another stake, you might consider a novel approach:

Consider the Stakes

1. Thorny problems pose threats (vv. 7,8)
2. The cross of Christ removes threats (vv. 9,10)

EIGHTH SUNDAY AFTER PENTECOST

The Scriptures

> Old Testament — *Amos 7:10-15*
> Epistle — *Ephesians 1:3-14*
> Gospel — *Mark 6:7-13*

The Text — Ephesians 1:3-14

This Sunday is the first in an eight-week succession of Epistle readings from Ephesians. A more extended overview of the letter would seem to be in order. It belongs to that group of Paul's letters known as the Prison Epistles. It shares this distinction with Philippians, Colossians, and Philemon. The Prison Epistles get their name from the fact that they were written while Paul was under house arrest in Rome, awaiting the outcome of his appeal to Caesar (Acts 25:11; 28:30). This would date them somewhere between 59 and 62 A.D. Ephesians was probably written in the middle of this period, since it makes no reference to Paul's trial or his expecting to be released.

Ephesians was most likely written as a general letter written for circulation among the churches in the vicinity of Ephesus, a congregation in which Paul had labored for more than two-and-a-half years. This would explain the absence of personal touches in the letter and the fact that many of Paul's readers seem to know him from reports rather than from personal acquaintance (1:15; 3:2).

What makes Ephesians such a remarkable letter is its exalted vision. In it, Paul sees life from a cosmic perspective, giving us a God's-eye view of things. He begins by seeing the individual Christian's life in the light of eternity. Our present faith has an eternal cause, God's gracious choice of us in Christ before the foundation of the world. It leads us to an eternal goal, that we may live forever to the praise of his glorious grace.

In chapter 2 Paul gives us the tragic vision of what humanity is without Christ, and the glorious vision of what the new humanity is with and in him. We are the body of Christ, united in him with God and with each other. In chapter 3 Paul speaks about the key role played by himself and the other apostles in making known this new revelation of God's will.

In the final chapters of the letter Paul urges his readers to live from their new identity in Christ. This means remaining one in faith and love with the body of Christ, recognizing and appreciating the gifts Christ gives to his church, growing mature in our knowledge of Christ and serving one another in our lives of personal ministry. Noteworthy in chapters 4 and 5 is the way in which Paul frames moral issues in absolute terms. Living the new life is not a matter of finding which shade of gray is the most comfortable for us, but a struggle between light and darkness, the old and the new, in which there can be no compromise offered and quarter given.

In a particularly beautiful section at the end of chapter 5 and the beginning of chapter 6, Paul speaks of our earthly roles and relationships with each other as being shaped and regulated by our individual relationship with our Lord Jesus. Jesus is the power behind and the pattern for our expressions of love to one another as husband, wife, parent, child, slave, and master.

In the final section Paul takes us beyond the surface cut-and-thrust of everyday life to see the cosmic forces locked in combat. Our struggle is not against mere human beings but against the spiritual forces of evil in the heavenly realm. Only by putting on the full armor of God and depending on his power will we be able to stand firm.

From this brief overview we can see that Paul clearly wants to teach the readers of this letter to look beneath the surface of life and understand its true nature. Life's true nature is known only to God, summed up in Christ, and revealed to us through the apostolic word. The impressive depth and breathtaking vision of the letter is all the more remarkable in view of Paul's confinement while writing it. Only faith in the promised love of God can soar to such heights or sound such depths.

The sermon text views believers from the vantage point of God's selection of them in Christ before the foundation of the world. The particular challenge for the preacher is to present the doctrine of election as gospel, which it is. It was not revealed as grist for the mills of speculation or debate, but as a joyful truth to be announced so as to bolster faith. To miss this is to miss the tone of Paul's message. Election is gospel history viewed in eternity's light.

v. 3 — *Praise be to the God and Father of our Lord Jesus Christ, who has blessed us in the heavenly realms with every spiritual blessing in Christ.*

Paul begins by leading his readers in a hymn of praise. The praise of our lips is to be accompanied by the praise of our lives. This praise is not found in some generic hymnbook, acceptable to anyone who believes in a Supreme Being. It is directed to the God who is the Father

214

of our Lord Jesus Christ. Jesus is the only way we can approach God, trust in him, and discern his eternal purpose for us.

In Christ, God has blessed us with every spiritual blessing. There is absolutely nothing outside Christ's gift, and nothing to gain by looking for another giver. The blessings he gives are spiritual, which means they are grasped by faith and not by sight. They are in the heavenly realms and so are kept secure from "the dust and the rust and the ruin that names us and claims us and shames us all."

vv. 4-6 — *For he chose us in him before the creation of the world to be holy and blameless in his sight. In love he predestined us to be adopted as his sons through Jesus Christ, in accordance with his pleasure and his will—to the praise of his glorious grace, which he has freely given us in the One he loves.*

Before the world was born, God set his heart on having me as his own forever. Not only did he determine to embrace every human being by the redeeming death of his Son, he also selected me personally and individually in Christ before time began. He chose me, not *because* I was holy and blameless, but *that I might be* holy and blameless before him. All the world can condemn me, the devil may accuse me, and my own conscience convict me. But God has determined that in Christ I am holy and blameless before him. No other verdict matters. In these words I find a place in which to lose a guilty conscience, on which to build a new life.

God's choice can be approached from several directions for better understanding. We can consider the *attitude* in God's heart which prompted his choosing. Paul says he did it "in love" and "in accordance with his pleasure and will." In other words, it was a free act of love on God's part. It was not prompted by anything God saw in me, but a loving resolve in which God's will alone was active (cf. Jn 1:13).

This means the *act of choosing* itself was one of pure grace. What makes God's grace so amazing is just this that we can detect no cause for it in ourselves. The fact that the choosing occurred "before the foundation of the world" underscores the same truth, since it tells me that I was chosen before I existed, before I was someone who could choose, or think, or do anything. Overwhelmed by God's unconditional love for me, I can only "praise his glorious grace" (v. 6).

God did not choose us to be saved in some capricious or arbitrary way, but in connection with the redeeming work Christ would do. God chose us "in him." Adoption is "through Jesus Christ." His grace is given to us "in the One he loves." Look at Jesus living and dying for you in history, and you will understand the *nature of God's elec-*

tion in eternity. It was not the act of a god soft on sin, but the act of God by which he determined to deal with sin completely in Christ. It was not the act of a bored, disinterested god casually deciding our fate. It was the act of God who loved all the lost. He resolved to send his Son to become one of us and die for us.

There are many things about God's eternal will which are hidden and inscrutable. But Christ's death on Calvary is supremely scrutable. From this direction alone do we approach God's choice of some to be his own in eternity.

The content of election, as far as we are concerned, is seen in the phrase "to be adopted as his sons." Adoption (υἱοθεσία) was a common practice in the Greco-Roman world. The literal meaning of the Greek is "setting into sonship." It was a legal procedure by which someone with no claim of membership in a family or clan was taken into the family or clan as a son. Afterwards, the one adopted had the full legal status of a son, and full inheritance rights.

Jesus, of course, is the "natural" Son in God's family, who has also (as true man) earned the right to hear his Father say, "This is my son, whom I love; with him I am well pleased" (Mt 3:17). We had no such right, since we are sinful. But Jesus earned God's fatherly approval for us. By faith we receive the status of being children and heirs of God. We have the same rights as the "natural" Son (Ga 3:26; 4:4-6).

Adoption includes the gift of the Spirit, by whom we call out to God in the complete freedom of faith, "Abba, Father!" The full blessings of our adoption will reach fulfillment when our bodies are raised free from sin and death at the return of Christ (Ro 8:15,23). Then we will inherit the kingdom prepared for us from the foundation of the world. From all this it is clear that God chose us in eternity to be his children, determined that we would receive the gift of faith and the Spirit in time and resolved to bring us safely through every trial—including death—to our inheritance in heaven. From eternity to eternity we have every reason to praise his glorious grace!

> vv. 7-10 — *In him we have redemption through his blood, the forgiveness of sins, in accordance with the riches of God's grace that he lavished on us with all wisdom and understanding. And he made known to us the mystery of his will according to his good pleasure, which he purposed in Christ, to be put into effect when the times will have reached their fulfillment—to bring all things in heaven and on earth together under one head, even Christ.*

We note some of the same themes in this section that we noticed in the previous one: the resolve of God's will, God's grace, the christocentric nature of election and so on. No further comment is necessary on these points.

What we will want to take a closer look at are some of the distinctive notes Paul sounds here. Our election was not some abstract process which began and ended in the clean white halls of heaven on that eternal morning. It included redemption in blood, the cost of the forgiveness of sins. Ἀπολύτρωσις is the act of securing the release of someone who is enslaved or whose life is forfeit. Redemption sets the person free from the slavery and the punishment by a substitutionary payment.

As "objects of wrath" (Eph 2:3), our lives were forfeit. We deserved nothing but the consuming fire of God's anger. We lived out our lives enslaved by wretched desires for wretched, unfulfilling things. By giving his Son over into the utter poverty of death, God lavished the riches of his grace on us—all undeserving.

Paul praises the "wisdom and understanding" of God's resolve to save us. The Almighty knows things as they truly are, and plans accordingly. His wisdom and understanding for us "little children" is clearly seen in that he comes to us not as he is in his unclothed majesty, but clothed in the humanity of Jesus (Mt 11:25-30). He hides his wisdom deep in the apparent foolishness of the cross and the proclamation of the cross (1 Co 1:18-31).

This "mystery" of his will (τὸ μυστήριον = a secret, to be known only by revelation) has been made known to us through the apostolic Word. The Word is the delivery system by which God gives to us in time what he planned for us in eternity.

Paul brings this section to a close by describing God's plan in terms of its final outcome: "to bring all things in heaven and earth together under one head, even Christ" (v. 10). These are extraordinary words. Ἀνακεφαλαιόω means "to sum up," to put a list of things under one organizing head. God planned that Christ would break down the barriers between heaven and earth and eliminate the divisions which alienated one human being from another. Christ is the sum and substance of history, the final crashing chord uniting all its dissonant strains into perfect harmony. In a world of confusion, where things do not add up, Christ makes sense of everything.

vv. 11-14 — *In him we were also chosen, having been predestined according to the plan of him who works out everything in conformity with the purpose of his will, in order that we, who were the first to hope in Christ, might be for the praise of his glory. And you also were included in Christ when you heard the word of truth, the gospel of your salvation. Having believed, you were marked in him with a seal, the promised Holy Spirit, who is a deposit guaranteeing our inheritance until the redemption of those who are God's possession—to the praise of his glory.*

"We" in verses 11 and 12 refers to Paul and his fellow countrymen, the Jews. "You" in verse 13 refers to the people of the Gentile nations, among whom Paul preached and for whom he had been appointed an apostle. The basic thrust of the passage is to tell us that God decided from eternity to unite Jew and Gentile believers in Christ, to form one people who would be his "treasured possession" (Ex 19:5). Paul unfolds this truth more fully in chapters 2 and 3.

The Jews attain their true nature as a people formed "for the praise of his glory" by centering their hope in Christ. Gentiles become part of God's people through faith in the same Lord. They share the same purpose in life, which is to live to praise God's glory. They wait for the same inheritance: the perfect freedom of heaven. Contrast this with the desperate state and grim destiny of the unbeliever, as outlined in 2:1-3.

All this happens "according to the plan of him who works out everything in conformity with the purpose of his will" (v. 11). The plans of men fail, and all our personal visions of the future fade, but God's resolution concerning us cannot fail. We can proceed serenely through life, knowing that we are lords of all in Christ, and that everything must serve us. Nothing can happen outside God's loving will for us. Others may rebel and oppose him, but he will mold, fashion, and shape everything that happens—even the wicked plans of evil men—so that they further his gracious will.

Paul reminds us of the point in time at which God's eternal plan intersected with our personal histories by the words, "You also were included in Christ *when you heard the word of truth*" (v. 13). God delivered our salvation to us in time by calling us to faith through the gospel.

By means of the same gospel he will preserve us in faith until we reach our glorious goal. To assure us that the inheritance of heaven will be truly ours, he sealed us with the gift of the Holy Spirit. Just as a seal serves to mark out an object as belonging to an individual, so the Holy Spirit is God's "seal of ownership on us" (2 Co 1:22).

Paul further characterizes the Holy Spirit as God's "deposit guaranteeing our inheritance" (v. 14). He uses ἀρραβών, familiar to his readers from the world of commerce as a technical term. It is variously translated as first installment, down payment, or pledge. It is a payment which obligates the contracting party to make further payments. Here it serves once again to emphasize the absolute certainty of our salvation in Christ. By giving us the Holy Spirit, God has obligated himself to release the complete inheritance to us on the last day.

Praise his glorious grace!

Homiletical Suggestions

Spend some time giving the book's setting and historical background. It certainly doesn't have to come across as a dry lecture. A prisoner who writes a letter such as this surely must strike answering chords in the hearts of those who feel themselves trapped by the uncertainties of this life. The stress of everyday demands can reduce our forward vision to practically nothing, so that our best hope becomes surviving the next few minutes. Paul gives us some certainties to proclaim here, and a vision broader than the oceans.

One angle of approach:

A God's Eye View of Your Future

1. Secured by God's decision (vv. 4,5,11)
2. Signed, sealed, and delivered (vv. 7,9,11,14)
3. For the praise of his glory (vv. 3,6,14)

In these days when self-esteem building is regarded as the most important task of psychology, and the highest mission of the church, we might do well to preach a sermon in which Christians are encouraged to appropriate their full identity as children of the triune God:

By God's Grace, I Am

1. Chosen to be my Father's child (vv. 3-6)
2. Set free by the blood of Christ (vv. 7-10)
3. Sealed by the promised Spirit (vv. 11-14)

Finally, if one wishes to preserve the hymnlike quality of the section, he can adapt Paul's words in verse 6 to formulate the theme:

Praise God for His Grace

1. He chose me for his own (vv. 3-6)
2. He redeemed me by his blood (vv. 7-10)
3. He sealed me with his Spirit (vv. 11-14)

THE NINTH SUNDAY AFTER PENTECOST

The Scriptures

Old Testament — *Jeremiah 23:1-6*
Epistle — *Ephesians 2:13-22*
Gospel — *Mark 6:30-34*

The Text — Ephesians 2:13-22

In the first ten verses of this chapter Paul speaks the most beautiful message ever heard, the gospel. He makes no distinction between Jews and Gentiles, because both groups were in the same spiritual boat, dead. Both groups came to believe in the same way, by grace. There is only one way to be saved, by God's grace in Christ Jesus. That applies to all, both Jews and Gentiles. That is the one thing that all believers have in common.

v. 13 — *But now in Christ Jesus you who once were far away have been brought near through the blood of Christ.*

The old order has passed away; a new order has appeared. Before, Gentiles were excluded, foreigners, without hope. Now they have been "brought near." Ἐγενήθητε is aorist passive, indicating that their nearness was not their accomplishment. It was done for them by God. How did God do that? In these four verses (13-16) Paul uses six different phrases to emphasize that Jesus accomplished this. Here he starts out by saying, "in Christ Jesus," then ends the same verse with, "through the blood of Christ."

The one and only One who supersedes all human barriers, tears down all human walls, and unites all people regardless of race, color, sex, national origin, or spiritual aptitude is Jesus. In the world, people who have these differences may be far apart, but in Christ they are "near." His work of saving mankind is the one historic event that made the difference, destroyed the old order and set up a new order where Jew and Gentile are no longer separate but united.

v. 14 — *For he himself is our peace, who has made the two one and has destroyed the barrier, the dividing wall of hostility*

Jesus is the peace between two races. He is the one person who destroys everything that separates and divides, who brings the two cultures together as one united church. Literally, he is "the one who made the two one and loosed the dividing wall of the fence of hostility." As strong, seemingly permanent, and divisive as the wall was,

Jesus brought it down. No matter how strong the prejudices are, no matter how deep the animosity, no matter how set the hatred, Jesus can bring down any wall. The next two verses tell us more about how Jesus did this:

v. 15 — *by abolishing in his flesh the law with its commandments and regulations. His purpose was to create in himself one new man out of the two, thus making peace,*

What had fueled this enmity? What had kept this barrier strong and divisive? "The law with its commandments and regulations," the law which God gave to his Old Testament people made this wall solid. So, the way to break down that wall was to abolish the law. That's exactly what Jesus did. In one act, once for all (aorist active participle), Jesus abolished that law.

He did this "in his flesh." He made himself subject to the law, fulfilled all its commands and demands, and suffered for all transgressions against the law.

Now follows the clause of intended result, which continues into verse 16. His first purpose, which he achieved, was "to create one new man out of two." It took nothing less than God's creative power (κτίσῃ) to destroy the old divisions and create one new person. Jesus exerted that power, "thus making peace."

v. 16 — *and in this one body to reconcile both of them to God through the cross, by which he put to death their hostility.*

This is the second part of the intended result clause. Jesus' purpose was to "reconcile both of them to God," and he accomplished that. Basic in ἀποκαταλλάσσω is the idea of change. There was no need for God to change. There was no way for man to make the necessary change. In Christ, God changed our status. See 2 Corinthians 5:17-21.

"In this one body" does not refer to Christ's body. Rather, Jesus reconciled both peoples in one body—together. Recall τὰ ἀμφότερα ἕν (v. 14) and τοὺς δύο κτίσῃ . . . εἰς ἕνα (v. 15).

The cross was the one historical event that abolished the law, reconciled God and man, and destroyed the hostility. What hostility did Jesus put to death? First of all, the hostility between God and man. Then also the hostility that man has for other men.

There is a certain redundancy in these four verses, redundancy for the sake of emphasis. Paul wants the Ephesians to know for certain that there is no more hostility.

v.17 — *He came and preached peace to you who were far away and peace to those who were near.*

Here, Paul quotes the Old Testament to prove that he is not teaching a new doctrine but one that the prophets have already proclaimed. Already in the Old Testament, God reminded the Israelites that salvation was not intended only for them. In Isaiah 57:19 we read, "'Peace, peace, to those far and near,'" says the Lord. 'And I will heal them.'" Compare also Zechariah 9:10.

Paul repeats the word "peace" in both phrases to show that the message to the Jews and to the Gentiles was exactly the same. Both Jews and Gentiles have peace, and peace from the same source, Jesus the Savior. He doesn't use a generic term of telling, proclaiming, or declaring. He uses εὐαγγελίζω.

v. 18 — *For through him we both have access to the Father by one Spirit. Both Jews and Gentiles have the same access to God through Jesus.*

The point should be made that all people of all time are saved in the same way through Jesus. The Old Testament people weren't saved because they were Jews who could trace their physical ancestry back to Abraham or because they followed certain customs. They were saved through believing in the "Seed" whom God promised as a blessing to all nations. That is the only way in which anyone in Old Testament times was saved. That is also the only way in which New Testament believers are saved. With the blessing of salvation goes the privilege of approaching God, "access to the Father."

What does the phrase ἐν ἑνὶ πνεύματι mean? The two possibilities are: 1) "By the one Holy Spirit," who brings about this access to God, or 2) in one spirit, both Jewish and Gentile believers approaching the Father in one spiritual attitude. The NIV obviously chooses the former, as do many good commentators. The context directs us toward understanding this phrase as "in one spirit." In discussing unity Paul has cited "one new man" (v. 15), "one body" (v. 16); now it is "one spirit."

v. 19 — *Consequently, you are no longer foreigners and aliens, but fellow citizens with God's people and members of God's household,*

At one time the Gentiles were "separate from Christ, excluded from citizenship in Israel, foreigners to the covenants of the promise, without hope and without God in the world" (2:12). Now, based on all he wrote in verses 13-18, Paul can say, "No longer." You are no longer what you were—foreigners and aliens—part of God's family. Gentile Christians are no longer people without rights, outsiders.

Rather, they are "fellow citizens with God's people." Συμπολῖται are citizens who dwell in a place with all rights and privileges. They belong there. It is their home. They are full-fledged citizens. They are also "members of God's household," part of the family, with all the rights, privileges, and responsibilities thereof.

v. 20 — *built on the foundation of the apostles and prophets, with Christ Jesus himself as the chief cornerstone.*

Now Paul uses a third picture to illustrate the unity which Jesus has established: bricks in a building. The foundation on which Christians are built is "the apostles and the prophets." In 1 Corinthians 3:11 Paul says the foundation upon which we build is Christ. Is there a contradiction? When Paul talks about "the apostles and prophets," he is not speaking about them as men, but as the ones who wrote down God's Word, of which Christ is the heart and core. To be founded on the Scriptures ("the apostles and prophets") is to be built on Christ.

In Paul's illustration here, what part does Jesus play in this building? He is called ἀκρογωνιαίου; from ἄκρον, "the high point, top" and γωνία, "the corner." There are two possible ways of understanding the term: 1) the cornerstone, the first stone laid in the foundation, the stone which gave every other stone its direction and placement; 2) the capstone, the last stone set in an arch, holding it secure.

Either definition provides an excellent picture of Christ and his relation to the church. As "cornerstone" Jesus is the stone used to mark and measure all other stones. He is the one to whom we always look to determine what shall be our direction. As "capstone" Jesus holds his church together securely.

This verse specifies the two things needed to build Christ's church: Scripture and Christ. We are founded on the Scriptures. Through Christ we have the strength to believe and to follow his will for our lives.

v. 21 — *In him the whole building is joined together and rises to become a holy temple in the Lord.*

Συναρμολογουμένη is a present participle which denotes a continuing process. Building Christ's church and fitting it all together is a continuing process, as we grow closer to him and to one another. The building fits together, grows together, to become "a holy temple in the Lord." Jesus puts us here. Jesus helps us to grow together. The temple exists to serve Jesus and to bring glory to him.

v. 22 — And in him you too are being built together to become a dwelling in which God lives by his Spirit.

This "you" does not designate either Jew or Gentile, as it did in the other verses. For now there is no difference. We are all one, and the "you" denotes all of God's people, Jews and Gentiles together.

"You are being built together" is again present, indicating a continuing process. You are all components in the building of Christ's church, "a dwelling in which God lives." Each of us plays a part in that dwelling, each has a certain place and function, each has a right (and a need) to be there.

Paul concludes with ἐν πνεύματι. Only the Holy Spirit can affect a change in us. Only the Holy Spirit could convert us from "dead objects of wrath" into living saints. Only the Holy Spirit can soften our attitude toward people who in this world might be regarded as threats or enemies. Only the Holy Spirit can help us grow in faith so as to be built up in Christ's church and take our place with the rest of the "bricks." Only the Holy Spirit can give us the courage and the ability to bring others to Jesus.

Homiletical Suggestions

In the Old Testament lesson, God condemns the shepherds of Israel for scattering his sheep. He promises to send his own shepherds who will rescue and tend his flock, and none will be lost. In the Gospel for the day Jesus tries to get away from the crowds so that he and his disciples can get some rest. But when the crowds come to him and appear to be a sheep without a shepherd, the Good Shepherd has compassion and takes time to teach them.

Adapting the Shepherd idea to the Epistle lesson and using a phrase from the Old Testament lesson, we suggest:

There Will Be No Missing Sheep

1. Many people are lost (vv. 13,19)
2. Jesus brings them back (vv. 14-18)
3. God's people accept them (vv. 19-22)

Or, talk about God's church and how it grows, using only verses 19-22:

God Builds His Church

1. The foundation is the Scripture (v. 20a)
2. The cornerstone is Christ (v. 20b)

3. The bricks are God's people (vv. 21,22)

For a sermon emphasizing the unity of Christ's church try:

When the Walls Come Tumbling Down

1. Some walls seem too solid (vv. 13,19)
2. Jesus has destroyed all the walls (vv. 14-17)
3. All Christians are now one people (vv. 18-22)

TENTH SUNDAY AFTER PENTECOST

The Scriptures

Old Testament — *Exodus 24:3-11*
Epistle — *Ephesians 4:1-7,11-16*
Gospel — *John 6:1-15*

The Text — Ephesians 4:1-7,11-16

One of four letters written by Paul while he was a prisoner in Rome, Ephesians is a positive epistle sent to edify a congregation where he had spent more than two years. The blessedness of membership in the church of Christ and the obligations of that membership comprise the two main parts of the letter. The text under consideration begins the second part with an admonition to preserve the unity which Paul has described in chapter 2, a unity which has broken down the old barriers between Jewish and Gentile believers.

v. 1 — *As a prisoner for the Lord, then, I urge you to live a life worthy of the calling you have received.*

Following the doxology in the previous verse, οὖν clearly starts a new section. Paul is appealing to his readers to live appropriately as members of the church because of their gracious "calling" to faith by the gospel (cp. Ro 12:1). As a prisoner for this faith he can speak with the authority and credibility of the Lord he serves.

v. 2 — *Be completely humble and gentle; be patient, bearing with one another in love.*

Turning to the subject of unity, Paul cites the attitudes necessary to maintain it. Humility, gentleness, and forbearance are each rooted in Christian love (ἀγάπη).

v. 3 — *Make every effort to keep the unity of the Spirit through the bond of peace.*

The first three verses are one sentence in Greek. A participle dependent on the first two verses, σπουδάζοντες, is translated as an imperative: "Make every effort." "To keep" (τηρεῖν) means to guard and preserve so that something precious is not lost. That precious possession is "the unity of the Spirit," which is the theme of this section. It is a oneness established by the Holy Spirit when he calls people to a common faith in Christ as Lord and Savior. It is based, as we shall see (vv. 5,13,14), on agreement in doctrine. "The bond of peace" sustains the cohesiveness of this unity.

vv. 4-6 — *There is one body and one Spirit—just as you were called to one hope when you were called—one Lord, one faith, one baptism; one God and Father of all, who is over all and through all and in all.*

Three triads form the basis of this unity. Within each triad appears a Person of the Holy Trinity: Spirit, Lord (Jesus), Father.

"One body" refers to the church, the *Una Sancta* confessed in the Creed, further described as to its nature and function in verse 16. "One Spirit" corresponds to the idea of one body; the two fit together. The Spirit of God indwells the body of believers. And their "one hope" is the same sure hope of salvation to which they were called in Christ.

"One Lord, one faith, one baptism" are also connected. We are joined with the Savior, Jesus Christ, by believing in him and his Word, through the means of grace, particularly the sacrament of Baptism (Jn 15:5,7; Gal 3:26,27).

God is the Father of all who are in the family of Christ (cf. 2:19) and his relationship to them is multi-dimensional—"over, through, in." In other words, it is all-encompassing. Thus the inspired writer impressively depicts the true spiritual unity of the Christian church (cp. Jn 17:20,21).

v. 7 — *But to each one of us grace has been given as Christ apportioned it.*

"But" introduces a new thought, explaining how this unity can be retained amid the diversity of gifts bestowed upon the church. "Each one" has received a gift of grace (χάρις) from Christ who has ascended on high to rule over the world for the benefit of his church as the parenthetical thought of vv. 9 and 10 (not included in the Epistle Lesson) and 1:20-23 make clear.

v. 11 — *It was he who gave some to be apostles, some to be prophets, some to be evangelists, and some to be pastors and teachers,*

In addition to the spiritual gifts mentioned in other letters (Ro 12:4-8; 1 Co 12:1-11), various offices are mentioned as Christ's gifts for preserving the unity of the church. This passage has been used many times to define special functions which the Lord has provided to spread the good news of salvation in Christ as his messengers and sent out to proclaim the Word of God and to guide and instruct his people. Regardless of how the work is described today, or what titles they hold, these people are gifts to be received with thanks by the church.

v. 12 — *to prepare God's people for works of service, so that the body of Christ may be built up*

The primary work which the aforementioned gifted people have to do is "to prepare God's people" (ἀγίων), equipping them, outfitting them "for works of service." The concept of lay ministry is a scriptural principle, not merely a maxim of "church growth." For every member of the church is a servant according to this verse. Their purpose and function is to build up the body of Christ. Christians are "body-builders" in this sense, as they use their gifts for the corporate good of the church.

v. 13 — *until we all reach unity in the faith and in the knowledge of the Son of God and become mature, attaining to the whole measure of the fullness of Christ.*

The desired result will be achieved when all believers are united in a mature understanding of the faith which is embodied in the fullness of Christ, who is plainly identified as "the Son of God." Such a lofty goal will hardly be reached before we are raised with him and joined with him forever in heaven. Nevertheless, we strive for it.

v. 14 — *Then we will no longer be infants, tossed back and forth by the waves, and blown here and there by every wind of teaching and by the cunning and craftiness of men in their deceitful scheming.*

A striking image reminds us of our present condition: babies, bounced around like buoys on a wind-swept sea. The subtle subterfuge and saccharin sentiments of false doctrine can easily sway us, ripping us loose from our moorings, unless we are tethered securely to the truth of God's word.

v. 15 — *Instead, speaking the truth in love, we will in all things grow up into him who is the Head, that is, Christ.*

As we, motivated and governed by love, instruct and encourage one another, there will be growth. The truth will nourish and strengthen us so that we become ever more obedient to and imitative of him who is the Head of the body, Christ.

v. 16 — *From him the whole body, joined and held together by every supporting ligament, grows and builds itself up in love, as each part does its work.*

228

Again employing his beautiful "body" language Paul concludes this section by tying it all together with the theme of unity with which he began. The church is a unit, like a body comprised of many members, held together and working together by and in the love of Jesus Christ. As 1 Corinthians 12:12-31 demonstrates so graphically, each part is essential to the good of the whole.

Homiletical Suggestions

In an age when church unions are effected by "agreeing to disagree," this text is a welcome reminder of the true unity we possess in Christ through the Holy Spirit. It is a oneness he produces by means of the teachings of God's Word. Christians who are in doctrinal agreement express this fellowship. This doctrinal unity is our real strength in a visible church.

The diversity of the church, the variety of gifts the Lord bestows on its members, also has one purpose: to build up the body of Christ. Fulltime professionals and part-time volunteers work together in this ministry. We are called by God to this Christian life, which is typified by humble, patient love for one another "as each part does its work."

These thoughts lead to the following outlines:

The True Unity of the Church Is:

1. Produced by the Spirit of God (vv. 1-6,13-16)
2. Promoted by the gifts of God (vv. 7,11,12)

Christ's Gifts to His Church

1. Come in different packages (vv. 7,11,12)
2. Keep us working together (vv. 1-6)
3. Help us grow stronger (vv. 13-16)

Using a coin with the inscription, *E pluribus unum,* as an object lesson, you might provide a more striking theme:

Out of Many, One

1. We have different gifts in the body of Christ (vv. 7,11,12,16)
2. We work together in the unity of the Spirit (vv. 1-6,13-16)

Adapting Paul's admonition for the theme, and utilizing only verses 1-6, try:

Keep the Unity of the Spirit

1. The unity is God's gift (vv. 3b-6)
2. The keeping is our responsibility (vv. 1-3)

ELEVENTH SUNDAY AFTER PENTECOST

The Scriptures

> Old Testament — *Exodus 16:2-15*
> Epistle — *Ephesians 4:17-24*
> Gospel — *John 6:24-35*

The Text — Ephesians 4:17-24

Paul did not write this letter to the Christians in Ephesus to address any particular error or heresy that had arisen within the church, but to broaden his readers' understanding of God's gracious, eternal plan for them and all people. He hoped to lead his readers to a deeper appreciation of God's high goals for his people. In the early chapters of this letter Paul has reminded his readers that God has an eternal plan for them (1:4ff.) who were once lost in sin (2:1). He has assured them that they are now saved, thanks to God, by grace alone through faith (2:8,9).

Paul continues his letter by pointing out that people who know God's grace will demonstrate their knowledge by the way they live. In appreciation for the free gifts of forgiveness and life eternal, they will constantly seek to live a life of thanks to their merciful Savior. To live in any other way would indicate they no longer consider Jesus' saving work as the most important reality of their lives.

It is with these things in mind that we come to the words of the text. Paul speaks of the Christian's sanctified life and contrast it with the "old" way of life—life without Christ.

> v. 17 — *So I tell you this, and insist on it in the Lord, that you must no longer live as the Gentiles do, in the futility of their thinking.*

Paul is God's spokesman. At the beginning of this chapter he wrote, "As a prisoner for the Lord, then, I urge you to live a life worthy of the calling you have received" (4:1). Now his urging progresses to insistence. He testifies on behalf of the one true God and relates his will and purpose by commanding his readers not to live as the Gentiles do.

Paul uses the term "Gentiles" to refer to unbelievers. Many of the Ephesian Christians were "Gentiles," but after their conversion their ethnic background no longer matters. They are entirely different people now from what they were before.

Without Christ there is no life. There is only futility (ματαιότης, "vanity, emptiness"). In contrast to the life they now live in Christ, Paul reminds these Christians of the emptiness they used to call "life," the kind of futility in which their unbelieving neighbors were still living.

The unbeliever's goal is "happiness." His mind is filled with countless thoughts of how to obtain his goal, but because Christ is not in his thoughts they will never lead to happiness.

vv. 18,19 — *They are darkened in their understanding and separated from the life of God because of the ignorance that is in them due to the hardening of their hearts. Having lost all sensitivity, they have given themselves over to sensuality so as to indulge in every kind of impurity, with a continual lust for more.*

Paul traces the futile thinking of the unbelievers back to their darkened understanding. Their thoughts are futile because their minds have been totally corrupted by sin. It's impossible for unbelievers to have even one godly thought. Their sinful, corrupted nature has made them total strangers (ἀπηλλοτριωμένοι) to the spiritual life that God gives.

Whose fault is all this? Satan is no doubt the agent of the passive participles (darkened, separated) but, as is the case with all sin, the unbeliever must share equally in the blame. The unbeliever makes his heart callous or hard. He has ignored the natural knowledge of God and the law written in his heart for so long that his perverse thinking and conduct no longer bother him.

As Paul describes the conduct of unbelievers, he uses words such as "sensuality" and "impurity." Ἀσέλγεια is unrestrained living. Ἀκαθαρσία is uncleanness, or filthiness. Some limit the thought here to sexual sins, but ἀκαθαρσία is general enough to cover sins of every kind. People who have no sense of right or wrong go from one sin to another in an attempt to satisfy their insatiable cravings (πλεονεξία), no matter what the cost. Like drug addicts, they cannot get enough of the sinful pleasure that manages to bring only fleeting satisfaction.

Ironically, the unbeliever's darkened understanding of happiness must sooner or later lead to misery. Already in this life, without realizing it, the unbeliever suffers the consequences of living apart from God. He lives without the comforting peace that comes from being right with God through faith in Christ. If the unbeliever remains without this peace during his life here, then physical death will seal his separation from God for all eternity.

vv. 20,21 — *You, however, did not come to know Christ that way. Surely you heard of him and were taught in him in accordance with the truth that is in Jesus.*

Paul has been speaking about the conduct of the unbeliever. He now makes it clear to his readers that the individual who has come to know Christ will no longer live or act like an unbeliever. To come to know Christ means much more than becoming acquainted with him and his teachings. It means embracing him and his saving accomplishments by faith.

Εἰ serves to remind the Ephesian Christians that they heard the truth of Jesus. In effect the apostle is saying, "If indeed you heard . . . and certainly you did. . . ." By God's grace we, like Paul's first readers, have come to trust in the saving truth about Jesus—how he lived and died and rose again for us. When we came to know and believe this truth, we did not at the same time learn that we could serve and thank such a Savior by living like the unbelievers around us.

v. 22 — *You were taught with regard to your former way of life, to put off your old self, which is being corrupted by the deceitful desires;*

Paul says that Christ is served only when the Christian puts off the old, sinful nature which resembles the unbeliever in every way. By bringing us to faith, God has put off the "old" for us. Because of Christ's work the sin of our old Adam, along with his bad reputation and his insatiable desire for evil, is no longer charged against us. Appreciating what Christ has done, we will not want to give the "old" nature the upper hand in our lives. In our service to Christ and in our desire to remain in his truth, we will want to drown the "old self" continually through daily contrition and repentance.

How important it is for Christians to recognize the old nature as a constant and deadly threat to our salvation! It is a constant threat because it can never be reformed. It is "being corrupted" (φθειρό-μενον), Paul says. Note the present tense. The sinful nature never cleans up its act. In fact, it only gets worse as time goes on.

The Christian will want to realize this because the old nature is something that he will carry with him as long as he lives in this world. The old nature is a powerful threat because it is always ready and willing to be deceived by its deceitful desires. Deceitful desire, using an old trick of Satan, stirs up the old self by telling it half-truths. It leads the old nature to think only of the pleasure or the apparent gain to be had by sinning. It says nothing of the consequence of sin and the destruction to which it leads.

This deceit is very clever at times, even leading the Christian to believe that God overlooks a believer's sins because he or she is a believer. The truth that is in Jesus assures that God never overlooks sin for any reason. He does forgive sin for the sake of his Son's innocent suffering and death on behalf of all sinners.

Former Secretary General of the United Nations Dag Hammarskjold once said: "You cannot play with the animal in you without becoming wholly animal, play with falsehood without forfeiting your right to truth, play with cruelty without losing your sensitivity of mind. He who wants to keep his garden tidy doesn't reserve a plot for weeds." Paul's reminder and warning concerning the old nature will lead each Christian to ask, "Am I reserving a plot for weeds?" As the Christian is led by God to see his "weed beds" of sin, he will bring them to God in confession, plead for his forgiveness and, assured from the gospel that he has it, ask for God's strength that he may put off the old and put on the new.

vv. 23,24 — *to be made new in the attitude of your minds; and to put on the new self created to be like God in true righteousness and holiness.*

In these two verses Paul presents us with the good news that we Christians have a new self according to the gracious work of our God who motivates and empowers us to live in such a way that the new self controls our thoughts, words and behavior.

'Ανανεοῦσθαι, present passive infinitive, and κτισθέντα, present passive participle, remind us that the new person is not something we could produce or create. God is the agent of these two passives. The new self is his work. He makes new that attitude of the Christian's mind which serves to guide the believer, just as futile thinking directs the actions of the unbeliever. God continually renews this attitude through his life-giving means of grace.

It is this God-worked, attitude-renewing faith that supplies the Christian with the power and the desire to strive to live the holy life that God freely credits to him for Jesus' sake. Paul expresses this same truth in Galatians: "I have been crucified with Christ and I no longer live, but Christ lives in me. The life I live in the body, I live by faith in the Son of God, who loved me and gave himself for me" (2:20).

In appropriating this truth to the lives of Christians, we do well to make a distinction between δικαιοσύνη and ὁσιότης. Here, δικαιοσύνη is God's unchanging love of right. With the image of God renewed in him, the Christian will love what is right, just as God does. 'Οσιότης (not ἁγιωσύνη) might best be explained as God's unchanging aversion to sin. The two words together express a similar thought, one from the positive aspect and the other from the negative. Paul adds emphasis to this thought by employing both words.

Homiletical Suggestions

The Old Testament selection and the Gospel for the day have a definite connection. In the Gospel Jesus speaks of himself as the Bread of Life. In so doing he compares himself and his work with the manna that God furnished the Israelites in the wilderness. What is interesting is that in both these readings there were people who believed they knew just what it was that would bring them satisfaction and make them happy in life. In the Gospel he explains that he has something greater to offer them: life with God!

In our text Paul makes clear that it is the sinful nature which will always take the unbelieving sinner down countless avenues in search for pleasure and satisfaction, all to no avail. The constant pursuit of sinful earthly pleasure is the chief characteristic of the life of the unbeliever. While he lives in this world, the Christian still possesses that same sinful nature, and he must contend with the same characteristic in himself.

Throughout the text Paul speaks of how and why the old self can be put off by each and every Christian. The Christian can put off the old and put on the new because God has brought him to the knowledge of the truth that is in Jesus, and through that truth called the sinner to faith. God makes him a new creature who possesses spiritual life and the spiritual strength he needs to serve, honor, and thank his gracious God for the gift of new life.

This text will be preached near the end of the summer months, when attendance is often at a seasonal low and when the congregation is "gearing up" for its busier Fall schedule of classes and events. It's a fitting time of year to remind our flocks that we do not find true rest and pleasure in what the unbelievers are pursuing. Rather, we find it through our daily walk with God as we spend time in his truth and there find the strength we need to serve him.

Possible themes:

Live in the Knowledge of Jesus

1. Put off the old (vv. 17-22)
2. Put on the new (vv. 20-24)

You Are a New Creation

1. Made holy (vv. 20,21, 24b)
2. To live holy (vv. 17-19, 22-24a)

Ignorance Is Not Bliss!

1. It results from hardened hearts (v. 18)
2. It separates souls from God (v. 18)
3. It leads to a life of lust (vv. 17,19)
4. Its cure is knowing Christ (vv. 20-24)

TWELFTH SUNDAY AFTER PENTECOST

The Scriptures

Old Testament — *1 Kings 19:4-8*
Epistle — *Ephesians 4:30—5:2*
Gospel — *John 6:41-51*

The Text — Ephesians 4:30—5:2

Paul did not have a special agenda in writing to the Ephesians as he had when he wrote to the Galatians and the Corinthians. There don't seem to have been any special problems that needed correction. Nor was he writing to them to encourage them in the face of severe persecutions. In fact, the letter is quite free from personal references that could be tied to a specific congregation. This leads some to conclude that it may have been intended as a general epistle to all of the churches in the province of Asia.

Though he had no problem to correct, Paul did desire to build up the Christians in the faith and thereby strengthen their hold on eternal life. So he wrote them a letter describing the nature of the Christian church in the first half and the behavior of its members in the second half. Our text, coming from the second half of the letter, deals with the behavior of Christians.

4:30 — And do not grieve the Holy Spirit of God, with whom you were sealed for the day of redemption.

Here and in 1 Thessalonians 5:19 Paul talks about being careful not to cross the Holy Spirit. In the latter he says, "Do not put out the Spirit's fire." Here he says, "Do not grieve the Holy Spirit." Λυπεῖτε means vex, irritate, or make sad. He goes on (v. 31) to list the actions that would cause such a reaction in the Holy Spirit.

Before we deal with those actions, though, there is another expression in verse 30 that commands our attention. The apostle says to the Christians, ἐσφραγίσθητε. That means they were marked with a seal as a means of identification and protection. The brand on a herd of cattle or a craftsman's hallmark might be so described. The Holy Spirit, imparted to Christians through baptism, is the seal of identification that will mark them for salvation on the day of redemption. Since that is the case, they do not want to grieve the Holy Spirit of God. Rather, they will want to do as Paul suggests.

v. 31 — Get rid of all bitterness, rage and anger, brawling and slander, along with every form of malice.

The terms he lists all have to do with anger expressed in loud speech and quarreling. The picture is of a bitter person who has allowed his anger to increase while it is pent up inside him. When it finally bursts forth, the torrent of invective is loud, angry, malicious, and sometimes slanderous. It may even lead to brawling.

This is the kind of hateful confrontation Jesus hoped to head off when he advised Christians in Matthew 18:15, "If your brother sins against you. . . ." Paul warned against the problem with very practical advice earlier in this chapter, when he said, "In your anger do not let the sun go down while you are still angry and do not give the devil a foothold" (vv. 26,27). Is there a married couple anywhere who could not benefit by Paul's advice?

v. 32 — *Be kind and compassionate to one another, forgiving each other, just as in Christ God forgave you.*

Readers familiar with the KJV may remember and prefer the translation "tenderhearted" for εὐσπλάγχνοι. It conveys the idea of a heart that is not hard like stone and impervious to any human needs, but one that is sensitive and open to the needs of others.

Such a heart is the result of kind, compassionate, and forgiving treatment from our loving God. In Christ he has forgiven us, and his forgiveness moves us to act in the same way toward others. It is not the merit of the one who needs forgiveness that compels us. According to our human way of thinking, we would be perfectly justified in not loving a person who has sinned. No, it is the undeserved love of Christ for us that moves us to love another who does not deserve our love. Χαριζόμενοι is based on χάρις and means to "deal graciously," i.e., to forgive. Jesus Christ gave himself into death to pay for our sins when we deserved nothing but damnation. That love also moves us to give freely of our love when others do not deserve it either.

5:1 — *Be imitators of God, therefore, as dearly loved children*

Μιμηταί: We are to "mime" God, to act as he does in our dealings with each other. Since we are dearly loved children, we ought to love each other dearly. Τέκνα ἀγαπητά are the objects of the love which has no ulterior motives. It holds no hope of gain for itself. It simply desires to do something good for someone else. It is the word used in John 3:16.

v. 2 — *and live a life of love, just as Christ loved us and gave himself up for us as a fragrant offering and sacrifice to God.*

In the walk of life (περιπατεῖτε) let love be the state in which you live (ἐν with dative, connoting sphere). That's what Christ has done for us by giving himself over to death for us "as a fragrant offering and sacrifice to God." "He sacrificed for their sins once for all when he offered himself" (He 7:27). God smells the sacrifice, and it removes the stench of sin from his nostrils. Paul also uses this picture in 2 Corinthians 2:14,15. The offensive odor is replaced by the sweet smell of Christ, and we are saved.

Homiletical Suggestions

How the counseling load of the pastor would be lessened if God's people were more diligent in following Paul's advice! The bitter and malicious arguments between spouses would not occur. The angry infighting that goes on in so many workplaces would not exist. The gossipy backbiting that plagues so many congregations wouldn't be a threat to God's work. This text affords an opportunity to teach again and to encourage the Christian way of maintaining relationships.

The preacher will want to be careful to avoid the pitfall of simply lecturing a captive audience about the "dos" and "don'ts" of family relationships. Even if the advice does come directly from the Word of God, it is not enough to preach the law to direct a Christian's actions if we do not preach the gospel which moves him to action.

The text lends itself well to preaching the gospel, as do all of Paul's writings. In these five short verses Paul assures us of God's love in Christ in no less than four ways. He reminds us that we are "sealed for the day of redemption." He reiterates that "in Christ God forgave you." He refers to us as "dearly loved children." He repeats that "Christ loved us and gave himself up for us." Paul seems never to have been able to say or write very much without repeating the gospel. We are well advised to do the same.

An outline that treats each of these gospel statements:

Christians, How Can You Be Angry People?

1. You are sealed in the Spirit for the day of redemption (4:30)
2. You are forgiven by God in Christ (4:31,32)
3. You are God's dearly loved children (5:1)
4. You are saved by Christ's sacrifice (5:2)

Using the apostle's words as the theme, you can divide the text as follows:

Be Imitators of God

1. Do not grieve the Spirit with angry rage (4:30,31)
2. Forgive each other as dearly loved children (4:32; 5:1,2)

Let another of the apostle's words serve as the theme:

Walk in Love

1. Avoiding all bitterness so as not to grieve the Holy Spirit (4:30,31)
2. Forgiving each other as God forgave us in Christ (4:32)
3. Imitating Christ, who gave himself up for us (5:1,2)

THIRTEENTH SUNDAY AFTER PENTECOST

The Scriptures

> Old Testament — *Proverbs 9:1-6*
> Epistle — *Ephesians 5:15-20*
> Gospel — *John 6:51-58*

The Text — Ephesians 5:15-20

These words from God through the Apostle Paul fall in the middle of a large section on Christian living and relationships. We who were dead in our sins and unbelief have been made alive with Christ. By grace we have been saved! A good question is: "How does the God who saved me from my sins want me to live?" Paul, under the inspiration of the Holy Spirit, answers that question for us and our people in the wider context and in our text.

In our sermon text alone, in the six verses of the original Greek, we find five imperatives—five injunctions to guide us in our life of grateful response to the Lord's love and salvation. And there are five participles which add flesh to the imperative "skeleton." God certainly doesn't leave us in the dark as to how he wants us to live as his children.

v. 15 — *Be very careful, then, how you live—not as unwise but as wise,*

The οὖν causes us to look back to the previous verse and paragraph. There Paul urges us to live as children of light, to find out what pleases the Lord, to expose the fruitless deeds of darkness and to realize that by a miracle of God's grace we are spiritually alive. Our Savior shines on us with his love and forgiveness. God has placed the precious gift of salvation in our hearts and hands.

But this gift can be lost, foolishly tossed away and discarded as if it were worthless garbage. Who could do such a thing? We and our hearers could! That's why Paul emphasizes, "Be very careful."

Being wise means that we can discern between what is valuable and vital and what is not. It means, too, that we recognize the constant danger we face as Christians living in a hostile environment. We "walk in danger all the way." Therefore we step carefully, mindful of Satan's mine fields and protective of the precious gift of salvation cradled in our arms. And in wisdom we view wisdom itself as another priceless gift of God.

v. 16 — *making the most of every opportunity, because the days are evil.*

It doesn't take a top-notch detective to find evidence that the days we live in are indeed evil. Just read your newspaper or watch the nightly news. Dark violence, pale apathy, red lust, and green greed stand out as giants in the land. Even many churches and religious citadels have become rotten to the core, promoting homosexuality, abortion, and other evils while avoiding any worthwhile Bible teaching and instruction. It's a fact: the days are evil!

Since this is so, Paul encourages us to make the most of every opportunity. You might recall the KJV's rendering of this expression: "redeeming the time." Ἐξαγοράζω means "to buy up for one's use." What are we to buy up for our use? Paul answers, τὸν καιρόν, the right time to do or accomplish something. As shrewdly as we attempt to buy an item on sale and take advantage of its lowest possible price, so shrewdly are we to watch for and snatch up opportunities.

Opportunities to do what? First of all, since the days are evil and we are in danger of being sucked in by that evil vacuum, Paul wants us to seize every opportunity to be strengthened and built up by the means of grace. Then he encourages us to make the most of every opportunity to spread the gospel and so to snatch someone else from evil and the evil foe. He is leading us to "overcome evil with good" (Ro 12:21)

v. 17 — *Therefore do not be foolish, but understand what the Lord's will is.*

For emphasis God's apostle repeats himself. "Do not be foolish" matches up with the "not as unwise" of verse 15, and "understand what the Lord's will is" corresponds with "live . . . as wise."

The Lord doesn't want his people to be ostriches with their heads in the sand. He wants us to be people with our heads in the Book, the Bible. For that is the only way we gain an understanding of what God wants for us and from us. From the Word we learn that the first item on "God's Will List" is for sinners to be with him in heaven. For this reason Jesus came from heaven to earth and allowed himself to undergo hell's torments as our sinless substitute. Eternal blessings are what the Lord wants for us. And what does he want from us? He wants our hearts, trusting in our Savior and responding to his grace in grateful service.

v. 18 — *Do not get drunk on wine, which leads to debauchery. Instead, be filled with the Spirit.*

Here Paul cites one specific example of foolish living—drunkenness. What's wrong with it? In the eyes many, nothing! Overdrinking, in fact, is considered by many to be fun and funny, glamorous and exciting. But the Scriptures pull off the grinning mask of drunkenness and expose its hideous face. Drinking to excess wastes people, their time, talents, and treasures. It wastes people and ruins relationships. The alcohol becomes the master, and debauchery can result, a lifestyle that is heading for the gutter and the sewer. And all because people are looking for a "high"!

There is a good "high" to be had. "Instead, be filled with the Spirit." The Spirit is the Comforter and Counselor. He gives joy in the midst of sorrow and suffering. He heals wounds and gives peace. He brings us to a spiritual "high" that has no regrets and lasts forever! Again, the tool of the Holy Spirit to do all this wonderful work inside of us is the word and promises of the Lord God. Paul could just as well have said, "Be filled with the word."

v. 19 — *Speak to one another with psalms, hymns and spiritual songs. Sing and make music in your heart to the Lord,*

The Greek text shows three present participles: speaking, singing, and making music. The present tense indicates the ongoing nature of these activities. They become a way of life and are not a one-time occurrence. That they are participles and not main verbs shows their dependence on the preceding verse. Being filled with the Spirit results in speaking, singing, and making music.

Music is a treasured gift of God. We can use ψαλμοὶ and ὕμνοι and ᾠδαὶ πνευματικαί as a way to teach and encourage one another in public worship. But we might also at times sing by ourselves as we go about our daily tasks. It may even be a little tune we make up and hum to ourselves, expressing our joy and happiness in having such a good God!

v. 20 — *always giving thanks to God the Father for everything, in the name of our Lord Jesus Christ.*

Εὐχαριστοῦντες is the fourth present participle in a row. This time its ongoing nature is brought out explicitly by the addition of "always" and "for everything." In other words, Paul is calling for a life of thanksgiving, not a mere Thanksgiving Day! He is calling for non-stop thanksgiving, not only at times of success and at happy events, but for everything!

"Everything" includes everything from a car accident to job loss to health problems, and the list goes on and on! But "everything" also

242

covers all the rich spiritual gifts showered on us daily through the saving work of our Lord Jesus Christ. Forgiveness, peace, joy, love, and hope are everyday realities in and through Jesus. Because Jesus was punished for our sins by his Father, we can claim God as our loving and caring Father. We know that our Father will work out everything, even life's disasters and distresses, for our good (Ro 8:28). Thus we are blessed with a constantly grateful spirit, "In the name of our Lord Jesus Christ."

Homiletical Suggestions

What a beautiful text on sanctified Christian living! When so many are striving to have "the good life," hold before your eyes and your people's eyes the joys and beauties of "the wise life." The Old Testament lesson with Wisdom's call and the Gospel reading featuring Jesus' words of wisdom give the service a unifying "wisdom" theme. Keying off verse 15 of our text, issue this call:

Live the Wise Life

1. Understand the Lord's will (vv. 15,17-20)
2. Make the most of every opportunity (vv. 15,16)

Another approach stresses the importance of possessing the Spirit-given wisdom of knowing why we are alive, physically and spiritually alive as believers. When so many have no sense of purpose in life, we can proclaim:

Christian, You Are Alive for a Good Reason

1. Greet each day thankfully in the Lord (vv. 19,20)
2. Spend each day wisely for the Lord (vv. 15-18)

FOURTEENTH SUNDAY AFTER PENTECOST

The Scriptures

> Old Testament — *Joshua 24:1,2a,14-18*
> Epistle — *Ephesians 5:21-31*
> Gospel — *John 6:60-69*

The Text — Ephesians 5:21-31

As he often does in his epistles, Paul uses the second half of the letter to elaborate on sanctified living. After speaking of the grace God has shown us in Christ, Paul goes on to point out how we can respond appropriately to that grace by patterning our lives according to God's will. In the verses before us, Paul will speak specifically of God's will regarding the relationship between husband and wife. Parallel passages are found in Colossians 3:18,19 and 1 Peter 3:1-7.

v. 21 — *Submit to one another out of reverence for Christ.*

In the Greek text this verse begins with the last of four participles modifying the imperative of verse 18: "Be filled with the Spirit." Although verse 21 is translated as an independent imperative in the NIV and connected with the verses which follow, it is still part of Paul's definition of Spirit-filled living. A Christian's willing submission to his fellowman is a manifestation of the Spirit's indwelling.

This verse presents a general rule for the Christian's attitude and conduct, consistent with Paul's words in Philippians 2:3 and Jesus' words in Matthew 20:26. Such humble submission will be motivated not by a servile fear but by a filial "reverence for Christ."

v. 22 — *Wives, submit yourselves to your husbands as to the Lord.*

The middle ὑποτάσσομαι, inferred from the previous verse, literally means "to place oneself under someone, to be subordinate to." The word indicates that an order has been established. But that order is not necessarily determined on the basis of quality or importance. For example, when the truck driver submits to the 14-year-old crossing guard by stopping his truck when the guard's hand goes up, the truck driver is not showing himself to be weaker, less intelligent, less gifted, less important, or in any way inferior. He is, however, submitting. The driver recognizes that because of the order of authority, established by the government for the good of drivers and pedestrians alike, he must submit to the will of the crossing guard. Submission has to do with order, not value.

244

Paul here applies the principle of ὑποταγή to the relationship between women and their own husbands: τοῖς ἰδίοις ἀνδράσιν. He is encouraging Christian wives to submit voluntarily to the God-given authority of their husbands. Their willing submission is rendered "as to the Lord" himself.

It is interesting to note that Paul, in a literary way, takes the women to one side and talks to them separately about their role in marriage. Later, he does the same thing with the men. This is Paul's way of countering the natural inclination to be more concerned about "what my spouse should be doing" than about "what I should be doing." The preacher does well to use Paul's approach by encouraging each wife to focus on her role, not the role of her husband, and to address husbands according to the same mode.

vv. 23,24 — *For the husband is the head of the wife as Christ is the head of the church, his body, of which he is the Savior. Now as the church submits to Christ, so also wives should submit to their husbands in everything.*

With the ὅτι clause the apostle clearly states the reason why wives are to submit to their husbands. Wives are to submit because God has appointed the husband to be the head of the wife. God already established this principle in the Garden of Eden (Ge 2:18,22,23; 1 Ti 2:12,13).

Yet the relationship between husband and wife is not comparable to a master-slave relationship. Rather, a Christian marriage is modeled after the relationship between Christ and his church. He is the Savior of the church. He sacrificed his life to save miserable sinners like us. The fact that he has proven his unconditional love for us, in addition to the fact that he would never ask us to do anything that is not in our best interest, gives us reason to subordinate ourselves willingly to him. As members of Christ's body, we do not resent his headship. We appreciate it. We willingly submit to him as our perfect Lord and God-given Head. God tells the Christian wife to maintain the same attitude toward her God-appointed head, even though he is not perfect.

v. 25 — *Husbands, love your wives, just as Christ loved the church and gave himself up for her*

Having spoken to Christian wives, Paul turns his attention to Christian husbands. The fact that the inspired writer devotes more space to the role of the husband than to the role of the wife should underscore how vital a husband's love is in the overall well-being of a Christian marriage.

A husband's love for his wife is to be like Christ's love for the church. Ἀγάπη in the New Testament is love for the unlovable. It is sacrificial, unconditional love. It is the love which Jesus showed by laying down his life for a world of people who hated him (cf. Ro 5:8; 1 Jn 3:16). Christ's love not only serves as the model for a husband's love. It is also the motivation for such love. Only when we understand how much Christ has loved us, in spite of our failings, can we in turn love our spouses, in spite of their failings. When Christ is the model, the husband's attitude will not be, "How can I better rule my wife?" but, "How can I better love my wife?"

vv. 26,27 — *to make her holy, cleansing her by the washing with water through the word, and to present her to himself as a radiant church, without stain, or wrinkle or any other blemish, but holy and blameless.*

With three consecutive ἵνα clauses the apostle probes deeper into the purpose of Christ's sacrificial love. The Savior's purpose was to set apart (ἁγιάσῃ) a people for God. He did this, literally, "by means of the bath of water in connection with the spoken word." This cannot be anything but a reference to Holy Baptism. Even though Reformed commentators grant the reference to baptism, they still seek to characterize it as a merely symbolic ceremony performed by man in obedience to God. Such an interpretation fails to take into account that the subject of ἁγιάσῃ is Christ. *Baptism is a means by which Christ cleanses us.* Thank God for such an instrument of his grace!

Although Paul's reference to baptism may initially seem to be a digression from the subject at hand, it is still an appropriate proof of Christ's love for the church, his bride. Paul's choice of words brings to mind the picture of a groom turning an ugly, filthy "Cinderella" into his perfect bride by washing her and clothing her in a spotless wedding gown. Such was the love which Christ showed to filthy sinners by washing them in his blood and dressing them in his righteousness, so that they might be holy and blameless when they are presented before God on the Last Day.

v. 28 — *In this same way, husbands ought to love their wives as their own bodies. He who loves his wife loves himself.*

From the analogy of bride and bridegroom Paul returns to the head and body picture of verse 23. Notice the progression of his thought: If the husband is like Christ who is the Head and if the wife is like the church which is his body, then the husband is to consider the wife as his own body—and care for her as such. Christ's care for his body, the church, is the standard for a man's treatment of his body, his wife.

vv. 29,30 — *After all, no one ever hated his own body, but he feeds and cares for it, just as Christ does the church—for we are members of his body.*

Here Paul appeals to a self-evident fact. People work hard to care for their own physical needs. Jesus works harder than all to care for the needs of his body, the church. So, husbands have an obligation (ὀφείλουσιν, v. 28) to care for the physical, emotional, and spiritual needs of their "own bodies," their wives. Such a spirit of caring flows from the Christians' status as "members of his body."

v. 31 — *For this reason, a man will leave his father and mother and be united to his wife and the two will become one flesh.*

Paul's whole argument regarding the close connection between husband and wife is ultimately based on God's declaration in Genesis 2:24. The words, "For this reason," do not connect with anything in the preceding verses. They are simply part of the quotation from Genesis. The passage brings out the intimate union which God created and intends between one man and one woman in marriage. That union finds its most complete physical and psychological expression in sexual intercourse, and the phrase "one flesh" reflects that, although it includes the whole relationship of one man and one woman in marriage.

Homiletical Suggestions

Premarital pregnancies, troubled marriages, no-fault divorces, overbearing or abusive husbands, "women's rights" wives, and families caught in the crossfire of the war between the sexes—these are just a few of the reasons why this portion of God's Word is so applicable to life in today's Christian congregations. Of all the advice offered by secular counselors, newspaper columnists, and talk-show hosts, none compares to the marriage guidance which God gives in his Word. Who can better define the roles of husband and wife than he who created them in the first place?

Even though the respective roles of men and women may be the subject of controversy, we dare not sidestep it. An outline which would allow us to clearly summarize God's perfect plan for marriage would be:

Consider God's Plan for a Healthy Marriage!

1. God says, "Husbands, love your wives" (vv. 25-31)

2. God says, "Wives submit to your husbands" (vv. 22-24)

Because this text contains some very specific law statements, any sermon based on it has the potential to leave husbands and wives feeling guilty about their past failures and feeling frustrated by the poor prospects for meeting God's high standards in the future. Therefore a generous helping of the good news of Christ's unconditional forgiveness and power for Christian living will be necessary to insure that listeners walk away recharged and renewed rather than deflated and discouraged. An outline that can help meet that goal is:

In Christ You Can Make Marriage Work

1. Jesus is the model (vv. 21-25,28,29,31)
2. Jesus is the motivation (vv. 23, 25-27, 30)

FIFTEENTH SUNDAY AFTER PENTECOST

The Scriptures

> Old Testament — *Deuteronomy 4:1,2,6-8*
> Epistle — *Ephesians 6:10-20*
> Gospel — *Mark 7:1-8,14,15,21-23*

The Text — Ephesians 6:10-20

This epistle concludes the pericopes from Ephesians in this series. These readings have given the measurement of God's praise in the church through redemption, peace, unity, purity, love, spirituality, and submission. This final reading identifies the source of power for living such praise-filled lives in Christ, especially as we encounter the opposition.

The Epistle complements the Old Testament and Gospel readings for the day. The Old Testament lesson engenders obedience to the true Word of God with its promise of wisdom. The Gospel addresses the purity of the Word of God to hearts polluted with impurity and the words of men. The Epistle speaks of the power of the Lord and his word by which we stand as Christians.

v. 10 — *Finally, be strong in the Lord and in his mighty power.*

"Finally" strikes the exclamation point to everything Paul has written in this letter, as well as those things left unsaid. All can be summed up, finally, with the words "be strong in the Lord and in his mighty power." They echo the command and promise to Joshua (Jos 1:6-9) as well as the proclamation of the prophet: "Yet their Redeemer is strong; the LORD Almighty is his name" (Jer 50:34).

"Be strong" is a simplified translation of the passive ἐνδυναμοῦσθε. A more literal translation would be "be strengthened." The NET translates: "Let the Lord and his mighty power make you strong." This verb is the key word in the text from which the rest flows. We therefore must understand the whole counsel of God: strength belongs to God (Ps 46:1), by ourselves we have no strength (Jn 15:5), God wants us to be strong and makes us strong (2 Co 12:10). Κράτος is "strength" in action and is related to ἰσχύς, which is "might" in possession, whether put into action at the moment or not. Consider it God's way of strengthening us so that we have a claim on his strength and can use it when needed (1 Co 10:12).

vv. 11,12 — *Put on the full armor of God so that you can take your stand against the devil's schemes. For our struggle is not against flesh and blood, but against the rulers, against the authorities, against the powers of this dark world and against the spiritual forces of evil in the heavenly realm.*

God outfits his army with his πανοπλία, the full armor of a soldier. Emphasis needs to be placed on the fullness of this armor, the completeness of the outfit. It is not the author's intent that we should wear one piece without every piece in place. This becomes obvious as Paul later details the armor's components, piece by piece.

In an effort to alert us to the real need for the whole armor Paul speaks of the devil's schemes and methods. While many today deny the reality of the devil as a personal being, his personality and power are seen best in the crafty ways in which he works destruction. Whereas God has a panoply he will give to people for their eternal protection, the devil has his wily ways for working people's destruction.

Paul describes the nature of our struggle. Our wrestlings go beyond "blood and flesh" (note the Greek word order). The apostle sees that underneath and behind what is human and sinful, Satan himself is active.

The use of ἀρχάς ἐξουσίας, κοσμοκράτορας τοῦ σκότους, and πνευματικὰ τῆς πονηρίας indicates the organization of the devil's kingdom, denoting the chiefs and heads of groups. The words imply attacking power, ruling powers, and wicked power in this great number of spirit beings. In 1:2 Paul spoke of the "ways of this world and the ruler of the kingdom of the air—the spirit who is now at work in those who are disobedient." By God's grace in Christ we have been released from them to live lives of faith to do the good works which God has prepared for us to do. It seems appropriate that here Paul reminds us all that although we are freed from them, the devil's forces are still there and waiting for the next battle when they reclaim us. This is all the more reason to be armed for this battle with the armor God provides.

v. 13 — *Therefore put on the full armor of God, so that when the day of evil comes, you may be able to stand your ground, and after you have done everything, to stand.*

The urgency of arming ourselves is stressed because we do not know when the day of evil, when we have to do battle, will come. Even as people today enlist in the armed forces, endure rigorous training, and are issued equipment for an undetermined future battle, so it is with us.

Paul is not speaking of the day of death, still less the day of judgment, not every day in general. He speaks of the day or time in life when the forces of evil deliberately mount their attack on us. These forces have their day (Job 1). They will attack and accuse (Ro 8:33,34). Thank God it is not every day. Thank God that he arms us for those days (2 Co 4:7-9), that it is his will for us that we will stand in the battle and in the end be victorious.

> vv. 14-17 — *Stand firm, then, with the belt of truth buckled around your waist, with the breastplate of righteousness in place, and with your feet fitted with the readiness that comes from the gospel of peace. In addition to all this, take up the shield of faith, with which you can extinguish all the flaming arrows of the evil one. Take the helmet of salvation and the sword of the Spirit, which is the word of God.*

Now we come to the armor itself, a picture perhaps evoked by the sight and constant presence of the soldiers guarding Paul as he wrote this.

There is the belt, actually a girdle or waist belt, much wider than the belts we wear to hold up our trousers. Perhaps it is mentioned first because it protected the most vulnerable parts of the body, the target of the sword thrust in ancient warfare. The sword was thrust upward into groin and abdomen, through stomach and lungs, and into the heart. The girdle protected that area. It also kept the armor in place and supported the sword. Paul uses this belt as a picture of truth. This is the objective truth revealed in Jesus Christ (Jn 14:6) and in the faithful Word of truth (Jn 17:17). The Word of truth is the most essential armament of our inner being.

Next comes the breastplate of righteousness, that righteousness from God (Ro 3:21-26) which is ours by faith (Ge 15:6). Such righteousness is our breastplate, closest to the heart and protecting it.

The third item of military gear are the war sandals which gave firm footing and gait. Paul defines them in terms of what the Christian needs for his walk of faith: "the readiness that comes from the gospel of peace." Here lies a paradox: that the gospel of peace equips us for battle. We follow Jesus who came to bring peace (Eph 2:14) and the sword.

Now the shield of faith must be taken in hand. Rather than the small, round shield, Paul has in mind the scutum, which was four feet long and two and one-half feet wide. When the soldier was in battle stance, the scutum protected his entire body. The shield of faith is God's gift which apprehends salvation (2:8), effects the forgiveness of past sins (1:10), affords access to God (3:12), assures eternal life by the deposit of the Holy Spirit (1:13,14), rendering us holy and without blame (1:4).

The warrior was not to hide his head behind the shield. He needed to look over it to face his opponent. For that reason he was also equipped with a helmet to cover his head. On the Christian's helmet is written, "Salvation." The reference to salvation is a general one. Salvation protects the Christian and helps him to hold up his head with confidence and joy.

That brings us to the one offensive weapon, the sword of the Spirit, which is the Word of God. How foolish to think of a soldier without a weapon. How ridiculous to picture the Christian without one—especially because he has one. The sword of the Spirit is made by the Spirit and given by the Spirit. It is the powerful Word of God (He 4:12,13), the revelation of the Holy Spirit (2 Pe 1:20,21), and it is the best offensive weapon for the man of God (2 Ti 3:16).

> vv. 18-20 — *And pray in the Spirit on all occasions with all kinds of prayers and requests. With this in mind, be alert and always keep on praying for all the saints. Pray also for me, that whenever I open my mouth words may be given me so that I will fearlessly make known the mystery of the gospel, for which I am an ambassador in chains. Pray that I may declare it fearlessly, as I should.*

A well-equipped soldier also needs a "battle-cry" to speak and shout as he takes the field. The Christian soldier has his: prayer in the Spirit. As Jesus Christ teaches his disciples what and how to pray (Mt 6:9-13; Lk 11:2-4), and as they "pray continually" (1 Th 5:17), so let prayer be there on the battlefield—all kinds of prayers and requests. As the saying goes, "The power of prayer doesn't need to be proven; it needs to be practiced."

With this general call to prayer, Paul specifically directs intercessory prayers on behalf of all the saints and especially for himself. While prayer is personal it should never be self-centered. Think about the other soldiers and saints and expect them to think about you. And let these prayers be centered in the gospel. Paul asks his readers to ask God to give him the opportunity, the courage, and the clarity that will serve the gospel's purpose even while he himself is in prison. Rather than bemoaning his fate as a prisoner he considers the grace given him as an ambassador of Christ. For a corollary to this prayer consider Paul's testimony of how his chains advance the gospel (Php 1:12ff.).

And, dear reader and preacher, accept the prayer here offered for you: God give you the courage and clarity needed to equip his saints today!

Homiletical Suggestions

Are we strong enough to stand in the face of temptation? To find daily renewal in our baptism? To withstand the evil spirits of evolutionism, spiritualism, materialism, narcissism, commercialism, sexism, Satanism, and others? The Lord calls on us to be strong and at the same time makes us strong. He does it through the preaching of texts such as this one.

Paul uses imagery taken from the equipment of the best soldiers in the world of his day, the Roman legionaries. These soldiers conquered the world for Rome and maintained the Roman Peace. What made them invincible in their day was discipline and valor. What makes Christ's soldiers invincible in peace and war is their divine armor.

Let the Lord Make You Strong

1. Strong against the devil and his works and ways (vv. 10-12)
2. Strong in the Lord with the full armor of God (vv. 13-20)

Am I a Soldier of the Cross?

1. Look at your enemies (vv. 11-13)
2. Put on God's armor (vv. 14-20)
3. Stand your ground (vv. 10,11,13,14)

The struggles that confront many of us can happen to any of us. The question is not, "Will it happen?", but, "What do I do when it happens?" The Lord gives the answer:

Be Strong

1. Not in yourself—you'll find only weakness
2. Not in this world—you'll find only the devil and destruction
3. But only in the Lord and his mighty power—he'll give you the victory

SIXTEENTH SUNDAY AFTER PENTECOST

The Scriptures

> Old Testament — *Isaiah 35:4-7a*
> Epistle — *James 1:17-22,26,27*
> Gospel — *Mark 7:31-37*

The Text — James 1:17-22,26,27

James, most probably "the Lord's brother," wrote this epistle to Jewish Christians who were scattered among the heathen nations. These Christians were subjected to many trials and their Christian faith was severely tested. The purpose of this letter from James is to encourage these Christians in their faith and admonish them for their shortcomings in Christian living. The text begins with encouragement.

> vv. 17,18 — *Every good and perfect gift is from above, coming down from the Father of the heavenly lights, who does not change like shifting shadows. He chose to give us birth through the word of truth, that we might be a kind of firstfruits of all he created.*

Temptations that lead God's children away from God do not come from God. When Eve was tempted, the temptation did not come from God (1:13). Only good things come from God. Evil has a different source. The good and perfect God can give his children only what is good and perfect (Lk 11:11-13).

James uses two words for the gifts that come from God. Δόσις is the act of giving. Δώρημα is the thing given. The act of giving demonstrates the Father's goodness. Every gift the Father gives is perfect. His greatest gift to us from heaven is salvation.

This salvation is a reality because it comes from God the Father, "who does not change like shifting shadows." When the sun moves, it produces shadows that shift and change. God the Father, however, never changes. Therefore his good giving and his perfect gift of salvation never change.

It does not matter how evil the world becomes. It does not matter that the world's evil is constantly knocking at the Christian's heart and demanding an invitation to enter. There still is only one changeless salvation which comes to us from heaven. It comes to us through the good act of giving on the part of God the Father and the perfect gift of Jesus which the Father gave.

God willed (βουληθείς) to bring us into his eternal life through the means of his "word of truth." This will of God was in effect even before he created the world (Eph 1:3,4). Why would God change his mind and send temptations to lure us away from his perfect gift of salvation? Instead, he sends the "word of truth" which instructs us in the redemption of Jesus so that faith in Jesus is created and sustained in us.

The intended result of God's good giving and perfect gift of salvation is that "we might be a kind of firstfruits of all he created." The firstfruits are the first of the crop to be gathered and put safely into the storehouse. More fruits will follow until the entire harvest is safely stored. God used the gospel to gather these Christians, along with James, into his eternal storehouse in heaven. More blood-bought souls would be gathered through the means of the gospel. It remains the means which the Holy Spirit uses to gather the harvest of souls for heaven. We are also beneficiaries of this perfect gift of God.

> vv. 19-22 — *My dear brothers, take note of this: Everyone should be quick to listen, slow to speak and slow to become angry, for man's anger does not bring about the righteous life that God desires. Therefore, get rid of all moral filth and the evil that is so prevalent, and humbly accept the word planted in you, which can save you. Do not merely listen to the word, and so deceive yourselves. Do what it says.*

James begins a new line of thought with the tender greeting, "My dear brothers." The next phrase of this greeting is better taken to refer to the previous verses than to the following verses. James urges these Christians to take note of the gifts God has given them and to understand that God chose them to receive these gifts of salvation. With this understanding they would be willing to hear the instruction of James to avoid whatever would prevent them from possessing these gifts of salvation which come through the Word of truth.

Those hearing the gospel are to be "quick to listen" and "slow to speak." One cannot hear when his mouth is open. How often haven't parents and teachers had to remind children to stop talking and start listening? James teaches the same thing to God's children. We can't learn the gospel well if we are talking while it is being taught to us.

James continues by saying Christians are to be "slow to anger." People easily become angry with each other when they stop listening to each other and start talking. When they disagree, they are not inclined to listen but to talk more. Arguments erupt and anger results. When Christians stop listening to the gospel and tell others what they think the Word of God says, the result is an argument that results in anger.

Such anger does not work God's righteousness. When one is angry he is not receptive to the message of God that he has declared us right before himself through Jesus. Thus the instruction of James: Be "slow to become angry."

Christians are to get rid of everything that opposes God's righteousness. There is more evil in this world than we know what to do with. Get rid of it all and live opposite to the world by humbly accepting the Word of truth that the Holy Spirit uses to bring you to faith. The Word is valuable because it can save you. So be willing to avoid whatever would prevent the Word from coming to you.

James, however, is not satisfied that the Christian only hear the Word. To accept the Word is more than hearing it. Too often Christians are satisfied to be only hearers of the Word.

This was a great fault of the Jews of Jesus' day. They heard the Word on Sabbath after Sabbath. But most failed to believe in the subject of the Word, Jesus Christ. They were deceived by the trap of Satan. "Listen and God will be pleased. Go to church and that is all that is necessary." How many Christians today are deceived by this trap of Satan? James teaches that it is necessary to do the Word.

To do the Word is to believe and live accordingly. When Christians do the Word, their lives will be a demonstration of the true saving faith in their hearts, for they will perform the works that please God. James is not teaching work-righteousness here or anywhere else in this letter. He is teaching how true saving faith, which is worked in the heart by the gospel, makes us doers of the Word. As doers of the Word, "we are God's workmanship, created in Christ Jesus to do good works, which God prepared in advance for us to do" (Eph 2:10).

vv. 26,27 — *If anyone considers himself religious and yet does not keep a tight rein on his tongue, he deceives himself and his religion is worthless. Religion that God our Father accepts as pure and faultless is this: to look after orphans and widows in their distress and to keep oneself from being polluted by the world.*

James refers back to his words about the tongue in verse 19, where he told the Christians to be "slow to speak." Those who consider themselves to be true worshipers of God, but at the same time allow their tongues to be out of control like an unbridled horse, are deceiving themselves. They do not practice a religion that expresses the saving truth.

James concludes this portion with two examples which demonstrate the types of works a true believer does in response to the saving gift of salvation he receives from God. The first is a work of love: "to look after orphans and widows in their distress." These were people who were forgotten by society. Even today, those who are poor and homeless are often forgotten by those who are blessed with many possessions, along with the gift of salvation. God has not forgotten these people, and neither should God's people forget them (1 Jn 3:17).

The second response of the Christian is a work of faith: "To keep oneself from being polluted by the world." The Christian strives to live so that none of the world's evils permanently resides in his heart. He also has an eye of faith on Jesus, who cleanses him from all impurity and sin (1 Jn 1:7).

Homiletical Suggestions

The Old Testament reading from Isaiah says that the ears of the deaf will be unstopped by the gospel and that the tongue of the dumb will shout for joy when the gospel is heard. The Gospel reading relates an incident when Jesus made a deaf and dumb man hear and speak. The people were amazed by this miracle and cried out, "He even makes the deaf hear and the dumb speak." Jesus still opens ears to hear the message of the gospel and gives the will and strength to speak that message in this world. Our text is a lesson from James that teaches the Christian how to use his ears and tongue in ways that glorify the God of salvation who has blessed him with eternal life.

An outline suggested by the words of the text:

God's Kind of Religion

1. Quick to listen (vv. 17,18,19a)
2. Slow to speak (vv. 19b-22,26)
3. Eager to do (vv. 21,22,27)

Another suggestion emphasizes what God looks for as his children's response to the gospel:

Don't Talk So Much!

1. Listen and learn (vv. 17-19a)
2. Learn and do (vv. 19b-22,26,27)

SEVENTEENTH SUNDAY AFTER PENTECOST

The Scriptures

Old Testament — *Isaiah 50:4-10*
Epistle — *James 2:1-5,8-10,14-18*
Gospel — *Mark 8:27-35*

The Text — James 2:1-5,8-10,14-18

James wrote to believers in Jesus. Like the rest of his epistle, this text preaches the law, with a view to instructing believers in Christian living and also to show us where we still sin. In this section James instructs us as disciples of Jesus to be intent on carrying out God's will by treating everyone in the church impartially. Such equal treatment will be a demonstration of our faith in the Lord Jesus, who was impartial in his treatment of others.

v. 1 — *My brothers, as believers in our glorious Lord Jesus Christ, don't show favoritism.*

The negative particle μή with the present imperative ἔχετε has the connotation of "stop holding." A literal translation of the Greek text is: "My brothers, do not continue holding the faith of our glorious Lord Jesus Christ in favoritism." Apparently the Christians James is addressing had been showing favoritism in their midst. But their faith in Jesus was to be free of such partiality, which had the effect of bringing disgrace on the Christian faith and the glorious Lord Jesus Christ.

vv. 2-4 — *Suppose a man comes into your meeting wearing a gold ring and fine clothes, and a poor man in shabby clothes also comes in. If you show special attention to the man wearing fine clothes and say, "Here's a good seat for you," but say to the poor man, "You stand there" or "Sit on the floor by my feet," have you not discriminated among yourselves and become judges with evil thoughts?*

James sets before his readers an example of how they may have been showing partiality in their midst. The subjunctive verbs followed by the passive indicative in these verses indicate a general condition.

James refers to a situation which may have arisen when his Christian readers met for worship. The word "meeting" is the Greek συναγωγή, referring to the gathering of the congregation for worship or instruction. In the example a rich man and a poor man enter the assembly. The congregation "looks intently" upon the rich man. James uses ἐπιβλέπω and the prefix intensifies the meaning "look" or "see" to "look upon intently." We might say today, "Their eyes got big when they saw the rich man." Thus, the NIV's "show special attention."

The special attention includes pointing the rich man to one of the best seats in the meeting. But the poor man is merely told to stand or sit on the floor. The brothers' treatment of the two men reveals that they have made a distinction between them. They have passed judgment on them, διεκρίθητε, showing partiality to the rich. They have become "judges with evil thoughts," literally "of wicked reasoning or design" (διαλογισμῶν πονηρῶν).

v. 5 — *Listen, my dear brothers: Has not God chosen those who are poor in the eyes of the world to be rich in faith and to inherit the kingdom he promised those who love him?*

Partiality to the rich over the poor does not agree with the will of God, for God has chosen the poor to inherit his kingdom by grace. Following God's will, the Christians also are to be gracious to the poor. But when they show partiality to the rich, they show their mind is set not on the things of God but of men. For the very ones whom God has chosen are the ones they consider the less desirable in the church.

v. 8 — *If you really keep the royal law found in Scripture, "Love your neighbor as yourself," you are doing right.*

God's law of love is royal because it is his. As such, it is the highest law, embracing all commandments. When Christians actually carry out (τελεῖτε) that law, they do (ποιεῖτε) what is good and right, καλῶς. Their observance of that law shows their mind is set on doing the will of God, even as Jesus, in whom they believe, did the will of God.

v. 9 — *But if you show favoritism, you sin and are convicted by the law as lawbreakers.*

God's will revealed in the law, "Love your neighbor as yourself," forbids partiality of some over others. But those who show partiality to some show their mind is not set on that will of God; they commit sin, and the law of love points them out as lawbreakers who have missed the mark established by God's will: ἁμαρτίαν ἐργάζεσθε.

v. 10 — *For whoever keeps the whole law and yet stumbles at just one point is guilty of breaking all of it.*

Some might argue that showing partiality is an insignificant infraction of the will of God. But God's will as expressed in the law of love is a unit. As cutting a ring at any one point ruins the whole ring, as breaking a vase in one place destroys the whole vase, so breaking any one point of God's law breaks the whole law. Whether the infraction be partiality, adultery, or something else, the result is the same: that person is a lawbreaker.

The perfect γέγονεν indicates the lasting result. From then on that person has become and remains guilty of having broken the whole law. He has failed to carry out God's will perfectly.

> vv. 14-16 — *What good is it, my brothers, if a man claims to have faith but has no deeds? Can such faith save him? Suppose a brother or sister is without clothes and daily food. If one of you says to him, "Go, I wish you well; keep warm and well fed," but does nothing about his physical needs, what good is it?*

Saving faith is proven by what it does to carry out God's law of love toward one's neighbor. Works of love are fruits of faith. The "faith" some claim to have but which does not work in love for the well-being of others is worthless. Of what value are well-wishes when the person expressing them does nothing to alleviate the suffering he sees? Such loveless "faith" cannot save, for it shows an absence of the true saving faith.

> vv. 17,18 — *In the same way, faith by itself, if it is not accompanied by action, is dead. But someone will say, "You have faith; I have deeds." Show me your faith without deeds, and I will show you my faith by what I do.*

Following upon the example of a Christian who wishes another well but then sends him away uncared for, James writes οὕτως, which here means "in this manner." Lovelessly ignoring the needs of others reveals a dead faith. True saving faith no longer exists in that person who claims to be a Christian but fails to act in love. The challenge to that false Christian to prove the existence of his faith without deeds of love is a challenge he cannot meet. For true faith is seen by the very deeds of love it does to carry out the will of God.

Homiletical Suggestions

Prophetically, the Old Testament reading reminds us that by his perfect obedience to the will of God Christ Jesus redeemed us. By his perfect active obedience he fulfilled the law of God for us so that we may be clothed with the robe of his righteousness. By his perfect passive obedience throughout his passion he delivered us from the guilt of our sins and saved us from the curse of the law.

The Gospel, Mark 8:27-35, shows the promised Christ resolutely setting out to accomplish this. Now we who believe in him for our salvation may express our thankful love to him and our heavenly Father who sent him. The sermon text says that we are to do that by setting our minds on fulfilling the law of love as he himself did.

The text is all law, instructing us believers in the Lord Jesus Christ how we are to treat one another. Especially, however, it convicts us as lawbreakers, who have failed to keep the royal law of love. It reminds us that we have made distinctions between people and have shown preference to some over others. It further brings to mind that we have failed to extend loving help to others at every opportunity. As such lawbreakers we are deserving of eternal punishment.

The only glimmer of gospel is found in the words "our glorious Lord Jesus Christ." Those words imply all that our Redeemer is as the God-Man who delivered us from the guilt of our sins against God's law of love, and saved us from the eternal punishment we deserve. Those words are fleshed out by what Isaiah 50:4-10 and Mark 8:27-35 say about him.

When that law and gospel have been expounded, this text may be applied from the viewpoint of the third use of the law. In thankful love for our redemption we are guided to live according to God's will, loving one another. A suggested basic outline for the entire text is:

Let Us Fulfill the Law of Love

1. Let us not show favoritism (vv. 1-5, 8-10)
2. Let us help our fellow Christians in need (vv. 8-10)
3. Let us demonstrate our faith by whatever we do (vv. 14-18)

If you find the text too long to treat in its entirety, try:

Faith Without Deeds Is Dead

1. Dead faith does not fulfill the law of love (vv. 8-10)
2. Living faith proves itself in deeds of love (vv. 14-18)

EIGHTEENTH SUNDAY AFTER PENTECOST

The Scriptures

> Old Testament — *Jeremiah 11:18-20*
> Epistle — *James 3:16—4:6*
> Gospel — *Mark 9:30-37*

The Text — James 3:16—4:6

3:16 — For where you have envy and selfish ambition, there you find disorder and every evil practice.

In this section of his epistle, beginning with verse 13, James is making a contrast between two types of wisdom—that which a believer in Jesus exhibits and that with which unconverted man functions. In this particular verse James points out that disorder and evil actions can be traced back to individuals' seeking their own selfish interests. This statement rings true whether one is talking about government, business, church, or home. Taking private vacations at public expense, falsifying statistics in order to gain a promotion, or telling falsehoods about another person in order to advance oneself are examples of such corruption.

3:17 — But the wisdom that comes from heaven is first of all pure; then peace loving, considerate, submissive, full of mercy and good fruit, impartial and sincere.

This verse presents the antithesis to verse 16. When human beings do not follow their sinful self with a "me first" attitude, but rather follow God's thinking (ἄνωθεν σοφία), there is concord among human beings.

Wisdom from God is in the first place "pure." It has no additives mixed into it. It is what it is supposed to be. It seeks others' welfare first, not worrying that it will be left out in the cold. The Christian is ready and willing to "give in" for the sake of another. The Christian on the freeway doesn't have to cuss out the other driver for cutting him off. The Christian employee can carry out his boss' demands without sputtering under his breath or talking behind the boss' back. The Christian student doesn't have to put down a loner classmate in order to stay in the good graces of his peers. Christian siblings don't have to argue about whose turn it is to pick up the living room or clear off the table. And this attitude is one which the Christian exhibits to all, not just a chosen few. It is real, not a facade.

3:18 — *Peacemakers who sow in peace raise a harvest of righteousness.*

The NIV translators have decided in this verse to render the passive σπείρεται as an active verb and have converted the dative of agency τοῖς ποιοῦσιν with its object εἰρήνην into the subject. This rendition is possible, but easily obscures the genitive of source reflected in δικαιοσύνης. A literal translation of this verse would be: "The fruit from righteousness is sown in peace by those producing peace."

Jesus teaches in the Gospel of John that those declared righteous by him and therefore connected to him produce much fruit—good works. James approaches this same concept by using the terminology of "wisdom from above" and by making a list in verse 17 of specific characteristics which emanate from such wisdom.

Here in verse 18 James refers to all good works generically as "fruit from righteousness" which are scattered about by believers among all mankind with a mindset of bringing peace to others. These words certainly suggest that our society is not to be a "dog eat dog world" which is the creed of so many. What is more, the strengths and attributes with which God has blessed a particular Christian are not to be used to dominate over another who is not so blessed. Rather, the child of God seeks to help and befriend others that they might have peace in this life and be led to cling to Jesus for eternal peace.

4:1 — *What causes fights and quarrels among you? Don't they come from your desires that battle within you?*

James has said that the Christian's goal is to live a life of faith in peace. Now he addresses some of the snares into which a Christian can so easily plunge. Because Satan is alive and well, Christians often are led astray into quarreling with their fellow believers in places as intimate as the Christian church and home.

4:2 — *You want something but don't get it. You kill and covet, but you cannot have what you want. You quarrel and fight. You do not have, because you do not ask God.*

This verse provides a catalog of vices. The thought of self-seeking desire comes out again and again as one surveys the list. "Me, myself, and I" become the watchwords for conducting one's affairs. Some commentators seek to soften the term "murder" by making it into a hyperbole for hatred, since both sins are one and the same in God's eyes. Perhaps this is the case. On the other hand, James could mean what he says literally, for there have been Christians who committed murder.

The last portion of this verse suggests why these Christians are living with so many unfulfilled desires: There is something wrong with their prayer life. Verse 3 continues the thought:

4:3 — *When you ask, you do not receive, because you ask with wrong motives, that you may spend what you get on your pleasures.*

God's Word repeatedly warns against a show of religion. Jesus again and again pointed out this danger to the Pharisees and Sadducees. Here James ties into the last thought of the previous verse and describes sham prayer. Prayer is to be a heart-to-heart talk with God, with the implicit thought, "Thy will be done." When people pervert this into, "Lord, give me what I want right now!" the concept of God's good and gracious will for the believer's life is being derailed. Words of unbelief are being muttered at God and the petitioner leaves with nothing.

4:4 — *You adulterous people, don't you know that friendship with the world is hatred toward God? Anyone who chooses to be a friend of the world becomes an enemy of God.*

Beginning with this verse James lays down a line of demarcation, letting his readers know exactly where they stand. The Greek μοιχαλίδες is a substantive adjective used to denote both sexes, here translated with the phrase, "You adulterous people." This is a term which crops up again and again in the Scripture, both in the Old and New Testament. It is a term which is applied to individuals who should be acting like people of God, but are instead acting like unbelievers. God's people, his Church, are his Bride. When any of his own strays away from him and joins himself to other gods, such a person has committed spiritual adultery. Satan is the god of this sinful world, and anyone following Satan's lead is automatically at odds with God. Thus Jesus warns, "Live in the world, but don't be a part of the world." Many are the compromises which Christians of all ages make so that they blend in with the world—in entertainment choices, vocabulary, values, comments about social issues.

4:5 — *Or do you think Scripture says without reason that the spirit he caused to live in us envies intensely?*

There is a difficulty in this verse, as demonstrated in the critical apparatus. Did James use the aorist of κατοικίζω (cause to dwell) or the aorist of κατοικέω (dwell)? The NIV reflects the reading chosen by the UBS. The NET, opting for the aorist of κατοικέω and with an eye toward verse 6, translates: "The Spirit who dwells in us strongly opposes envy?" This rendering can be supported by the grammar of the verse and makes more sense in context.

Natural man craves and yearns to fulfill his sinful desires and be friends with the world, but the new man created by the Holy Spirit causes the Christian to crave and yearn for his God and his God's will.

4:6 — *But he gives us more grace. That is why Scripture says: "God opposes the proud but gives grace to the humble."*

For the children of God there is an avalanche of undeserved grace. God desires to draw his own ever closer to him and lavish them with his love. To augment this point James refers to a passage taken from Proverbs 3:34, which is reiterated elsewhere in the New Testament (Mt 23:12; 1 Pe 5:5). The sense is obvious. God wants people on his terms and only on his terms. The Christian humbly looks to Jesus for his all. The unbeliever wants everything and thinks he can have it all, but in reality finds himself at war with the Almighty and has nothing!

Homiletical Suggestions

There are many preaching values in this portion of God's Word. Nonetheless, in approaching this text as a whole, one immediately notices the dichotomy between following God's way and the world's. With this basic premise in mind, consider the following outlines:

Seek the Wisdom That Comes from Heaven

1. Worldly wisdom produces selfish living (3:16; 4:1-4)
2. God's wisdom produces spiritual living (3:17; 4:5,6)

Borrowing the theme from the summary statement of 4:7b and using the quotation in 4:6b for the parts, we have:

Submit Yourselves to God

1. God opposes the proud (3:16; 4:1-4)
2. God gives grace to the humble (3:17,18; 4:5,6)

NINETEENTH SUNDAY AFTER PENTECOST

The Scriptures

> Old Testament — *Numbers 11:4-6, 10-16, 24-29*
> Epistle — *James 4:7-12*
> Gospel — *Mark 9:38-50*

The Text — James 4:7-12

Although there has been debate over the authorship of James, over whether the letter has a clearly-structured outline, and even over its canonicity, one theme for the letter is generally agreed upon: Repent! With fifty-one imperatives (eleven of which appear in our text) James calls on Christians to turn from all evil to a holy God. He warns against backsliding, against sins connected with apostasy and against the temptations that arise from persecution. He shares what it means for the Christian to be one of God's people—how that truth shapes one's life.

Our text is part of a section which begins in chapter 3 and focuses on Christian humility as an expression of the true repentance which is being encouraged in this epistle. James tells his readers that this humility is actually a product of Christian wisdom (3:13). Unlike earthly wisdom which produces "envy and selfish ambition," and consequently "disorder and every evil practice" (3:14-16), Christian wisdom leads to humility and thus to peace and "a harvest of righteousness" (3:17,18).

This humility does not crave the life of pleasure which so often causes endless troubles (4:1-3). It does not crave the friendship of the world, for that would place one in opposition to God (4:4-6). Rather, true Christian humility expresses itself in submission to God, in sorrowful repentance and in purification of life (4:7-9). It is a humility which God exalts (4:10). Such humility will not permit the Christian to slander or proudly pass judgment on others (4:11,12).

v. 7 — *Submit yourselves, then, to God. Resist the devil, and he will flee from you.*

Ὑποτάγητε sets the tone for this entire portion of Scripture. Understood as a middle—"submit yourselves" the word carries the meaning of voluntarily placing oneself under another. In this case, James is encouraging Christians to place themselves under God—to place themselves in his ranks, under his leadership and his direction, under his will and his word. Such submission means giving oneself completely and totally, without hesitation or condition. It means denying self and taking one's will and desires and thoughts and words and actions and gifts and abilities—one's entire being—and placing all of it at the disposal of the Almighty God. And, of course, that sort of self-submission will express itself in the way the Christian relates to his God and to his fellowman.

At first glance it may appear that a new thought begins in the second half of the verse. However, James is simply stating the other side of what is really the same coin. Submission to God *means* resisting the devil, and vice-versa, for every evil working of Satan in his fight against Christ and the church, and every temptation which he throws like a snare before the feet of the Christian constitute nothing less than an attack on the lordship of the Almighty. Satan would like nothing better than to have Christians arrogantly throw off that lordship and claim it for themselves. He would like nothing better than to see God's people refusing to submit to the Lord. And so Satan will play on and take advantage of what is natural in every person alive, and that is the tendency to be proud and haughty, to do as one pleases, to thumb one's nose at God and his ways and his will for one's life.

The ferocity of Satan as he does daily battle against Christ's church dare not be underestimated. Scripture describes the devil as an entity to be feared—very powerful, very crafty, having many evil angel followers, and using any tool at his disposal which will help tear the believer from the ranks of the Almighty God (cf. Mt 4:1ff.; Eph 6:12; 1 Pe 5:8,9).

If one resists the devil and his vicious attacks, that person will overcome. Proper preparation means arming oneself with the spiritual weapons which God supplies (cf. Mt 4:1ff.; Eph 6:10ff.). It means submitting to God, to his will and his ways. It means following him, walking in his ranks, with his weapons in our arsenals. When Satan attacks, such a properly prepared person will be able to oppose him successfully. The devil will flee from that person.

vv. 8,9 — *Come near to God and he will come near to you. Wash your hands, you sinners, and purify your hearts, you double-minded. Grieve, mourn and wail. Change your laughter to mourning and your joy to gloom.*

With these words James is not encouraging unregenerate man to make some sort of decision for God and for Jesus Christ. Such a decision, of course, is impossible (cf. 1 Co 12:3). Rather, James is speaking to the Christian, encouraging him to submit himself (by the power of the Holy Spirit) to God by coming near in sincere repentance. Ἁγνίσατε, aorist imperative, calls for an action that is decisive.

James does not demand only a partial coming near, but one that is complete and final. He calls for Christians to approach God in humility, to acknowledge their total unworthiness and helplessness. He calls for them to acknowledge the fact that, although they claim to be the Lord's, they have turned away from the Almighty time and again, going their own way, trying to live without the Lord in this world, and bringing upon themselves the Lord's anger and the eternal consequence of their rebellion.

Finally, James calls upon Christians to acknowledge their inability to change this sad state of affairs. Having done this, the child of God can confidently await the Lord's coming near to him. Pardon, peace, righteousness, and glory are not too great for the God of grace to bestow on even the most unworthy people who call on him with their whole hearts and approach him in sincere repentance.

This repentance can be marked in several ways. James encourages Christians, "Wash your hands." True repentance presupposes (in fact demands) a putting away of the evil practice. There will be an outward renewal.

More important, there will be an inward renewal as well. "Purify your hearts, you double-minded." There is a change in the outward behavior of the penitent because there has first been a change in the mind and will. Sin is put away, not because it has simply been outgrown or because it may no longer be fashionable, but because the will of the penitent sinner is to do the will of the Lord alone. True repentance leaves absolutely no room for being double-minded, for having one's affections and devotion divided between God and the world. Rather, true repentance means discarding any love for the world and any adherence to the sinful philosophies which shape the thinking and practices of the world. God simply will not tolerate a divided heart (cf. Mt 6:24).

The three imperatives in verse 9 serve to further define genuine repentance. James calls for heartfelt sorrow and contrition over sins committed. He is not calling for a mere outward show, but for a sorrow over sin that is sincere, and that leaves one dejected (κατήφειαν, literally "a casting down of the eyes, a falling of the countenance") because he knows that sin offends a holy God and condemns the sinner to an eternity of torture and death in hell. It should be understood that James is not speaking against laughter and joy in general, but only against that laughter and joy which in the slightest way makes light of sin.

v. 10 — *Humble yourselves before the Lord, and he will lift you up.*

With ταπεινώθητε (aorist passive imperative understood in the middle sense), James is summing up the thoughts of the previous verses. He is again encouraging Christians to put away all arrogance, sinful pride, and self-righteousness. He exhorts them to resist the workings and ways of Satan, and to submit themselves humbly to God. This implies repentance, turning to the Lord in deep sorrow and remorse; never seeking excuses for sin, but presenting oneself to the Almighty with a broken and contrite heart—a heart that realizes its need for healing and longs for that healing.

To the one who humbles himself before the Lord, James offers a glorious promise: "He will lift you up." The lifting up or exaltation of which James speaks is that of God's pardoning grace. It is the lifting up which was experienced by the prodigal son (cf. Lk 15), the adulterous woman (cf. Jn 8:11), and many others. It is the lifting up which every true Christian has experienced and relishes. It is the lifting up of which Jesus so often spoke (cf. Luke 14:11; 18:14), and which he himself provided for all the world.

This "lifting up" involves two things. It involves, first of all, that God in his undeserved love for mankind accepts the payment which Jesus made for mankind's sinfulness. The Father has accepted Jesus' payment for sin—his suffering and torture and death on Calvary's cross—as if mankind had made it. The payment was vicarious, substitutionary. As a result, in the eyes of God mankind's sin is gone. The guilt is gone. The liability for punishment is gone. And the impending penalty of eternal death in hell is gone.

What is more, the "lifting up" to which Jesus refers also involves God, again in his undeserved love for mankind, crediting mankind with the perfect righteousness of Christ. As a result, the believer is not an outcast, but a privileged subject in God's kingdom. Christ, by his life and death, has brought about reconciliation between God and man. There is peace with the almighty God, and human beings have been exalted to the position of God's own children and heirs of the eternal treasures of heaven.

vv. 11,12 — *Brothers, do not slander one another. Anyone who speaks against his brother or judges him, speaks against the law and judges it. When you judge the law, you are not keeping it, but sitting in judgment on it. There is only one Lawgiver and*

Judge, the one who is able to save and destroy. But you—who are you to judge your neighbor?

The focus of James's discourse does not change with these verses. He continues in his encouragement toward godly humility by pointing out that such humility will be made evident by the love with which the believer treats others. This is true because humility demands that a person place himself under God's law, and that law in turn demands that he love his fellowman perfectly (cf. 1 Jn 4:20,21). Conversely, a lack of love for one's fellowman reveals a lack of true humility, for it is in essence an attack on God's law and evidence of one's unwillingness to live under that law.

James makes his point by focusing specifically on the subject of speech and on sins of the tongue. He could have chosen any infraction of God's law to make his point. The present tense of the negative imperative (καταλαλεῖτε) and the fact that sins of the tongue are the subject of a large portion of chapter 3 and were mentioned again in chapter 4, together indicate that sins of the tongue were a besetting sin among James's readers, at least a problem that needed attention.

When one speaks evil of another or judges him, not only is he showing lovelessness, but he is also showing a lack of godly humility. He is portraying an attitude which says that he knows better than God's law and therefore better than God, the Giver of the law. He imagines that he has a better understanding of what is acceptable. He does not keep the law, but by his criticism of the law, by his condemnation of it, by his claiming that the law has erred in what it demands and forbids, he sets himself up as judge of the law. In his sinful pride he usurps God's position and authority.

The text concludes with a final call to repentance. What has been described is the height of arrogance and rebellion—a terrible offense against the sovereign Lord. He alone (εἷς is placed at the beginning of the sentence for emphasis) is Lawgiver and Judge. There is only one, and it is he. How dare any feeble creature attempt to usurp this position! Such a person brings on himself the most severe condemnation.

Self-examination will reveal that no one is in a position to judge his or her fellowman (cf. Mt 7:1-5). A Christian, of course, can and must judge according to God's Word when he encounters a clear case of sin. God's Word demands this of him. But self-examination and a realization of one's own sinfulness and unworthiness will break the proud, self-righteous heart and will forbid anyone to pass judgment where he has no right to do so. Instead, he will be led to turn in humble repentance to the God who alone has the power "to save and destroy."

Homiletical Suggestions

One theme runs through the ILCW readings for this day: the humility and submission of man which God's sovereignty demands. In the Old Testament lesson one of the many examples of Israel's spirit of rebellion is shared. The nation murmurs against and questions and voices its dissatisfaction with the manner in which the Lord is displaying his providential care: he has allowed adversity (be it ever so light) to enter their lives. Moses, in turn, expresses his despondency over the burden which he has been asked to carry—the responsibility of leading this rebellious people. In both cases the Lord, by relieving the trouble, effectively and impressively demonstrates his glory and the submission which it demands.

The Gospel from Mark focuses on the way in which the Christian will demonstrate his submission to God. He will do so by filling the role of the servant. As such he will not be self-seeking in any way, but will seek the glory of God alone. This, of course, will mean an acceptance and favorable recognition of every deed which is done for the glory of God (a point which was also made in the Old Testament lesson). The Christian's life will also be marked by a selflessness and self-denial which always seeks the spiritual good of the other, even if that other is a mere child. In addition, the Christian will give evidence of his submission to the Lord by his sanctified life, living at peace with his fellowman.

Focusing on the natural tendency in people to rebel against and attempt to throw off the lordship of the Almighty, and to claim lordship for themselves, you might consider the following outline:

Let Go of Ego!

1. By submitting to the almighty God (vv. 7-10)
2. By dealing with your neighbor in love (vv. 12,13)

Keying on the term "double-minded" and on the misconception that a Christian may be one of God's own and still have a close and active association with the world and its ways, the following outline comes to mind:

Unconditional Surrender!

1. Through total denial of everything worldly (vv. 7-9)
2. Through total submission to God and his ways (vv. 10-12)

Another outline:

God Exalts the Humble

1. Their humility leads to repentance and purification of life (vv. 7-9)
2. Their humility leads them to deal with their fellowman in love (vv. 11,12)
3. Their humility receives an eternal reward (v. 10)

TWENTIETH SUNDAY AFTER PENTECOST

The Scriptures

Old Testament — *Genesis 2:18-24*
Epistle — *Hebrews 2:9-11*
Gospel — *Mark 10:2-16*

The Text — Hebrews 2:9-11

The writer of Hebrews was concerned about the effect that the message of certain Judaizers would have upon the Jewish Christians. They were trying to persuade these Christians to return to the laws and beliefs of the old covenant. As proof of their claim these Judaizers pointed to the persecutions which their Christian brothers were experiencing, stating that these were God's acts of judgment on them for forsaking their former way of life.

In Hebrews we find a message of encouragement, first given to these early Christians but also very applicable to us today. Christ is the focal point throughout the letter, as the case is made for the Christian life being better than our former sinful way of life. The Savior is better than what these Hebrew Christians once had.

The Epistle establishes the superiority of Christ. The first chapter of this letter points out that Jesus is better than even the angels in heaven. However, our Lord allowed himself to be made "a little lower than the angels" to rescue mankind from sin and damnation.

Man was created as the masterpiece of God's creation, with everything subject to him by God's command (2:6-8). Sin, however, has obscured our view. Instead of man ruling supreme, he allows himself to be ruled by sin, and "at present we do not see everything subject to him" (2:8).

The picture becomes much clearer when we look to God's Son. The sermon text goes on to describe what we do see in our Savior: one who took on humanity to save us from sin.

v. 9 — *But we see Jesus, who was made a little lower than the angels, now crowned with glory and honor because he suffered death, so that by the grace of God he might taste death for everyone.*

If we look to ourselves, we see nothing worthy of salvation. But when we look to God's Son, we see "Jesus." We see our Savior. His human name reminds us that God became a man like us to save us.

He came down from heaven, being made "a little lower than the angels," leaving his exalted state and becoming true man. We confess this fact in the Nicene Creed: "For us and for our salvation, he came down from heaven, and was incarnate by the Holy Spirit and the virgin Mary."

But we don't see a defeated Messiah. We see one who "is crowned with glory and honor." He accomplished his mission on earth and again resumed his heavenly throne (Php 2:5-11; Eph 1:20,21). God gave his approval to the work of his Son by exalting him once again to his right hand. Ours is a glorious and triumphant Savior.

Jesus earned his position of glory and honor. He "suffered death," taking the punishment that we deserved. God sent his Son to take our place. It was purely an act of undeserved love on his part. It was an act that made salvation possible and certain "for everyone" (2 Co 5:15). Jesus tasted death for all on Calvary's cross, and for this feat he now sits on his exalted throne in heaven.

v. 10 — *In bringing many sons to glory, it was fitting that God, for whom and through whom everything exists, should make the author of their salvation perfect through suffering.*

Our salvation is all God's doing. The only way of salvation is God's way. Only he is capable of bringing us to glory. In his plan we see his infinite wisdom revealed. God is in control of all things (Ro 11:36). Everything has come into existence through him, and everything works out for his glory. His plan of salvation was no different. His way of saving the world was no haphazard event. It was all part of his plan, even the cross itself. The Hebrew Christians were tempted to be offended by the fact that their Savior was put to death on such a cruel, detestable instrument of torture such as the cross. But they shouldn't be, because even the way our Savior died was part of God's plan. God knew what he was doing in sending his Savior to the cross.

Jesus is referred to as the "author" (ἀρχηγός) of salvation. He is the source, the originator of our way to eternal life. (5:8,9; Jn 14:6). God made his Son "perfect through suffering" (διὰ παθημάτων τελειῶσαι). He was a complete Savior, fully qualified to take our place, because he obeyed his Father perfectly and carried out his saving will. He had to be a suffering Savior. He had to suffer death. Without suffering death he would not have been a complete Savior, because the ransom for sin required that someone suffer and die for the world. The Old Testament spoke of a suffering Savior (Isa 53). Being our Prophet and our King would not be enough. Jesus also had to be our High

Priest and offer himself as the sacrifice for our sins. God made him a complete Savior by having him suffer and die for the world.

v. 11 — *Both the one who makes men holy and those who are made holy are of the same family. So Jesus is not ashamed to call them brothers.*

Commentators are divided as to which "family" the writer has in mind. Certainly it is not incorrect to say that through his suffering and death Jesus has brought us into the family of his heavenly Father and made us co-heirs of salvation (Ro 8:17). But if we stay with the line of thought of the previous verses, we see this is a reference to Jesus' becoming one of us, becoming part of the human race. This thought comes up again in verse 14. Jesus shares our human nature. He is truly one of us! By becoming one of us he was able to make atonement for our sins (2:17) and make us holy (10:10).

Our status has been changed. Once despicably corrupt and sinful creatures, we are now changed into beloved members of God's family—all because of the Savior's work! Jesus can now look upon us as his brothers and sisters (Mt 12:49,50 and parallels; Ro 8:29). Because of his redemptive work, we have been restored to the family of God.

Homiletical Suggestions

One can't help centering any sermon on these verses around the saving work of our Savior as he took on our human nature to do what we are unable to do. He lived for us. He died for us. Because Christ allowed himself to be humbled and fully completed his Father's plan of salvation, he now reigns from his exalted throne in heaven above, and we have the sure hope of joining him there someday.

One outline that brings out these points:

Jesus Calls Us His Brothers

1. He came as one of us (v. 9a)
2. In order to die for us (vv. 9b,10)
3. So that we could live eternally with him (v. 11)

Keeping our sights directly on the Savior:

See the Exalted Savior

1. Once he came to die (vv. 9b,10)
2. Now he lives on high (vv. 9a,11)

TWENTY-FIRST SUNDAY AFTER PENTECOST

The Scriptures

> Old Testament — *Amos 5:6,7,10-15*
> Epistle — *Hebrews 3:1-6*
> Gospel — *Mark 10:17-27*

The Text — Hebrews 3:1-6

Though the author of this epistle is unknown, the very title reminds us that it was written to Hebrew Christians. Our text is expressive of the general purpose of the letter, showing how Jesus fulfills the Old Testament promises and prophecies.

In Deuteronomy 18 Moses, by inspiration, had pointed ahead to The Prophet who was to come, to whom the people should listen. Here the author points to Jesus as the supreme mediator, compares and contrasts him with Moses, and demonstrates how Jesus is superior to Moses.

v. 1 — *Therefore, holy brothers, who share in the heavenly calling, fix your thoughts on Jesus, the apostle and high priest whom we confess.*

Our attention is immediately drawn to the titles applied to the readers: holy brothers who share in the heavenly calling. This is the only time ἅγιοί appears in the New Testament in combination with ἀδελφοί. We are holy because we are clothed with Jesus' righteousness and set apart for God's use, so that we even become the temple of God.

The term "brothers" is also significant because it reminds us that we, the readers, are children of God, born of the Spirit, brothers (and sisters) of Jesus as well as of each other.

The natural question to ask is, "What does it mean to share in the calling?" It could simply mean we are all going to share heaven, but it is the calling to faith that comes from heaven. We have been called by God as people whose ultimate destination is the heavenly home.

While we wait we are to consider, to keep our thoughts fixed on, Jesus. What a beautiful exhortation this is, combined with the two names given to Jesus here! Jesus is called the apostle and high priest whom we confess. The idea of Jesus as priest and high priest should be one with which we are familiar, though the writer will treat that concept in great detail later in this Epistle. While Moses never was a priest, Jesus serves as our high priest (cf. chapter 2) by shedding his blood on the cross, as a sacrifice that pays for our sins. The writer will bring out these thoughts in detail later. Recall the work of the high priest in the Old Testament: to represent God to the people and the people to God.

But how is Jesus the apostle? This is the only time in the New Testament where Jesus is specifically given this title. It means, of course, "the sent one." Though this is the only time Jesus is given this title, he does speak of himself as sent from the Father, sent into the world. For example, he says to his apostles: "As the Father has sent me, I am sending you" (Jn 20:21). Jesus is the ultimate "sent one," sent into the world to redeem the world. It is this apostle and high priest whom we confess because we trust him for our eternal salvation. Through him we live and to him we live.

The reason for the writer's appeal becomes apparent in the next verse:

v. 2 — *He was faithful to the one who appointed him, just as Moses was faithful in all God's house.*

Jesus and Moses were both found faithful to their appointed calling. Moses was the most admired leader of the Hebrew people. Jesus' calling is as apostle, sent from God to do God's saving work, and as high priest, the Mediator between God and men. Both were appointed by God. Now, Moses was found faithful in all God's house, the household of believers (cf. Eph 2:20ff.). When we read the books of Exodus through Deuteronomy, one of the characteristics of Moses which stands out is his faithfulness to God's commands, as well as his faithfulness in serving God's people. Moses was a servant: of God, of his Word, of his people.

vv. 3,4 — *Jesus has been found worthy of greater honor than Moses, just as the builder of a house has greater honor than the house itself. For every house is built by someone, but God is the builder of everything.*

Now we come to the point of comparison, or rather contrast. Jesus is worthy of greater honor than Moses. At first this might seem obvious to the believer, but remember to whom this was written. The Hebrews were people who took pride in their relationship to Moses. God spoke directly with him; he was the mediator of the Ten Commandments and the Law; under God, he led them through the wilderness to the promised land.

Jesus, as the builder of all things, the Creator, deserves more honor than Moses, who is simply a part of the building. This house of God, made up of all believers, existed, in fact, before Moses. God (also God the Son) founded it and supervises it. He established it and continues to build it up as his own house, made up of living stones. Jesus is greater because he is the Creator. We admire a great house, great architecture, but even more we praise the builder or designer.

The next verse adds an additional thought for consideration. Even the glory and honor of God should be judged this way. When we see the glories of nature, let us honor the God who made all things.

v. 5 — *Moses was faithful as a servant in all God's house, testifying to what would be said in the future.*

The comparison continues and the contrast will be brought out more fully: Moses was a faithful servant, particularly in speaking and writing down what God told him. Moses was indeed faithful as a witness testifying to truths to be revealed later. Think of all the various prophecies recorded by Moses, from the first promise (Ge 3:15) to his own prediction of Jesus coming as the Prophet (Dt 18:15). Consider Jesus' high opinion of Moses, when he said, "Moses wrote of me."

v. 6 — *But Christ is faithful as a son over God's house. And we are his house, if we hold on to our courage and the hope of which we boast.*

Like Moses, Jesus was faithful in carrying out his assigned work, saving the world of lost sinners. The contrast is now strengthened in two ways. First, the author switches from the name Jesus to the office and title "Christ." Then Christ is designated "son" in distinction from Moses the "servant."

If Jesus is superior to Moses in God's household—as the son is superior to the servant—then we should not let anyone persuade us to look to Moses in place of or in addition to Christ. Such attempts were being made among the Hebrew Christians at the time this Epistle was written. Today, too, the devil works through many religious leaders and sects to direct our trust to our own works and worth instead of trusting Christ alone.

The author closes out this section by encouraging us not to give up in the face of persecution or problems, but to remember that we are a part of God's house or building, that we are brothers of Christ and Moses, that it is Christ alone who can enable us to remain faithful to him and confess him under all circumstances. We are to hold on to our courage and the hope of which we boast: eternal life, forgiveness, heaven, glory, rest, eternal joy.

Homiletical Suggestions

Keeping in mind the author's insistence on Jesus' superiority to all that came before him, and his urging that we fix our thoughts on him, we suggest two outlines:

Christ Is Greater than Moses

1. Moses faithfully proclaimed God's law
2. Jesus faithfully fulfilled God's promises

Fix Your Thoughts on Jesus

1. He is faithful, as Moses was (vv. 1,2)
2. He is worthy of greater honor than Moses was (vv. 3,4)
3. He is the fulfillment of what Moses said (vv. 5,6).

TWENTY-SECOND SUNDAY AFTER PENTECOST

The Scriptures

Old Testament — *Isaiah 53:10-12*
Epistle — *Hebrews 4:9-16*
Gospel — *Mark 10:35-45*

The Text — Hebrews 4:9-16

To study Hebrews is to have the living and active Word of God penetrate even to the dividing of the soul and spirit, joints and marrow. It is to have the thoughts and attitudes of the heart judged just as surely as if one stood in the consuming fire of God's own presence. Yet, it is even more to have one's thoughts and hopes directed heavenward. There the Son, having made the perfect sacrifice for our sins, having opened a new and perfect way, is seated at the right hand of God and is constantly interceding for us, his brothers. It is to be drawn close to God through Jesus, the great High Priest, who mediated a new and better covenant than the law.

This moves the preacher, moreover, to express his faith in Christ Jesus in word and action. Using Scripture, he reminds God's people again and again what great things God has done for them through Christ Jesus to gain their salvation. He shows by careful exposition of Scripture how salvation by grace through faith in Christ was always God's plan and man's only hope. And he also warns, reproves, rebukes, and instructs in righteousness. The specific text before us contains all these elements.

vv. 9,10 — *There remains, then, a Sabbath-rest for the people of God; for anyone who enters God's rest also rests from his own work, just as God did from his.*

As with every aspect of the Old Covenant (tabernacle, priesthood, sacrifices), so it was true of the Sabbath Day and the resting place: their true significance was being lost in legalistic interpretation and mere outward observance. The spirit of the law was obscured, the letter was the thing, and the letter was killing everyone. It's no different today. How outward observance of religious ritual—be it Christian, Jewish, Muslim, Buddhist, Hindu—is held up for admiration by the world and sinful flesh! The spiritual significance of the Sabbath Day, as found in God's forgiveness through Christ, or the true resting place as a heavenly homeland for God's people—which is ours freely through Christ without merit on our part—that is despised and rejected.

Carefully follow the Old Testament Scripture, however, and you will see quite the opposite. Why does the Lord through David in Psalm 95 (cp. Heb 4:7) warn the people of David's day about the danger of not entering the promised rest, if it was the earthly promised land that was meant? In David's day that is where they all lived. Yet the warning was still needed. Obviously, "there remains, then, a Sabbath-rest for the people of God," where the rest will be like that of God himself.

If ever there was a relevant message, it is that of our remaining, promised rest in heaven. How we are brought to glory is what almost everything leading up to our text is about. As ready and waiting as that rest is, however, access to it has been denied to the disobedient among God's people in the past, and it could be denied to us. Therefore, the admonitions and warnings which follow are in order.

> vv. 11-13 — *Let us, therefore, make every effort to enter that rest, so that no one will fall by following their example of disobedience. For the word of God is living and active. Sharper than any double-edged sword, it penetrates even to dividing soul and spirit, joints and marrow; it judges the thoughts and attitudes of the heart. Nothing in all creation is hidden from God's sight. Everything is uncovered and laid bare before the eyes of him to whom we must give an account.*

No one can read Hebrews and come away believing we enter heavenly rest by anything but the obedience which is faith. At the same time it is made perfectly clear that entry can be forfeited by disobedience. The first chapters explain how we get into heaven in the first place. Our text warns of the distinct possibility of "falling" from heaven.

Perhaps the sinful flesh of a Christian is the opposite of that of a work-righteous Jew: it wants to do nothing at all. It needs exactly the medicine of these verses. It needs to hear that treating the commands of God in a cavalier manner will get it where it got the mass of Israelites whose bodies fell in the desert. It needs to hear the exhortation to effort in godly living, in faith, in testimony. It needs to hear that the Word will not be deceived by any hypocrisy or show, but will cut right through to reveal all. Our God is living and active, and so is his Word.

Τραχηλίζω is a verb unique to Hebrews. It is rather hard to translate exactly, but probable meanings are chilling in their implications:

our necks exposed like those of offenders or sacrificial animals, whose necks are literally on the line.

Consider ἐνώπιον and its corresponding Old Testament expressions: "in the sight of," "in the eyes of," or "before" (the Lord). To us, many of those Old Testament kings who did evil "in the sight of" the Lord would have looked little different from Noah or David, both of whom found grace "in the eyes of" the Lord (Ge 6:8; Ac 7:46). It is not to us, however, that they had to give account.

If our hearers are comfortable in their pews after hearing us expound these verses, we have "missed the boat." If, in their struggles, we do not bring them the help and strength of the remaining verses, we have likewise failed. What help is at hand!

v. 14 — *Therefore, since we have a great high priest who has gone through the heavens, Jesus the Son of God, let us hold firmly to the faith we profess.*

Our help is in the name of the Lord who sent his own Son to become our high priest. Jesus, the Son of God, has not entered through the curtain of an earthly place of worship into the symbolic presence of the all-knowing, all-seeing God before whom nothing is hidden. He has gone through the heavens themselves, directly to the throne of God—for us! While the writer does not fully explain the symbolism of the Old Testament priesthood until later in his letter, this is already his third reference to Jesus as high priest.

See what he has done! How can we be slack, shrinking back, cowering in the corner, sitting on the sidelines? "Let us hold firmly to the faith we profess." Study κρατέω: how the Jews "held on" to their traditions (Mk 7:3,4,8), how some in Pergamum "held on" to the teachings of Balaam (Rev 2:14), how some Christians need to "hold on" to their Head (Col 2:19) and to his name (Rev 2:13) and to the teachings they have received (2 Th 2:15; Rev 2:25) so that no one will take their crown (Rev 3:11). Study ὁμολογία: how well John 12:42 and Romans 10:9 show that it is the vital companion to faith in the heart. It is a big word for the understanding of Hebrews. See also Hebrews 3:1, 10:23, 11:13, and 13:15.

We have a great high priest. What gospel content can be conveyed! How relieved and happy our hearers can be!

v. 15 — *For we do not have a high priest who is unable to sympathize with our weaknesses, but we have one who has been tempted in every way, just as we are—yet without sin.*

As exalted and radiant and superior as our high priest is, he is our brother. This verse says it all. Endear their Lord ever more to your hearers by constantly interplaying and contrasting his two natures, as does Hebrews. When the writer has put our Lord Jesus on the highest pedestal he can, then he interjects a verse like this, which we are amazed to hear—so human does it reveal our Lord to be. Yet it is done without turning him into a tragicomic demigod for our entertainment: "yet he was without sin."

In view of his true humanity the invitation in the closing verse of our text seems completely natural.

v. 16 — *Let us then approach the throne of grace with confidence, so that we may receive mercy and find grace to help us in our time of need.*

The approachability of our God prompts the exhortation to approach. The phrase "throne of grace" shows that God is not only accessible but ready and waiting for sinners to come. We can approach this throne μετὰ παρρησίας. Most translators say "boldly" or "confidently." Luther says "joyfully." We know what lay behind Luther's choice of words: he never could get over the joy of finding out that all the human rituals and intermediaries and personal efforts he had been told were necessary were in fact not necessary.

The halls, courts, and thrones of worldly powers are largely closed to us today. Or, they are accessible only through ritual, red tape, and countless—mostly unsympathetic—intermediaries. Approach to the throne of grace requires an intermediary, too, but no more red tape and ritual. And our intermediary knows exactly what we're experiencing.

Homiletical Suggestions

Why do Christians fall? Is it primarily because of full-frontal attacks by Satanism, gross sin, or materialism? Is it not rather by "lifestyle" decisions, confusion of priorities, gradual conformity to the world, or negligible transformation of mind? Why is a Christian elementary school's sports program sometimes of more interest in the life of a congregation than the children's mission offering or evangelism training or seeking the straying? Are all the things pastors need really necessities? Why is it hard to get experienced pastors to take mission calls? Do children need the latest video game systems, ballet lessons, and tennis shoes? Can prospective pastor and teacher trainees see anything truly different in the lifestyles of their pastors and teachers? Materialism imperils us all.

Our text empowers us. The thoughts and attitudes of our hearts can be penetrated and judged by verses 9-13. Our lifestyles can be laid bare and our necks put on the line. Longing for our Sabbath-rest can be reawakened. And our great high priest is still interceding for us! In this text spiritual renewal is at hand. Jesus faced those lifestyle questions all along the way, from his birth in a stable, through his meager life, to his miserable death. The kingdoms of this world were real temptations for him too. We can go to him. Urge your hearers:

Recognize the Great Realities in Your Lives

1. The perils (vv. 9-11)
2. The power (vv. 12-16)

Another possibility:

There Remains a Sabbath-rest

1. This is a real rest, like God's, for his people (vv. 9,10)
2. There is help for the helpless to attain it (vv. 11-16)

TWENTY-THIRD SUNDAY AFTER PENTECOST

The Scriptures

> Old Testament — *Jeremiah 31:7-9*
> Epistle — *Hebrews 5:1-10*
> Gospel — *Mark 10:46-52*

The Text — Hebrews 5:1-10

Hebrews was written to a body of Christians of Old Testament Jewish background. Some of their number had been suffering persecution already, and it seemed that more persecution was to be expected. Some were beginning to wonder whether faithfulness to Christ was really worth the effort and distress. The context and content of the letter suggest that a number of them were tempted to go back to Old Testament Judaism with its temple worship, sacrifices, high priests, and ceremonies.

The purpose of this letter is to show them that to return to the Old Testament worship and ceremonies was not the right thing to do. The letter was to show them that Jesus was the fulfillment of all those ceremonies and sacrifices, and of the high priesthood. He was the promised One who would come to take away sin by his sacrifice once and for all. More than that, he was far superior to the angels (1:4—2:18) and far superior to Moses (3:1—4:13), through whom the Old Testament worship, sacrifices, and ceremonies were given.

Beginning with last Sunday's Epistle reading (4:14-16) the writer showed that Jesus is *the* great high priest, far better than all the other high priests since the time of Aaron. In this text we see the reasons why Jesus is a better high priest than the Jews ever had, why he is the *great* high priest. We also see Jesus' qualifications to be *our* great high priest.

v. 1 — *Every high priest is selected from among men and is appointed to represent them in matters related to God, to offer gifts and sacrifices for sins.*

To show how Jesus' office of high priest is far superior to that of Old Testament successors to Aaron, the writer makes a number of comparisons between Jesus and the high priest of Jewish worship. Through these comparisons he shows the tasks and qualifications of a high priest.

The high priest was chosen by God as "a man among men." The purpose of his office was to be in charge of the "things pertaining to

God" (τὰ πρὸς τὸν θεόν) on behalf of the people. The phrase "to offer gifts and sacrifices for sins" is appositional, telling us what the "matters related to God" were. This he did especially on the great Day of Atonement, as explained in Leviticus 16.

Already here we see how Jesus was far superior to those Old Testament high priests. The verbs used in this verse are present tense, indicating the continued, repeated actions of the high priests. The Old Testament priests since Aaron were continually being replaced because of their mortality. Their offerings for the sins of the people were done repeatedly, day after day, year after year. How unlike Jesus, the eternal Son of God, who made the "once for all" (ἐφάπαξ) sacrifice for our sin (7:27; 10:10)!

> vv. 2,3 — *He is able to deal gently with those who are ignorant and are going astray, since he himself is subject to weakness. This is why he has to offer sacrifices for his own sins, as well as for the sins of the people.*

One important reason why the high priests were chosen from among men was so that they could deal in a gentle manner with their fellow sinners who sinned in ignorance or who had carelessly strayed into sin. Because the priest was a man just as they were, he could easily understand why they could give in to some temptation and foolishly fall into sin. He had the same weaknesses and foolishly fell into sin just as they did.

But there was a drawback to the humanity of the Old Testament priests. Because they were sinners just like the people they served, they had to first make sacrifices for their own sins before they could make sacrifices for the sins of the people (Lev 16:11-14,17). How unlike Jesus, who was "without sin" (4:15; 7:26,27; Jn 8:46 and 1 Pe 1:18,19)! He had no need to make sacrifices for his sins first, since he had no sin. As the sinless Son of God, he was far superior to those Old Testament priests. There was no need to go back to those Old Testament priests and their sacrifices.

Like the Old Testament high priests, Jesus can also deal gently with us who are ignorant and are going astray, not because he has been guilty of the same sins but because he "has been tempted in every way, just as we are" (4:15). He knows and understands how difficult it is for us to resist the temptations from Satan and a sinful world around us, since he also had to battle them.

Incidentally, we learn by example from the Old Testament and Jesus how to deal with our fellow believers. We are also to be gentle and compassionate with them when they stray into sin and are trapped by it. Without tolerating or condoning sin, we avoid undue harshness and severity in dealing with the sinner. We, too, have committed sins of ignorance and weakness and have experienced the gentle care and forgiveness of a loving Savior. This, however, is not the writer's main point in his comparison of Jesus and the Old Testament high priests.

> vv. 4-6 — *No one takes this honor upon himself; he must be called by God, just as Aaron was. So Christ also did not take upon himself the glory of becoming a high priest. But God said to him, "You are my Son; today I have become your Father." And he says in another place, "You are a priest forever, in the order of Melchizedek."*

Another qualification of the Old Testament priesthood was that the high priests were appointed by God himself. No one took the position for himself. God chose them, through the succession of Aaron. That gave them their authority and power.

Again we see the comparison to Christ and his superiority over the other priests. Like them, he was called and chosen by God. The quotations from Psalm 2 and Psalm 110 prove that Jesus was not an impostor, coming to deceive the people. He had God's special calling and choosing. Jesus himself testifies to this in John 8:54 as he tells the Jews how he obtained the honor and glory of his position as the Christ, the promised Messiah: "If I glorify myself my glory means nothing. My Father, whom you claim as your God, is the one who glorifies me."

How much more glory and honor Jesus had than the Aaronic priesthood! He was not a temporary priest, serving only the few years of his lifetime here on earth. Instead, he was "a priest forever, in the order of Melchizedek." Jesus holds his position forever. And his position is that of a king-priest, like Melchizedek (Ge 14:18-20). Melchizedek is the only Old Testament figure who is both king and priest. Like Melchizedek, Jesus did not inherit his office through a successions of priests. More important, like Melchizedek, Jesus has no successor. Both are superior to Aaron, and Christ is superior to all. His office is eternal and his work will not, need not, ever be repeated.

Since Jesus is the eternal high priest, there is no need to go back to the Old Testament priesthood and worship. In Jesus we have the best, everything God wants us to have. We have the eternal Son of God himself. For more on Melchizedek and the parallels between him and Jesus, see Hebrews 7.

v. 7 — During the days of Jesus' life on earth, he offered up prayers and petitions with loud cries and tears to the one who could save him from death, and he was heard because of his reverent submission.

Now we see how Jesus faithfully and perfectly obeyed the call of his Father so that we might have a priest who made the perfect sacrifice for sin. The writer takes us back to the time of the Savior's ministry. We are especially reminded of the wrestling and agony of Gethsemane. We see the intensity of his praying in the piling up of terms: not only petitions (δεήσεις) but also ἱκετηρίας, urgent and earnest requests. Those prayers and petitions were offered with κραυγῆς ἰσχυρᾶς, loud outcry, made in grief and agony. Along with those loud cries were tears (δακρύων) that showed the anguish of soul he was experiencing.

Jesus' prayer to the Father in the Garden was that the Father's will, the salvation of mankind, would be accomplished. His prayer for himself—and us—was heard because of his reverent, godly fear, his submission to the Father's will. In answer to his prayer God sent an angel from heaven to strengthen him for the great task that lay ahead at the cross. Here is a high priest who not only prays for the people, but also puts himself in their place and willingly prays according to God's saving will.

vv. 8,9 — Although he was a son, he learned obedience from what he suffered and once made perfect, he became the source of eternal salvation for all who obey him

Already as a child Jesus knew what obedience was all about, and he rendered it perfectly. But in the agony of Gethsemane and Calvary we are shown the full extent of his obedience. As Paul says in Philippians, he "became obedient to death—even death on a cross" (2:8). There, as the great high priest, Jesus obediently gave himself as the perfect sacrifice for our sin.

Through his obedience he "reached the goal," which is a better translation of τελειωθείς than the NIV's "made perfect." The goal was his death on the cross as payment for all sin, his resurrection from the grave, and his return to the complete glory of heaven. There he sits at God's right hand, ruling all things in the interest of his church and acting as our intercessor.

As a result of his obedience, both active and passive, our eternal salvation has been earned. The work is complete. Nothing—no ceremonies and no sacrifices—needs to be added to it. Forgiveness for our sins and eternal life in heaven is God's free gift on the basis of Jesus' redeeming work.

That salvation becomes the personal possession of "all who obey him." Such obedience is not good works by which we earn Christ's forgiveness. Rather, "obedience" is "submissive hearing" (ὑπακοή), which is faith. Through faith Christ's redeeming work becomes our own. Our sin is forgiven. Salvation is ours as God's free gift. It belongs to all those who believe in Jesus as the Son of God and the Savior of the world who was obedient to death for them.

v. 10 — *and was designated by God to be high priest in the order of Melchizedek.*

With the work of redemption accomplished, God puts his stamp of approval on all that Christ has done as the great high priest. He is a priest like Melchizedek (cf. v. 6). His work goes on forever, never to end.

To sum up, Jesus is a much better priest than Aaron and his successors ever were. Those priests were temporary. Jesus is eternal. Their sacrifices had to be made repeatedly and could never pay for sin. Jesus' sacrifice was once for all time and made the perfect payment for sin. For the original readers of this letter to go back to the Old Testament priests, worship, and sacrifices was not only foolish, it would be disastrous. They would be throwing away the Savior and salvation God intended them to have, all of which he had pictured for them through the old priesthood. Jesus is all that is needed.

Homiletical Suggestions

At first glance the preacher might have difficulty seeing the relevant, practical applications in this text for modern hearers. Few, if any, have any desire to go back to Old Testament Judaism. Most really have no idea what that would mean, having little knowledge of the priesthood, Melchizedek, or the significance of Old Testament worship regulations for our salvation in Christ.

While that may be true, the Jewish way of thinking that the individual must make personal sacrifice of obedience to satisfy God's justice is common. People need to see that God has given them a real high priest, who rendered the obedience and made the sacrifice for them. They need to see in Jesus a Savior who understands and cares about their problems, trials, and temptations; who not only can understand but can also deal gently and decisively with them by his redeeming work. They need to see that Jesus is their source of eternal salvation and be led to a greater faith in him. These needs lead to a number of sermon suggestions:

Jesus Gives Us What We Need

1. He understand our temptations (vv. 1-3)
2. He delivers us from our sins (vv. 4-10)

Jesus Is the Source of Eternal Salvation

1. This is true in his praying (v. 7)
2. This is true in his suffering (v. 8)
3. This is true in his attaining (v. 9)

Because the concept and importance of the high priest are unknown to most of our hearers, it might be good to preach a sermon that provides that information and its relevance.

Jesus Is Our Great High Priest

1. He represents us before God (vv. 1,4-6)
2. He understands our human weaknesses (vv. 2,3)
3. He gained salvation for us by his sacrifice (vv. 7-10)

TWENTY-FOURTH SUNDAY AFTER PENTECOST

The Scriptures

Old Testament — *Deuteronomy 6:1-9*
Epistle — *Hebrews 7:23-28*
Gospel — *Mark 12:28-34*

The Text — Hebrews 7:23-28

This Sunday we continue to highlight the beautiful comfort found in the assurances that Jesus Christ is our great high priest. The emphasis of this particular text focuses on the ability of our high priest to meet our every need. In a world where the unbeliever runs from place to place futilely trying to answer needs he feels but doesn't even fully understand, in a world where even we as believers are often tempted to look elsewhere to answer the needs of our lives, the author of Hebrews holds up our great high priest as the all-sufficient answer to our every need. Just as the first readers of this letter found encouragement here in the reminder that there is no other place to run in time of need, so we find that same encouragement and reminder in these verses.

vv. 23-25 — *Now there have been many of those priests, since death prevented them from continuing in office; but because Jesus lives forever, he has a permanent priesthood. Therefore he is able to save completely those who come to God through him because he always lives to intercede for them*

Were the author's first readers tempted to return to the Levitical priesthood and the security of their ancient sacrifices and rituals? The author reminds them that they would be trading the only permanent priesthood for a very poor substitute.

Only Jesus had a priesthood to which they could turn forever. Only his priesthood was ἀπαράβατον. That word comes from the same root as the word for "trespass." Jesus occupies a high-priestly office that could never be "trespassed against," never broken or violated. He who lives forever is their eternal high priest who will never fail them.

The author then applies the comforting truth that Jesus remains forever as our high priest. We do not have to be searching constantly for a high priest we can depend on. Since he lives forever, we are able to depend on him every day for the salvation which we so desperately need. He has opened up for us the path to our Father in heaven (Jn 14:6). All who come to God through this high priest may approach "with freedom and confidence" (Eph 3:12). And the reverse is also true: without him there is no salvation (Ac 4:12).

What is more, not only does our high priest open up for us the path to the Father, he is also constantly interceding for us. He has entered the heavenly Most Holy Place with the sacrifice of his own blood, and because of that sacrifice the Father will forever hear him as he speaks in our defense (Ro 8:34).

Who would turn aside from such a high priest? Could there be any need we have that he could not meet?

v. 26 — *Such a high priest meets our need—one who is holy, blameless, pure, set apart from sinners, exalted above the heavens.*

The author answers the question we just raised. In Jesus Christ, the Father supplied us with exactly the high priest who would meet our every need. For, as the first three terms reveal, he is everything we are not. He is the one and only one whose holiness and blamelessness match the requirements of the law which the Gospel and Old Testament readings hold before us this Sunday. The beauty and comfort of that truth come to us when we understand that God's plan from all eternity was that "in him we might become the righteousness of God" (2 Co 5:21). Since this high priest was our God-ordained representative and substitute, "holy, blameless [and] pure" are words that will describe us before the throne of God.

As Jesus humbled himself under the law he lived that perfection for us. Now, however, the author goes on in his description of our perfect high priest to speak about his exaltation. The perfect participle κεχωρισμένος speaks of what is the continuing result of his being lifted up beyond the heavens. The aorist participle γενόμενος speaks of the one-time act of his being lifted up. Paul offers us inspired commentary on the conclusion of this verse in Ephesians 1:20-23.

v. 27 — *Unlike the other high priests, he does not need to offer sacrifices day after day, first for his own sins, and then for the sins of the people. He sacrificed for their sins once for all when he offered himself.*

Did these early Jewish Christians really want to go back to the Levitical priesthood and the old sacrifices? Here again the author shows how pitifully incomplete and imperfect those sacrifices were.

We can picture with him the countless sacrifices of Israel, day after day and festival after festival. From one Great Day of Atonement to the next (Lev 16:6) Aaron and his successors offered first a sacrifice for their own sins and then a sacrifice for the sins of the people. Again and again that sacrifice had to be repeated. That was necessary because those sacrifices were always imperfect and only a shadow of a much greater sacrifice to come.

But why go back to the shadow when the perfect and final sacrifice has come for us? Our "holy, blameless [and] pure" high priest, who had no sins of his own for which to sacrifice, made our sins his own as he performed the once and for all sacrifice of sacrifices. In this sacrifice he functioned not only as priest but also as the sacrificial offering.

Therefore by offering himself—once and for all time—he has indeed forever opened up the path to the throne of God. Because the "holy, blameless [and] pure" high priest took the place of all of us who were the exact opposite of him, the Father does indeed hear and accept his intercession for us and therefore forever accepts us.

Talk about what we need!

v. 28 — *For the law appoints as high priests men who are weak; but the oath, which came after the law, appointed the Son, who has been made perfect forever.*

The section closes out with one more reminder that we don't need to put our trust in any weak and sinful human mediators when we have the Son of God himself.

A better translation at the end of the verse would be "the Son, who has been brought to his goal (τέλος)." The Son who came and lived a perfect life, died an innocent death, rose and was exalted to the right hand of God, has reached the goal the Father gave him. As the great and final and permanent high priest he has completed our perfect sacrifice and now lives to assure us of the enjoyment of its blessings. He will not fail us until he has brought us to our eternal goal with him.

Homiletical Suggestions

Christians today are just as capable of becoming discouraged as were the Christians to whom this book was written. Today, as then, we can be tempted to look elsewhere for what we feel we need in this life. The exact temptation may be different. Who of us feels a yearning to sacrifice a few lambs or bulls? But the temptations are similar, as a host of human and earthly answers to our real or imagined needs appeal to us.

From the wisdom of the world, which so often seems to offer just the practical help we need in this life, to the "self-help" craze in the churches which directs us to our own "inner resources," there are always plenty of places to seek to satisfy our needs. Also, as we mis-diagnose what is really wrong with us, how often don't we go seeking answers in things physical for needs spiritual!

But there still is only one who meets our needs. He who sacrificed himself for each of us and who now lives to intercede for us without ceasing is the answer to our every need. There is no one and nowhere else worth turning to.

With those thoughts in mind we see a possible division of the text into theme and parts:

Your High Priest Meets Your Needs

1. Once by offering himself for you (vv. 26-28)
2. Now by interceding for you (vv. 23-25)

Another way of expressing those same thoughts would be:

Only Jesus Can Meet Your Needs

1. As the sacrifice who once died for you (vv. 26-28)
2. As the priest who lives to intercede for you (vv. 23-25)

One more way to express these thoughts emphasizes the permanency of our great high priest as compared to the transiency of all the helpers who fail us:

He's Always There to Meet Our Needs!

1. Always there with his cross (vv. 26-28)
2. Always there with his prayer (vv. 23-25)

294

TWENTY-FIFTH SUNDAY AFTER PENTECOST

The Scriptures

Old Testament — *1 Kings 17:8-15*
Epistle — *Hebrews 9:24-28*
Gospel — *Mark 12:41-44*

The Text — Hebrews 9:24-28

Every period of the church's history has had its particular troubles and temptations, which Satan has used in an effort to keep God's children from reaching faith's goal, salvation. These eras are characterized by persecution or by great doctrinal struggles. The devil's goal is always the same, to lead believers away from pure devotion to Christ.

The Christians for whom this letter was written also experienced their own troubles and temptations. They lived during the time of transition between the Old and New Testaments. While the redemptive work of Christ brought about a definite and immediate change from the Old Covenant to the New (Mt 27:51), the transition in practice took time, as various incidents in Bible history illustrate (cf. Ac 10:9ff.; Gal 2:11ff.; Ac 21:17ff.). The change of focus from the symbolism of the Old Covenant (Heb 9:9) to the realities of the New (9:11) was understandably difficult for the Jewish Christians. One does not change religions as easily as changing hats. Though not yet resisting "to the point of shedding blood" (12:4), these new Christians were under severe pressure to turn back to their old Jewish faith.

With earnest and heart-felt pleading the unknown author urges them not to "ignore such a great salvation" (2:2) as the New Covenant offers. He shows them again and again how the covenant of which Jesus is mediator is superior to the old one (8:6).

The verses of our text focus on the comparison of two things found in both the Old and New Covenants. First, heaven is greater than the man-made tabernacle. Then, Christ's sacrifice of blood is greater than the sacrifices made by the Old Testament high priests. To see how these comparisons fit into the author's train of thought the preacher should carefully read through chapters 8 and 9 and the first half of chapter 10.

v. 24 — *For Christ did not enter a man-made sanctuary that was only a copy of the true one; he entered heaven itself, now to appear for us in God's presence.*

With all the descriptive words in this verse, the two which beg for our immediate attention are "for us" (ὑπὲρ ἡμῶν). How often in the Scriptures does not the Holy Spirit put this preposition and this pronoun together to proclaim the glorious gospel. If we overlook these two words, we will miss the personal aspect of these verses. Then we might preach about salvation to our people, rather than proclaim *their* salvation to them. The Old Testament terminology in this epistle may seem irrelevant to the casual listener, but the preacher can immediately do away with such a notion when he emphasizes these two words. What Christ did, he did "for us."

When Christ our great High Priest entered the sanctuary of heaven, he fulfilled the role of the Old Testament high priest who went every year into the Most Holy Place. The priests of the Old Covenant entered a sanctuary made by human hands. The tabernacle, later the temple, were rightfully held in high regard by the Old Testament worshipers, but these buildings were properly understood only as "copies" of God's holy dwelling, heaven itself.

But what does this mean that Christ appears for us in God's presence? Why is this so important? The writer goes on to explain:

> vv. 25,26 — *Nor did he enter heaven to offer himself again and again, the way the high priest enters the Most Holy Place every year with blood that is not his own. Then Christ would have had to suffer many times since the creation of the world. But now he has appeared once for all at the end of the ages to do away with sin by the sacrifice of himself.*

The reason Christ appeared before our Father in heaven was to show himself to be the perfect and acceptable sacrifice for our sins. The benefit of his sacrifice becomes our own the moment the Holy Spirit brings us to faith. Believers are already in the heavenly Jerusalem (Heb 12:22; Eph 2:6). The blood of Jesus purifies us from all unrighteousness, so we can enter the Most Holy Place. Of course, now "we live by faith" (2 Co 5:7), but "when Christ, who is your life, appears, then you also will appear with him in glory" (Col 3:4).

Just as the man-made sanctuary was only a picture of the true one, so also the high priests of the Old Covenant served only as types of our great High Priest, Jesus Christ. This Epistle alone calls Jesus our High Priest. Here is an opportunity for the teaching pastor to re-emphasize this important office of Christ which his members learned about in their study of the Second Article. Here is an opportunity to show that the three offices of Christ (Prophet, Priest, King) are not just catechetical jargon but a meaningful revelation of what Christ has done for our salvation.

Two times each day the priests under the Old Covenant entered the tabernacle, once in the morning and once at night. But only once a year would the high priest enter the Holy of Holies to sprinkle the blood of animals on the Ark of the Covenant. This was on the Great Day of Atonement (Ex 30:10; Lev 23:26-32). Christ, our Great High Priest, did his work "once for all" (ἅπαξ). And, he came not with blood "other than his own," but with the blood that came "by the sacrifice of himself." As we sing during our celebration of the New Covenant, Holy Communion, ". . . offered was he for greatest and for least, himself the victim and himself the priest" (TLH 307,1). The "once-for-all" nature of Jesus' sacrifice is still subverted by the repeated "unbloody sacrifice" of the Roman Catholic Mass.

Just as there was a great contrast between the man-made sanctuary and the heaven which that building typified, so also there is an enormous contrast between the sacrifice of the Old Covenant high priest and the sacrifice of the Priest of the New Covenant, Jesus Christ. Christ brings his own blood! The writer now explains the full significance of this:

> vv. 27,28 — *Just as man is destined to die once, and after that to face judgment, so Christ was sacrificed once to take away the sins of many people; and he will appear a second time, not to bear sin, but to bring salvation to those who are waiting for him.*

Christ's sacrifice was so desperately needed because the sacrifices of the Old Covenant could not take away sin, could not enable us to face judgment without trembling in fear, could not bring salvation. One cannot help but feel the writer's heartfelt pleading with his Hebrew readers: "Do not be led astray by those who want to lead you back into the Old Covenant. There is too much for you to lose, too much to give up." The shedding of blood in the Old Covenant rites was significant as it symbolized the work the Messiah would do, but now the old has gone and the new has come! No more symbols, no more pictures and types. Now we have the real thing, full and glorious in Christ Jesus. His blood actually takes away your sin, so when he appears again he will bring salvation to all you who wait for your great and glorious High Priest to return."

Here the preacher finds color for the season. As we enter the last days of the Church Year, we bring to our people's minds and hearts words about Christ's return and thoughts of facing judgment. One can hardly find a more effective Scripture verse to bring us face to face with these realities than verse 27, where death and judgment are presented, one right after the other.

Thanks be to our Lord Jesus Christ we do not need to side-step these issues. On the contrary, with these words Christ calls upon his church to face boldly the reality of our own sin, death, judgment, eternity. While the world ignores such talk or pretends that these truths do not exist, we believe and confess that "Christ was sacrificed once to take away the sins of many people." This, of course, is not to say Jesus didn't take away the sins of all people. We can either understand the "many" to be in contrast to the "one" Savior or simply realize that all people are indeed many people. In either case, we know Scripture does sometimes use the word "many" even while it declares that "justification brings life to all men" (Ro 5:18,19). There is no limited atonement to be found in the Bible. Since Jesus is the Savior of all, we acknowledge our weaknesses and iniquities and then turn in faith to our Great High Priest of the New Covenant, who "brings salvation to those who are waiting for him."

Homiletical Suggestions

The goal of the preacher will be to help his people see that these Old Covenant pictures are not irrelevant. Rather, in them can be found magnificent pictures of the realities which Christ Jesus accomplished for us. The real blessings of the New Covenant are just too great for us to live again with only the pictures of the Old.

The sermon might do just what the text does, compare the old and the new:

The New Covenant Is Better

1. It leads to a better place (v. 24)
2. Because it brings a better sacrifice (vv. 25-28)

This outline takes the season of the Christian Year into account:

Christ Will Appear a Second Time

1. Not to do what he has already done (vv. 25-28)
2. But to bring us to what he has won (vv. 24,28)

TWENTY-SIXTH SUNDAY AFTER PENTECOST

The Scriptures

> Old Testament — *Daniel 12:1-3*
> Epistle — *Hebrews 12:25-29*
> Gospel — *Mark 13:1-13*

The Text — Hebrews 12:25-29

The unidentified writer to the Hebrews warns converts from Judaism against reverting to their former religion. He does so by emphasizing the supremacy and sufficiency of Jesus Christ as the one who revealed God's will and is the mediator of the new covenant. In chapters 11 and 12 we have his final plea to them, that they persevere in the Christian faith. Hebrews 12:25-29 is the concluding exhortation to listen to God and to worship him "acceptably with reverence and awe."

> v. 25 — *See to it that you do not refuse him who speaks. If they did not escape when they refused him who warned them on earth, how much less will we, if we turn away from him who warns us from heaven?*

Βλέπετε, present active imperative, directs the readers' attention to something important coming up, like our warning: "Look out!" μὴ παραιτήσησθε, aorist middle subjunctive, is a strong prohibition and warns them not to refuse the one who is speaking to them, Jesus Christ.

The conditional sentence which follows gives one reason no one should refuse Jesus. The writer points back, as he so often does in this epistle, to an event in Israel's history. He reminds the Hebrew Christians that the Israelites did not escape when they refused the one who warned them on earth, God's spokesman Moses. A recurring theme in the Old Testament is Israel's refusal to hear God and the punishment which resulted. Since God dealt that way with those who disobeyed the law, what will happen to any who turn away from the gospel which Jesus proclaims from his position of majesty at God's right hand? Jesus himself said that much will be demanded from those to whom much has been given (Lk 12:47,48). It will be better on Judgment Day for Tyre and Sidon than for those who heard Jesus and rejected him (Lk 10:14).

v. 26 — *At that time his voice shook the earth, but now he has promised, "Once more I will shake not only the earth but also the heavens."*

We recall how God shook the earth when he gave the law at Sinai, as recorded in Exodus 19:18. God will shake it again as prophesied in Haggai 2:6. The writer adds οὐ μόνον . . . ἀλλὰ καί to the quotation to emphasize that the future shaking will be more extensive than that at Sinai.

We are reminded of a consistent theme in Hebrews of the "better" and the "superior" as the writer often speaks of the supremacy of Jesus and the new covenant. Even the shaking will be greater in the cataclysmic events of the Last Day. How appropriate it is to reflect on this on the 26th Sunday after Pentecost, which focuses on the Last Day. The other Scripture lessons for this day help describe what the Last Day will be like.

v. 27 — *The words "once more" indicate the removing of what can be shaken—that is, created things—so that what cannot be shaken may remain.*

The writer interprets the Haggai passage in order to emphasize the purpose of the shaking on the Last Day. Those things which are shaken will be removed or changed: Μετάθεσις can mean either "removal" or "change." Whether they are removed or transformed, the purpose (ἵνα) is the same: "So that the things which cannot be shaken may remain." This verse reminds us of the permanence of heavenly treasures, compared to earthly treasures, and that our relationship with God is infinitely more important than the transitory and elusive.

v. 28 — *Therefore, since we are receiving a kingdom that cannot be shaken, let us be thankful, and so worship God acceptably with reverence and awe.*

The kingdom of God to which we belong is Christ's gracious rule in our hearts by means of the Word. We will fully enjoy this in heaven. Διό introduces an inevitable conclusion: Since we are receiving this unshakable kingdom, we are to do something in response.

We are to be thankful (ἔχωμεν χάριν). The NIV's "and so" renders δι᾽ ἧς, which refers back to χάριν. It is "through thanks" that we worship God acceptably.

Λατρεύωμεν can mean "worship" in the narrow sense or "serve by rendering religious service or homage." We prefer the latter because it encourages the reader to respond with his whole life and not in just one aspect of it.

How are those who are receiving an unshakable kingdom to serve
God? The acceptable manner is "with reverence and awe." What God
has done and will do for us generates a deep sense of awe and reverence which accompanies our worship and service to him.

v. 29 — For our "God is a consuming fire."

Our text concludes with a terse proclamation of the law, once
again warning those who are inclined to refuse God that there will be
terrible consequences of such an action. We are reminded of other
references to God as a consuming fire (Dt 4:24; 9:3; Isa 33:14). It
would not be good homiletical practice to quote this last verse as the
last words of a sermon. It should, however, have a place in the sermon to emphasize God's wrath on those who refuse. We recall that
Jesus could end a parable with someone being thrown into outer
darkness. Obviously, we should not use it in the expectation that it
will create a desire to serve God.

Homiletical Suggestions

Since this text is to be used at the end of the Church Year, the
preacher will most likely use it as a springboard to describe the
events and outcome of the Last Day. One of the main emphases will
be the purpose of the shaking: to remove or change the shakable
things so that only an unshakable kingdom will remain. But the
preacher would be remiss if he only described the Last Day and did
not proclaim the same exhortation the writer proclaims: do not refuse
him who speaks! The main emphasis of Hebrews, of chapters 11 and
12, and especially of this text, is a warning against backsliding and
refusing to trust in Jesus as the only Savior. Several basic outlines
come to mind which reflect this emphasis.

Do Not Refuse God!

1. He consumes those who do (vv. 25,29)
2. He gives an unshakable kingdom to those who do not (vv. 27,28)

If you prefer a more "catchy" outline:

When God Speaks, People, Listen!

1. Consider the consequences of refusing (vv. 25,26)
2. Consider that he will shake up the creation again (vv. 26,27)
3. Consider that he promises an unshakable kingdom (vv. 27,28)

If you want to emphasize the exhortation of verse 28, you may try:

Let Us Worship God in an Acceptable Way
1. Listen to him who shakes the earth (vv. 25,26)
2. Give thanks for his unshakable kingdom (v. 28)
3. Show him reverence and awe (v. 28)

TWENTY-SEVENTH SUNDAY AFTER PENTECOST

The Scriptures

> Old Testament — *Daniel 7:9,10*
> Epistle — *Hebrews 12:1,2*
> Gospel — *Mark 13:24-31*

The Text — Hebrews 12:1,2

The writer likens the Christian life to a great athletic contest. As in any race, the athlete must prepare himself, consider the obstacles and address the fatigue or weariness of pressing on toward the finish line. Here we find the wisdom and encouragement to run our race with perseverance.

> v. 1 — *Therefore, since we are surrounded by such a great cloud of witnesses, let us throw off everything that hinders and the sin that so easily entangles and let us run with perseverance the race marked out for us.*

The verse begins by looking back: "Therefore," because the foregoing is true. In the previous chapter part of the cloud of witnesses passed before the reader. The testimony about the heroes and heroines of faith—men and women who endured the difficulties of life, the temptation of Satan, and the abuse of the wicked people; yet who remained faithful—such a cloud of witnesses surrounds the believer.

We should not take this to mean that the spirits of Noah, Abraham, Moses, etc., hover over us or that they are seated in some sort of spiritual spectator stand. No, the spirits of the saints are with their Lord. They do not remain earth-bound, even to cheer on the current generation of believers. The cloud of witnesses surrounds us in another way. The testimony of their lives recorded in the Old Testament (cf. 11:2, ἐμαρτυρήθησαν), the witness recounted in chapter 11, these surround us.

Our text says that the cloud is "great." In 11:32 the writer had said, "I do not have time to tell you about Gideon, Barak, Samson. . . ." He could not detail every component of the "cloud." Since the time of his writing the cloud has expanded. The testimony of faithful New Testament believers has been added to it.

Therefore, since all this is true, what shall we do? Ἀποθέμενοι tells us what must be done to run the race successfully. "Having set aside" anything that hinders us, we run. The runner throws off any extra items or bulky clothing. God urges us to throw off anything that might hinder us, any unnecessary baggage.

What are the things that hinder us? We could think of many non-sinful things that hinder, obstruct, get in the way of a Christian. For example, a simple glass of wine with a meal is not sinful, but for the Christian struggling with alcoholism it may indeed cause problems. Working long hard hours to provide a certain standard of living may not be sinful, but when those long hard hours begin to cut in on worship or family Bible study, or attention to the family, then it's time to reduce hours. Socializing with family and friends is great fun, but if Sunday services no longer fit into the social schedule. . . .

We can think of many things that are not sinful but which may, nevertheless, impede spiritual progress. Perhaps the most obvious obstacles, however, are "the sins which so easily entangle." Christians, too, still have the natural tendency to sin. Satan knows this. He knows of our weakness, so he presents opportunities to sin. He sets traps in our path, sinful hazards. Then we walk right into them. We become tangled up. Because of our sinful nature we are easily entangled. The writer's advice? Put off that sin. Get rid of it. Stop allowing yourself to get tangled up. Verse 2 tells us how.

Put off the hindrance and run with perseverance. Perseverance is the ability to be under stress or pressure and not give up. In our Christian race it means to remain faithful, not to give up the faith or become angry with God when pressures mount.

The writer urges τρέχωμεν, "let us run," a hortative that encourages us to keep on going. Let's run the race marked out for us.

What is the race? What sort of course lies before us? Scripture helps us preview the Christian's race. Jesus told his followers that persecution lay in their future (Jn 15:20). Hebrews 11 lists some examples of the persecution that God's people faced. We too may expect persecution. Perhaps we do not face it right now, but seeing how rapidly governments change in this world, persecution or unfair discrimination may lie just around the bend. Scripture also speaks of the general cross that the Christian will bear in the form of trials or hardships (Ac 14:22; Jn 16:33). All of these things may be expected. We should not think it strange when they occur. We are not to look for glory before Paradise.

In the race marked out for us lie many hazards. The course is not an easy one. But Scripture points out that many reasons to rejoice lie in our path as well. The joy of seeing others grow in their faith (Php 1:4,5), the deep satisfaction of growing in wisdom and spiritual understanding (Eph 1:17), the warm unchanging love of the Lord

(Ro 8:28-39). Many reasons to rejoice, as well as pitfalls, lie in our path.

The race is laid out for us. The course is set. Where does it lead? Paul tells us in 2 Timothy 4:7,8. It leads to the crown of righteousness. That is the goal, the finish line of our race. One day all who persevere in the faith will receive the crown of righteousness. They will stand before the Ancient of Days (cf. Daniel 7:9,10—the Old Testament reading) as he takes his seat, and they will hear him say, "Not guilty." That is the goal or prize that awaits all who persevere.

> v. 2 — *Let us fix our eyes on Jesus, the author and perfecter of our faith, who for the joy set before him endured the cross, scorning its shame, and sat down at the right hand of the throne of God.*

In verse 2 we find the power to put off sin and run with perseverance. While the testimony of the cloud of witnesses encourages us, it is only by looking to Jesus that we are able to run the Christian race. We constantly look away from what hinders us and look toward Jesus.

How can we focus on Jesus? By being active in his Word. Regular worship, home devotions, group Bible studies, these help us fix our eyes on Jesus.

Who is this Jesus? He is "the author and perfecter of our faith."

First, he is the author. He is the one who gave us something to believe in. He, and what he did, are the object of our faith. What did he do? He endured the cross. Although he had committed no sin, Jesus endured the suffering of the cross. Our text says that he "thought down upon" (καταφρονήσας) the shame of the cross. Jesus did not consider the shame of the cross to be of such significance that it might keep him from carrying out his mission.

What was the shame of the cross? Certainly it was shameful to be hung out to die in full view of the public. But far more shameful was the curse attached to the cross (Gal 3:13). Jesus, the most holy one, allowed himself to become the cursed one. Surely this is the most shameful aspect of the crucifixion.

How did the Lord find strength to endure this? One thing that he did was to think about the glory he had left behind. Remember how Jesus prayed the night he was betrayed: "Father, glorify me in your presence with the glory I had with you before the world began" (Jn 17:5). Jesus focused on the joy that awaited him, the joy he had set aside to redeem humanity (Php 2:6-11), instead of on the shame of the cross.

Our text says that "he sat down at the right hand of the throne of God." The right hand of God is a metaphor meaning that Jesus received all authority in the universe. Jesus resumed his position of authority, so that every knee in heaven and earth would bow before him.

All this, all that Jesus did and said, is the object of our faith. He gave us something to believe in. He authored our faith.

We read that Jesus is also the perfecter of our faith. He is the one who will bring our faith to its goal. Paul tells the Philippians, "He who began a good work in you will carry it on to completion until the day of Christ Jesus" (Php 1:6). Jesus would mature their faith and maintain it to the very end. Jesus would give them what he had promised: the crown of righteousness, the joy of heaven. Surely he will do the same for us.

Only by looking to Jesus, fixing our eyes on him, will we be able to put away sin and run the race set before us.

Homiletical Suggestions

As we wait for the coming of the Lord, Satan tempts us to think that God is taking a long time. "Perhaps he will not come. Of what value is the faith?" "Give up," says the evil foe. The Old Testament reading (Daniel 7:9,10) reminds us that God has set a time for judgment. To some it may seem as if God will never come, but the day for opening the books is on his calendar. The Ancient of Days will take his seat. And so we run with perseverance the race set before us.

The Gospel (Mark 13:24-31) also speaks of the coming judgment. Signs will precede the Lord's coming. God's people are to take note and be prepared. Soon the angels will take the elect to glory, but a fearful cloud of judgment awaits the unbeliever.

The Epistle gives the Christian hope and encouragement as he awaits that day. Thus, all three readings lend themselves to the end-time focus.

Focusing on the idea of a race, we might present the text under one of the following outlines:

Let Us Run with Perseverance

1. Remembering those who have finished the race (v. 1)
2. Ridding ourselves of every handicap (v. 1)
3. Fixing our eyes on Jesus (v. 2)
4. Anticipating the joy that awaits us (v. 2)

Run the Race Marked Out for You
1. It is a test of endurance, won by many others (v. 1)
2. Throw off whatever hinders and fix your eyes on Jesus (vv. 1,2)

LAST SUNDAY AFTER PENTECOST

The Scriptures

Old Testament — *Isaiah 51:4-6*
Epistle — *Revelation 1:4b-8*
Gospel — *Mark 13:32-37*

The Text — Revelation 1:4b-8

In giving this revelation to John, Jesus wanted to show his servants what must soon take place (1:1). This is written in the form of a letter addressed to the seven congregations in the province of Asia. The sermon text includes the greeting to those congregations (vv. 4b,5a) and a doxology to the eternal Son (vv. 5b,6).

vv. 4b,5a — *Grace and peace to you from him who is, and who was, and who is to come, and from the seven spirits before his throne, and from Jesus Christ, who is the fruitful witness, the firstborn from the dead, and the ruler of the kings of the earth.*

This greeting is a variation of the standard greeting used in Greek letters. It is a very beautiful greeting in that it contains a summary of the gospel message—may all of the blessings of the gospel be yours!

Grace is the merciful Father's undeserved favor and love for sinners. Even though we were unlovable by virtue of our sins, God continued to love us and showed his love to us in sending Jesus into this world to be our Savior and by bringing us this message of reconciliation (Jn 3:16; Ro 5:8; Eph 2:8,9). "Grace" is a summary of all the gifts of God's love—forgiveness of sins, life, and salvation—that come to us through Jesus.

Peace is the effect which God's grace has brought about in us. It is peace for troubled consciences which flows from the forgiveness of sins (Jn 14:1; Ro 5:1; Php 4:7).

These gifts, grace and peace, come to us from the triune God. The designations for each Person of the Trinity include the work which they do for us. The terms for the Father present the first of many grammatical peculiarities found in the book of Revelation. Obviously, the preposition ἀπό governs the genitive case, but here it is followed by three nominatives. The first and last phrases consist of articularized participles (which is normal), but the second phrase consists of an article with a finite verb (which is not normal). John knows that he is not using normal grammar, as is evidenced by his proper use of the preposition in what follows.

These three terms may allude to and paraphrase Exodus 3:14, and they show the unchangeableness of the Eternal One, who has no beginning or end (Ps 90:2; Mal 3:6). John is using the terms as proper names. It is fitting that the unchangeableness of the Father be established right at the beginning of this book, which speaks of Satan's raging against the Lord and his church.

Why John uses the term "seven spirits" (NIV footnote: "sevenfold Spirit") is never explained anywhere in the book. From the arrangement between references to the Father and the Son it is clear that John has the Holy Spirit in mind. It may be that he has the sevenfold description of the Spirit in Isaiah 11:2 in mind: "The Spirit of the LORD will rest on him—the Spirit of *wisdom* and of *understanding,* the Spirit of *counsel* and of *power,* the Spirit of *knowledge* and of the *fear of the LORD.* . . ." It may also be that since seven is the number of completeness, John has in mind the pouring out of the fullness of the Holy Spirit (seven spirits) on the whole church (the seven congregations). The reference to God's throne expresses the truth that the Holy Spirit is continually in intimate fellowship with the Father and the Son.

Jesus is usually called the Second Person of the Trinity, but here he is listed third. We have another grammatical peculiarity, nominatives modifying a genitive, but the sense is unmistakable. Again, this points to the unchangeableness of his offices as Prophet, Priest, and King.

As the faithful witness Jesus fulfilled his office as Prophet, revealing God's Word to us. We can believe and trust his words through which he has brought us to the true knowledge of God.

As the firstborn of the dead he fulfilled his office as Priest, giving his own life as a sacrifice for all. He was the first to rise from the dead, never to die again (Heb 7:24). By his resurrection he has overcome death for us all.

As the ruler of the kings of the earth he fulfilled his office as King. He governs all other rulers and uses them to carry out his divine purposes. The church has been, and will again be, persecuted and oppressed by the rulers of this world, but all are under the power of Jesus as he rules in his eternal kingdom for the benefit of the church (Rev 11:15; Eph 1:22). The ragings of this sinful world cannot overcome our King, who watches over us.

Each Person of the Trinity works on our behalf, bringing us the grace and peace which is found in this opening greeting. It is not a vain wish, but one which is accomplished by the Triune God himself.

vv. 5b,6 — *To him who loves us and has freed us from our sins by his blood, and has made us to be a kingdom and priests to serve his God and Father—to him be glory and power for ever and ever! Amen.*

Here Jesus is praised in a threefold doxology. With the present participle (τῷ ἀγαπῶντι) John stresses that Jesus, who loved us before the beginning of the world and loved us while we were still sinners, lives and loves us now. His eternal love has been shown to us in the best possible way, freeing us from our sins by his blood. Λύσαντι is aorist, since he completed everything necessary to set us free from our sins. We had been slaves to sin but have now been released. We were subject to death but have been delivered from the punishment we deserved. The variant reading does not materially change the meaning, for it says that we have been washed clean by his blood.

Once more there is a grammatical peculiarity. After using two dative participles John follows with a finite verb. Not only has this Jesus in his love freed us from the result of our sins, he has also given us an exalted position—one which includes glorious privileges. He has made us into his kingdom; we rule with him. This is ours even now in the present age, even though to all outward appearances we are oppressed. All of our enemies are conquered, and we are heirs of an everlasting kingdom. Obviously this is a spiritual kingdom, not of this world (Jn 17:14-16;18:36; 1 Co 3:21,22).

As believers we are also priests who have the privilege of approaching God directly on our own behalf and in behalf of others. This is not an option, for it is an essential feature of the Christian life (1 Pe 2:9). As priests, our sacrifices are repentance, prayer, and praise, a life of service and thanksgiving. We are not to live as though defeated in this life, but to use our position as a kingdom of priests to serve God and our fellowmen even now.

Saying that we are priests for his God and Father brings out both natures of Christ. According to his human nature Jesus called him God, according to his divine nature, Father. It took both natures for him to accomplish our salvation.

For all of this, which Jesus has done for us, we are reminded to give him eternal praise, glory, and power. Besides giving him praise and glory through prayer and song, we are to praise and glorify him by revealing to others what he has accomplished for all. Amen at the end of the doxology is the exclamation point of the confident assurance of faith.

v. 7 — *Look, he is coming with the clouds, and every eye will see him, even those who pierced him; and all the peoples of the earth will mourn because of him. So shall it be! Amen.*

The exclamation, "Look," arouses the attention of the reader and points to what follows as especially important. What follows is the first prophecy of the book of Revelation.

The present tense, "he is coming," is used here in the prophetic sense, emphasizing the certainty of Jesus' coming. As he disappeared in a cloud at his ascension, so he will come again on the last day (Ac 1:11). The clouds are symbolic of his great majesty, power, and supremacy.

"Every eye will see him." No one will be able to shut his eyes to the fact that Jesus has returned in all of his majesty. This includes everyone who will have died before that day, including "those who pierced him." The latter are not only those who actually took part in his crucifixion, but all unbelievers who crucify him anew by their rejection. They will see him returning as judge. They will realize that they cannot escape, and that the time for repentance has passed. All that the unbelievers can and will do is to weep and mourn because of him, being terrified of the horrible fate which they see before their eyes. This is the solemn, dreadful truth.

On this last Sunday of the church year the theme for the service focuses on the Last Day, the day of judgment. All the unbelievers in the world will end up weeping and mourning because of Jesus' return. But for those who are Christ's kingdom and priests, this day is one of great victory and rejoicing. The triune God, who loves us and uses his almighty powers on our behalf, is guiding all of history to this glorious reappearing of Jesus on the last day. May we always be watching and praying for him because we do not know the day or the hour when he will come.

v. 8 — *"I am the Alpha and the Omega," says the Lord God, "who is, and who was, and who is to come, the Almighty."*

Here we have the first direct words of Jesus in Revelation (cp. Rev 1:17;22:13). We understand "the Alpha and the Omega" in the light of Isaiah 44:6, "This is what the LORD says—Israel's King and Redeemer, the LORD Almighty: I am the first and the last; apart from me there is no God." By using these words Jesus identified himself as the LORD God, κύριος ὁ θεός being the Septuagint and New Testament translation of the Old Testament JHVH ELOHIM. Now he is described with the same phrases as those applied to the Father in verse 4. Finally, the divine attribute of omnipotence is ascribed to him.

The point is that Jesus is the eternal, unchangeable, almighty God. As such no enemy is too mighty for him. Therefore, he is able to keep all the promises which he made to those who are his, and he is able to overthrow those who are not his. This is a great comfort for believers, since his love and concern for them will never change.

Homiletical Suggestions

Since this is the last Sunday of the church year, in which the theme for the service will center around Jesus' return to judgment, a number of possible treatments of the text suggest themselves. One possibility:

Every Eye Will See Him

1. Believers will rejoice (vv. 4a-6)
2. Unbelievers will mourn (vv. 7,8)

Since the times shortly before the Last Day will be so tumultuous, the comfort for believers which is found in these verses can be stressed in this way:

Trust the Almighty Ruler to Care for You

1. He has freed you from your sins by his blood (vv. 4a,5)
2. He has made you a priest in his kingdom (vv. 6-8)

Emphasizing the same comfort and encouragement:

Praise the Eternal Savior Who Watches over Us

1. He has demonstrated his love for us (vv. 4a-6)
2. He rules all things as the Almighty Lord (vv. 7,8)

REFORMATION DAY

The Scriptures

Old Testament — *Jeremiah 31:31-34*
Epistle — *Romans 3:19-28*
Gospel — *John 8:31-36*

The Text — Romans 3:19-28

The question of how one acquires righteousness before God was being answered incorrectly by some among the Christians at Rome. The Jews especially, who maintained their inbred reverence for the Mosaic Law, had difficulty grasping the monumental changes brought about by the life and death of Jesus Christ. Paul distinguished two "types" of righteousness, which may we call "law righteousness" and "gospel righteousness." In the first two-and-one-half chapters he discussed law righteousness and its utter inability to justify any human being, Jew or Gentile. Verses 19 and 20 of our text mark the transition to his teaching about the gospel righteousness, which is apprehended by faith alone.

vv. 19,20 — *Now we know that whatever the law says, it says to those who are under the law, so that every mouth may be silenced and the whole world held accountable to God. Therefore no one will be declared righteous in his sight by observing the law; rather, through the law we become conscious of sin.*

God's law speaks loudly and clearly to those who are ἐν τῷ νόμῳ. Every unregenerate person spends his life in the sphere of the law. His actions, words, and thoughts are all subject to that law and are condemned by it. God's law is comprehensive, and when our lives are examined under its microscope, no one can speak with pride or boasting—or in defense of how he has lived his life. This is in accord with God's intention that the law is to silence every mouth before God's judgment seat. No defense is possible or should be attempted. The whole world is ὑπόδικος, "under judgment."

Silence is the only appropriate response because the law makes us aware, painfully aware, of our guilt. Without the law we would not be so conscious of sin. Conscience might accuse us of being less than perfect, but it might also excuse us, reasoning that we are doing better than others. Then comes the mirror of God's law. Every spot, blemish, flaw, and defect is revealed.

v. 21 — But now a righteousness from God, apart from law, has been made known, to which the Law and the Prophets testify.

In this verse Paul introduces the gospel righteousness which Christ has fulfilled and which God has given. Because it is from God himself we may be absolutely certain that this righteousness is holy, perfect, without blemish. unchanging—and acceptable to God. It is χωρὶς νόμου. It is not in the least dependent on our sin-spoiled efforts to perform the deeds which the law demands.

This righteousness from God πεφανέρωται. It was necessary for God to "reveal" or "make manifest" the gospel righteousness because it was impossible for man to learn about it by his natural talents and abilities. It cannot be learned by solving a mathematical equation, watching for results in a test tube, or making astronomical observations. God has made it known plainly and simply in the gospel, so that even little children can believe.

The Scriptures testify, give witness to, gospel righteousness. That includes the same Old Testament Scriptures which the Jews in Rome appealed to in boasting about their superior level of law righteousness.

v. 22 — This righteousness from God comes through faith in Jesus Christ to all who believe. There is no difference,

We possess the gift of God's righteousness through the gift of faith in the gift of Jesus Christ. Our Savior earned this righteousness for us by his perfect obedience to the law. Though he was tempted as we are, he never fell into sin, never was enslaved by Satan. He went on to suffer and die as punishment for all our dismal failures in achieving righteousness.

All believers enjoy the gift of God's righteousness equally. Exactly the same righteousness belongs to the life-long believer and the last-minute convert, to Jew and Gentile, to the educated and the unlearned—"to all who believe."

vv. 23,24 — for all have sinned and fall short of the glory of God, and are justified freely by his grace through the redemption that came by Christ Jesus.

This is a classic passage of "universals." Universal condemnation and universal justification through universal redemption.

All are sinners and all deserve condemnation. All have missed the mark of God's absolute requirements. All have fallen to the temptations of the flesh, the world, the devil. All are enslaved by the devil, incapable of self-liberation.

But all are justified. All are declared "not guilty" in God's court because the punishment was suffered by our Savior. This has been done freely, out of God's grace and mercy. Christ has redeemed the whole race, setting us free.

vv. 25,26 — *God presented him as a sacrifice of atonement, through faith in his blood. He did this to demonstrate his justice, because in his forbearance he had left the sins committed beforehand unpunished—he did it to demonstrate his justice at the present time, so as to be just and the one who justifies those who have faith in Jesus.*

In the relationship between God and humanity, it was God who was offended. Yet God was the one who acted to bring about atonement. He acted on behalf of all humanity, which was not capable of acting on its own behalf.

He presented his Son as a sacrifice of atonement. Israelites were most familiar with the offering of sacrifices. Millions of animals had been killed through the centuries. Barrels of blood had been shed. On the Day of Atonement the high priest sprinkled blood on the atonement cover of the Ark of the Covenant. This restored the fellowship between Israel and God.

Now God himself has offered a sacrifice. The blood did not come from an animal but from God's own Son. This was the last sacrifice. Christ was presented as a ἱλαστήριον, literally a "place of atonement," but in its sense here the "sacrifice of atonement." In Christ, punishment was administered, guilt was expiated, judgment was carried out. God's justice was not compromised; the punishment was not forgotten.

Inasmuch as the punishment for all sins committed by all people of all time was inflicted on Christ, the sins of those who preceded Christ were not punished until the sacrifice of Golgotha. In one place, on one Person, God demonstrated his holiness which demanded justice and his grace which provided justification.

vv. 27,28 — *Where, then, is boasting? It is excluded. On what principle? On that of observing the law? No, but on that of faith. For we maintain that a man is justified by faith, apart from observing the law.*

Paul returns to the question of boasting. In view of man's universal sinfulness and God's universal justification there is no room for boasting. Boasting, after all, assumes that there are differences among people. It assumes that some have superior qualities or have achieved a superior performance. In the sight of the law, however, all are condemned. In Christ, all are redeemed. Faith in the same Jesus Christ brings the same justification to all.

Verse 28 enunciates the Reformation principle, "sola fide." This truth, on the basis of Scripture, we believe, teach, and confess. We are justified by faith alone, apart from works. That is the only way in which God has ever justified anyone.

Homiletical Suggestions

Reformation Day celebrates the victory of the truth of God's Word over error. The Deceiver has attacked the truth in many ways, at many times. But the truth has been preserved for us to this day. We encourage our people to value the truth as a heritage and treasure.

There is little difficulty in finding a sermon theme in verse 28. Combining it with the festival context and using the picture of the courtroom, try:

Justified by Faith Alone

1. "Guilty" in sin (vv. 19,20,23)
2. "Not guilty" in Christ (vv. 21,22,24-28)

If you are inclined to borrow hymn titles:

Dear Christians, One and All Rejoice

1. We once were doomed sinners (vv. 19,20, 23)
2. We now are declared righteous (vv. 21,22,24-28)

FESTIVAL OF HARVEST

The Scriptures

Old Testament — *Deuteronomy 26:1-11*
Epistle — *2 Corinthians 9:6-15*
Gospel — *Matthew 13:24-30*

The Text — 2 Corinthians 9:6-15

The congregation at Corinth had committed itself to take part in the offering for the impoverished Christians in Jerusalem. In fact, they "were the first not only to give, but also to have the desire to do so" (8:10). Paul had used the enthusiasm of the Corinthians to encourage other congregations to contribute generously. Many other congregations did follow the Corinthians' example and did contribute liberally.

Now, in chapter 9, Paul reminds the Corinthians of their commitment, so that when the delegation arrived at Corinth to receive their gift, the gift would indeed be ready. Thus there would be no embarrassment for the Corinthians, or for Paul.

In the verses of the text Paul gives the Corinthians some final encouragements for giving generously.

v. 6 — *Remember this: Whoever sows sparingly will also reap sparingly, and whoever sows generously will also reap generously.*

Paul uses a common proverb to encourage generosity. The meaning is clear: If you sow meagerly, don't expect big returns. If you want big returns, sow generously. Paul understood that the harvest is always in God's hands, but he was expressing himself in human terms. Humanly speaking, if a man sows sparingly, he shouldn't expect a bumper crop. But if a man sows bountifully, he can expect an abundant crop.

Literally, the word translated "generously" would be translated "upon blessing" or "toward blessing." It means sowing with an eye toward blessing, with a desire to reap a large crop. God has a way of blessing our efforts, not always in kind, and not always in a way we can see; but he does bless our labors for him. So Paul encourages his readers to be generous in their offerings.

v. 7 — *Each man should give what he has decided in his heart to give, not reluctantly or under compulsion, for God loves a cheerful giver.*

Προῄρηται is perfect middle indicative, literally "has chosen for himself in advance." The meaning is that this person "has chosen in advance what he wants to give, and that is now his commitment to his Lord."

The decision has been made in advance "in his heart." What Paul describes in these words is a person who with prayerful consideration and out of appreciation for what God has done for him had decided to give back to the Lord a certain amount. This is how the gift is to be given.

"Not reluctantly" (literally, "not out of grief or pain") and not "under compulsion" of any kind is the gift to be brought. God doesn't want his people "in pain" from giving. That's not the attitude God looks for from his people. Nor does God want our gifts offered out of some sense of "compulsion" or force, or necessity. No coercion of any sort! He doesn't want a gift because we "have to give." He wants our gifts, because we "want to give."

In fact, that's the next phrase Paul uses, "for God loves a cheerful giver." The word translated "cheerful" is ἱλαρός, "prompt to do something, glad to do something, cheerful, and glad." A person can be happy about giving to God only if his heart belongs to God.

Whenever the subject of motivation for giving comes up, there are often arguments about whether the law should be used and how law can be properly used. Some will point to this verse and say there must not be any law preached because the gift is to be given without compulsion.

When it comes to motivating Christian people to do good works, including giving, we have to realize that they have two natures. The evil nature is selfish, especially when it comes to "My Money." The evil nature will gladly spend countless dollars on things that satisfy the flesh but will begrudge even small amounts for God's work. Then our crafty old nature may remind us of this passage, "God loves a cheerful giver," and try to convince us that God would be happier with 10 cents from a happy Christian than $1.00 from a grouchy one.

There are times when we must convict that heart of the sin of greed and lovelessness. We need to preach the law with its full demands, just as we do against any sin. This, however, is not motivation to cheerful giving.

There are also times when the law in its third use is needed to teach about giving. Weak Christians need some guidelines, some examples and instructions from our God, so that we know what God wants and what opportunities for serving him exist.

The law does have a place in our talking about giving. Yet, we dare never stop with the law. The law can shame, or educate, or even beat down that old man into subjection. But only the gospel can melt our stony hearts of greed and motivate people to give cheerfully.

v. 8 — *And God is able to make all grace abound to you, so that in all things at all times, having all that you need, you will abound in every good work.*

Paul turns to God's goodness and his power to motivate his readers to generous giving. Paul uses forms and derivatives of πᾶς five times in this verse. The first four uses emphasize that God has given them and will continue to give them everything they need—indeed, far more than they could ever use up. The fifth appears in the purpose of God's generosity: "so that . . . will abound in every good work." God had blessed the Corinthians beyond compare. Now they are, in turn, to show love and compassion by their good deeds done to praise God and to help God's people.

v. 9 — *As it is written: "He has scattered abroad his gifts to the poor; his righteousness endures forever."*

Paul quotes Psalm 112:9 to prove the point he had just made in verse 8, that God does indeed give his gifts to his people. Note the connection between God's generosity and his δικαιοσύνη. Consider the gospel overtones, as Paul does in what follows.

v. 10 — *Now he who supplies seed to the sower and bread for food will also supply and increase your store of seed and will enlarge the harvest of your righteousness.*

Paul reminds the Corinthians that God is the supplier of everything for everyone. God will also supply and even "increase" their seed. Now, this "seed" Paul talks about can be either the physical blessings God will give to them or the spiritual blessings that will come to them, or both.

The last phrase, "the harvest of your righteousness," definitely refers to a harvest of spiritual blessings. The point that Paul makes is that all the blessings we receive, both the physical and the spiritual, are given to us to use for the purpose of gaining a spiritual harvest. We use the things we have to touch hearts of people and to bring them to Jesus.

v. 11 — *You will be made rich in every way so that you can be generous on every occasion, and through us your generosity will result in thanksgiving to God.*

The Corinthians were made rich "in every way," physically and spiritually. The present participle πλουτιζόμενοι adds the thought that this is still going on. God is still making them rich in all things.

The word translated as "generosity," ἁπλότης, has as its base idea, "singleness, simplicity, sincerity." So, instead of pushing the sense of "generosity," why not retain the main thrust of the word, that of "singleness of purpose and singleness of faith," as J. P. Meyer does in *Ministers of Christ*?

This gift is not just bringing some money to help those poor souls in Jerusalem. The Corinthians and all the other Christians were also giving themselves along with the money. This is a way of joining them all together as one. Thus, instead of translating it, "so that you can be generous on every occasion," the passage would read, "you are being made rich in every way for all singleness of spirit."

Through this act of "generosity," or "singleness of heart," many "thanksgivings" will be given to God. The gift and the unity of spirit that comes with it will cause people on both sides to thank and praise God. Those who were made rich so they could share their bounty with those in need, and the people in need who received the gifts from their brothers and sisters were both giving thanks and praise to God. The outgrowth of this gift was not to be the glory of men, but the glory of God.

v. 12 — *This service that you perform is not only supplying the needs of God's people but is also overflowing in many expressions of thanks to God.*

The Corinthians' service of giving would go far beyond merely "supplying the needs of God's people." It would also bring praises to God. This gift would cause many people to thank, praise, and worship God. That's the real reason for any good work.

v. 13 — *Because of the service by which you have proved yourselves, men will praise God for the obedience that accompanies your confession of the gospel of Christ and for your generosity in sharing with them and with everyone else.*

Verse 12 was a parenthetical remark that explained the fact that the "singleness of heart" was accomplishing thanksgiving to God. Now verses 13 and 14 continue the thought begun in verse 11, telling the Corinthians how this would be accomplished.

The eyes of the saints in Jerusalem and in Macedonia were on the Corinthians. The Corinthians had promised to give a generous gift. Would they be able to carry out this promise? Would their love for the

Lord and their love for the saints in Jerusalem prompt them to complete this task? Through the successful completion of the rest of this service (διὰ τῆς δοκιμῆς τῆς διακονίας) God will be glorified.

Their fellow Christians will praise God "for the obedience that accompanies your confession of the gospel." What will bring praise to God is how the Corinthians submit themselves to the gospel of Jesus and carry out this task of helping the brothers and sisters in Christ.

The second reason people will glorify God is "your generosity in sharing with them and with everyone else." Again, ἁπλότητι has "singleness" as its primary meaning. This fits well with the next word, κοινωνίας, which means "fellowship, communion, having a share with." The phrase would then read, "and for the singleness of the fellowship." What will bring praise to God is the close-knit fellowship these strangers have with one another. Even though they don't know each other, even though they are separated by miles and many cultural differences, yet they have a single fellowship. This close fellowship is "with them and with everyone else."

This close fellowship exists, not only between the Corinthians and the saints in Jerusalem, but among all who believe in Jesus.

The one thing that makes the world sit up and take notice of Christians is the love and oneness the church demonstrates. Where this unity and fellowship is demonstrated, people will recognize it and praise it. They may not believe the gospel or want to have anything to do with it, but they will respect it, and God's name will be glorified.

People will glorify God for the two reasons mentioned in this verse. Verse 14 supplies a third reason:

v. 14 — *And in their prayers for you their hearts will go out to you, because of the surpassing grace God has given you.*

The saints in Jerusalem will remember their brothers and sisters in Christ in their prayers. In fact, their hearts will go out to them. The word ἐπιποθούντων originally meant "miss one that is absent." Then with the prefix ἐπί added, it came to mean "long for, wish for, desire." The love and the singleness of fellowship behind the gift will cause a longing for these people that will never end (the present participle).

What will cause these saints in Jerusalem to "have their hearts go out to those people"? The money? No! Rather, "the surpassing grace God has given you." The gift of money is rather insignificant. What is impressive is how God could touch the hearts of people so that they would give generously, not only their money but themselves as well.

That's what God wants from us. Jesus tells us, "Let your light shine before men, that they may see your good deeds and praise your Father in heaven" (Mt 5:16). When Christians do good deeds, let God get the glory and the praise. This is the very point with which Paul ends this section:

v. 15 — *Thanks be to God for his indescribable gift!*

Paul thanks God for his gift to the Corinthians, a gift that defies description. To be sure, they were the ones who were giving the gift to the poor of Jerusalem. Yet it was God who had given the Corinthians the gift of their Savior and the gift to be able to be generous. So also, when we do good deeds, God gets the glory and the praise.

Homiletical Suggestions

To carry out the theme of the Harvest Festival, we could emphasize that we thank God not just by words from a church service, but also by our actions. Our theme could be:

Thank God with Words and Actions

1. God supplies you with all you have (vv. 8-11a)
2. God makes you rich so you can help others (vv. 6,7,11b,15)

To zero in on a stewardship theme, we could feature the maxim in verse 7:

God Loves a Cheerful Giver

1. Remember what God has done for you (vv. 8-11)
2. Remember that you get what you sow (vv. 6,7)

(This study originally appeared in *Sermon Studies on the Epistles — Series C,* Northwestern Publishing House, 1991).

MISSION FESTIVAL

The Scriptures

Old Testament — *Isaiah 62:1-7*
Epistle — *Romans 10:11-17*
Gospel — *Luke 24:44-53*

The Text — Romans 10:11-17

Paul's letter to the Romans proclaims the gospel as the power of God for salvation (1:16,17). In chapters 9 through 11 the apostle takes note of the special place of Israel as the people of the Promise. He speaks of his own personal sadness occasioned by the Jewish rejection of the Messiah, but he also makes it very clear that their rejection did not nullify God's promise of salvation for Israel. Rather, God created for himself a new Israel—Jew and Gentile—a new chosen people, not determined by human bloodlines but by faith in the redeeming blood of the divine Savior (1 Pe 2:9,10).

Even though the words of the text were written originally in regard to the Israelites, they apply equally to all who do not know Jesus as their Lord and Savior. It states very clearly that even in Old Testament times there was no salvation without faith and there can be no faith without hearing the message of God's salvation. It is therefore our privilege as people who know the Lord Jesus to help in proclaiming this message to others.

v. 11 — *As the Scripture says, "Anyone who trusts in him will never be put to shame."*

One thing is certain in this uncertain world. Everyone must face death and the accounting at the judgment of God. Just thinking about death and especially about the day of judgment produces anxiety in a great many people. But those who trust in Jesus as their Lord and Savior have no need for concern. They will not suffer shame. Their hope in Jesus will not be disappointed. They can be certain that they will receive the promised inheritance of heaven. Paul had quoted Isaiah 28:16 previously (9:33). In adding the πᾶς here, however, the inspired writer strengthens his assertion that salvation by faith is available not just for some but for all people. He substantiates his statement with the two verses that follow.

vv. 12,13 — *For there is no difference between Jew and Gentile—the same Lord is Lord of all and richly blesses all who call on him, for, "Everyone who calls on the name of the Lord will be saved."*

The Jews, as descendants of Abraham and bearers of the promise, considered themselves to be a nation with special status before God. Yet, although God preserved them as a people for the sake of his promise to Abraham (Ge 22:18), they will enjoy no special status on the day of judgment. Everyone, whether Jew or Gentile, has sinned (Ro 3:23). Therefore everyone can be justified in only one way, by faith in him who is Lord over all.

The NIV's translation of πλουτῶν εἰς πάντας, literally "being rich toward all," nicely brings across the sense of what Paul has written. Our Lord is indescribably rich (Ps 24:1). As the original and ultimate philanthropist (Ge 2:8,18; 3:15; Mt 5:45; Jn 3:16) the Lord cares for all, but he takes particular note of all those who call upon him in faith, granting them limitless mercy and grace, forgiving their sins (Ex 34:6,7), and providing for their eternal good (Ro 8:28). Ultimately, everything we receive from the Lord, whether good or bad in our limited perspective, is a blessing which he has showered on us from his abundant riches.

Verse 13 is a direct quotation from Joel 2:32, reinforcing Paul's claim that there is no difference among peoples so far as salvation is concerned, nor had there ever been in the past. Whoever turns to the Lord with simple trust will receive his help and guidance and, most important, eternal life. It is worthy of note that in quoting Joel 2:32 the apostle makes no distinction between the Lord Jesus and the LORD Yahweh of the Old Testament. As equal members of the Godhead they are one in essence, together with the Holy Spirit.

> vv. 14,15 — *How, then, can they call on the one they have not believed in? And how can they believe in the one of whom they have not heard? And how can they hear without someone preaching to them? And how can they preach unless they are sent? As it is written, "How beautiful are the feet of those who bring good news!"*

The Lord is so generous in bestowing his blessings that he places no restrictions on his recipients. But calling on his name is an act of faith, and the gift of faith is received in only one way, by the Holy Spirit's working through the means of grace, the gospel in Word and sacraments. If a person has had no contact with the gospel, there can be no faith. And without faith there is no hope.

Κηρύσσειν paints the picture of a herald voicing abroad the proclamation of his king or another high official. The herald's sole purpose

324

was to make known the words of his superior. He added no words nor interpretation of his own. All who want to heed the Lord's command to make disciples of all nations need to realize that the desired result can be obtained only by the faithful proclamation of his gospel. Only when his message is proclaimed are the hearers really hearing Jesus (Lk 10:16).

With today's technology and mass communications we have means that were not available to the apostles. Yet, there is no substitute for a real, live herald. Commercial spots may arouse interest. The broadcast media may be valuable aids for sustaining interest. Personal contact, however, remains the most effective way to make disciples. A remote and somewhat "generic" message cannot take the place of a concerned individual applying the balm of the gospel to the wounds of a sinner. In order to make and sustain personal contact, heralds must be not only trained but also sent and maintained.

The "beautiful" thing about the messengers' feet is not the feet themselves, but the fact that they carry the messenger who brings the good news of salvation. Thus, these words from Isaiah 52:7 may be applied not only to the feet of individuals doing the actual proclaiming of the gospel but also to those who support the cause of missions.

v. 16 — *But not all the Israelites accepted the good news. For Isaiah says, "Lord, who has believed our message?"*

The joy of those who bring the good news to others is often tempered by the knowledge that not everyone is as excited about the message as the messenger is. There remains in the heart of every individual the ability to reject the message of salvation (Mk 16:16). But such knowledge need not dampen our enthusiasm for getting the message out. If even God's chosen people rejected the message heralded by his great prophets (Paul is quoting Isaiah 53:1), and by Jesus himself (Jn 6:66), why should we despair when the message or the messenger is at times met with indifference or even hostility? We need to recognize that the hearers are rejecting not the messenger but the king the messenger represents (Lk 10:16). Nor does the king hold the messenger responsible for the results of his proclamation (1 Co 3:7-9). The Lord merely expects faithfulness in the heralding of the message (1 Co 4:2).

"The Israelites" is (correctly) supplied by the NIV to identify the πάντες who did not accept the good news.

v. 17 — *Consequently, faith comes from hearing the message, and the message is heard through the word of Christ.*

Since the Lord has not revealed any possibility of salvation without faith, and there can be no faith without knowledge of the gospel of the saving work of Jesus Christ, every human being needs to hear the words of Jesus. Salvation by faith is a wonderful gift of God (Eph 2:8,9), but there can be no faith without the gospel.

Homiletical Suggestions

Mission Festival is a special opportunity to remind Christians of how privileged they are not only to have the gospel of Jesus Christ for their very own but to be able to participate in spreading that good news of salvation to all the world. Although personal evangelism and worldwide mission work are themes that appear time and again in various texts throughout the church year, congregations are especially eager to hear further encouragement at an annual or semi-annual Mission Festival.

An emphasis on our privilege in being both hearers and heralds suggests:

The Christian Is Doubly Privileged

1. Privileged to hear the good news (vv. 11-13)
2. Privileged to herald the good news (vv. 14-17)

The universal nature of the Lord's gospel call and the recognition that his ascension directive is for all believers form the basis of another treatment:

The Gospel Is for Everyone

1. A comfort (vv. 11-13)
2. A challenge (vv. 14-17)

Here is an outline based on verses 13-15 only:

We Have a Message to Share

1. It is a beautiful message (vv. 13,15b)
2. There is a need for messengers (vv. 13-15a)

THANKSGIVING DAY

The Scriptures

> Old Testament — *Deuteronomy 8:1-10*
> Epistle — *Philippians 4:6-20*
> Gospel — *Luke 17:11-19*

The Text — Philippians 4:6-20

Paul had a special bond with the congregation in Philippi. His letter to them is filled with joy. Paul had not written because there were major problems in the congregation. Rather, he wrote to encourage them in their faith—not to be discouraged by his chains, to show Christ's humility to one another, to receive Epaphroditus back with honor, to place no confidence in their own works but to cling to the Savior and his gift of eternal life.

Paul closes his letter with instruction on thankfulness and contentment, on how we can be free from worrying and wanting.

> vv. 6,7 — *Do not be anxious about anything, but in everything, by prayer and petition, with thanksgiving, present your requests to God. And the peace of God, which transcends all understanding, will guard your hearts and your minds in Christ Jesus.*

Μεριμνᾶτε has as wide a range of meaning as our English word "care." Paul is obviously using it in a negative sense here: "to brood over something," "to be anxious about what may happen." The form is present imperative, "never be anxious." As God's children through Jesus, you and I never have a reason to be anxious about what may happen or to brood over what has happened. Matthew 6:25-34 explains why we don't have to be anxious.

Paul encourages the Philippians to let their requests, no matter how small or large, be known to God. As they present their requests they naturally are to give thanks for what God has already done.

It is hard to be anxious when you're thanking God. If we review the cornucopia of blessings which God has already given us, both physical and spiritual, the evidence is overwhelming that our God loves us and is able to care for us. Even the poorest believer has riches in heaven because of our Savior. The grace of free forgiveness is enough proof that our future is in good hands. So why worry?

Ultimately, God's forgiveness is what drives away our worry by giving us peace (Jn 14:27; Ro 5:1; Col 1:20). This peace from God and with God does surpass all our understanding. When a loved one dies, in a struggle against an addiction, or when a spouse has confessed adultery, the mind will say that there can be no peace. Yet the peace of God is able to fill our hearts with peace even when we think peace is impossible.

God's peace guards us. Φρουρέω is a military term, used with reference to guarding the city gates against hostile invasion and to keep the inhabitants of a besieged city from fleeing. In the same way God's peace through Christ will not let Satan overpower us, and it will prevent our bolting from our Savior to seek help in other places where there is no help.

vv. 8,9 — *Finally, brothers, whatever is true, whatever is noble, whatever is right, whatever is pure, whatever is lovely, whatever is admirable—if anything is excellent or praiseworthy—think about such things. Whatever you have learned or received or heard from me, or seen in me—put it into practice. And the God of peace will be with you.*

Don't think of this list as separate items, distinct from each other. Paul is describing different facts of the same category. "True" refers especially to the truth we find in Scripture, the pure teaching of God's Word. "Noble" is from σεμνός, a word which is linked with the gods in classical Greek. It has the idea of majestic and awe-inspiring, evoking reverence and worship. God's undeserved love for us is a good example of something that is σεμνά. "Right" and "pure" are two sides of the same coin, characterizing things that are in keeping with God's will and without sin. "Lovely" and "admirable" round out the list.

Paul summarizes his list with "excellent" and "praiseworthy." He tells us to *keep thinking* about such things. Λογίζεσθε is present imperative, meaning we are to keep doing this at all times.

We cannot produce peace with God or peace with ourselves. True peace is God's work and God's gift to us. We can, however, frustrate God's gift or obstruct his giving by what we think and do. Paul includes in his encouragement instructions on what to think and do in cooperation with the Holy Spirit as he fills us with peace.

We are both to think and do what is right. Paul encourages us to follow his example and put into practice all we can learn from him in word and action. With hands and hearts and minds centered on what is excellent and praiseworthy, all done by the power of the Spirit living in us, the God of peace will be with us, filling us with peace.

v. 10 — I rejoice greatly in the Lord that at last you have re-
newed your concern for me. Indeed, you have been concerned, but
you had no opportunity to show it.

Paul gives credit where credit is due. He doesn't point the Philippians to themselves to give them a pat on the back for their concern for
him. The Lord is the One who has moved them to support Paul with
their gifts. In the same way, as we give thanks to each other, especially among Christians, let it be obvious who deserves the praise:
the God who moves us and equips us to serve each other and him.

Ἀνεθάλετε, translated "you have renewed" by the NIV, conveys
the picture of a tree which appears dead during the winter but in
spring greens up, showing that life was always there. It isn't that the
Philippians haven't been concerned about Paul before (note the continuing action of the imperfects ἐφρονεῖτε and ἠκαιρεῖσθε,) but they
didn't have a chance to express their concern until Epaphroditus
came to Paul with their gifts.

vv. 11-13 — I am not saying this because I am in need, for I have
learned to be content whatever the circumstances. I know what it
is to be in need, and I know what it is to have plenty. I have
learned the secret of being content in any and every situation,
whether well fed or hungry, whether living in plenty or in want.
I can do everything through him who gives me strength.

Paul wants to make it very clear that he isn't looking for gifts for
his own personal gain. He has learned how to be content, no matter
what his circumstances. Paul's reason (and ours) for being content is
very different from any reason an unbeliever has. The Stoic philosophers of Paul's day reasoned that since worry wouldn't do any good,
why worry, why be discontent? We're content because we have a loving Savior who promises to take care of all our needs, not because
we're helpless to change our situation.

We're also different from the world because of why we trust our
God to take care of our needs. An unbeliever will worship his god,
whatever or whoever it is, because that god makes him feel good, satisfied, and cared for. If the god stops "providing," then the unbeliever
will either find a different god or work harder to serve his god because his god must be angry with him.

Paul's God has allowed him to go without many things. In
1 Corinthians 4:8-13 and 2 Corinthians 6:4-10, Paul recounts some of
his sufferings. But he has learned not to judge the power and love of
God by what happens in his life. Paul has learned, and his instruction is still benefiting him (the perfect μεμύημαι), that whether he has

more than he needs or goes hungry, his God will care for him by giving him strength to do all things.

It is interesting that Paul says he "learned" how to be content. Contentment is not an attitude we're born with. It is a lesson we learn as the Holy Spirit works trust in our hearts through the Means of Grace. Our society is growing more and more materialistic and dissatisfied with its possessions. We act as though we were drinking salt water: the more we drink, the thirstier we become. We need to proclaim boldly to our fellow Christians that the secret to being content is not what we have but whom we have: Jesus Christ. True contentment comes only through trust that Jesus loved me enough to die for me, that he lives, and that he will continue to care for me in every situation.

Paul has learned that there are no exceptions to God's strength and care. In *every* situation the Creator of the universe and the Savior of all strengthens him to be content.

> vv. 14-16 — *Yet it was good of you to share in my troubles. Moreover, as you Philippians know, in the early days of your acquaintance with the gospel, when I set out from Macedonia, not one church shared with me in the matter of giving and receiving, except you only; for even when I was in Thessalonica, you sent me aid again and again when I was in need.*

Paul doesn't want the Philippian Christians to misunderstand what he is saying, as though their gifts were a waste because of his contentment. In the last verses of the text (14-20) he shows why their gifts are important and good.

Their support of Paul is a good work in God's sight. God wants them to care for those who share the gospel with them (Gal 6:6). Paul has no false asceticism which places a phony value on fasting or other forms of self-denial. A Christian may fast, but hunger has no value in and of itself. Paul accepts their gift thankfully because, by providing for him, they are aligning themselves with him as partners in his present troubles.

Paul's troubles are not internal but external. Θλῖψις carries the idea of distress brought on by external difficulties and pressures. Certainly Paul's imprisonment in Rome is such a trouble.

Paul has not accepted gifts from other congregations so that they could not accuse him of preaching the gospel for profit. Yet he has accepted gifts from the Philippian congregation. If he had refused their gifts when they were so young in the faith (they had sent gifts before he left Thessalonica, the first city where he preached after visiting

Philippi), he would have hurt them in their faith. Sometimes the best gift is to let others give.

They have not given once, but "again and again." Christian love doesn't say, "I already gave." We naturally want to keep giving to our Lord because he keeps giving to us. And one of the ways we show our thanks to God is to care for his servants who share the good news with us.

> vv. 17,18 — *Not that I am looking for a gift, but I am looking for what may be credited to your account, I have received full payment and even more; I am amply supplied, now that I have received from Epaphroditus the gifts you sent. They are a fragrant offering, an acceptable sacrifice, pleasing to God.*

Paul continues to explain his attitude toward gifts. He has a much higher interest than personal gain.

Paul uses accounting terms. He is looking for a fruit of their faith (καρπόν) that could be credited to their account. This didn't mean they were to do this so they could earn merit with God. Rather, he wants them to fill their account with good works to show others how much they appreciate all that God has done for them.

They owe Paul nothing: Ἀπέχω was a technical term, "I receive a sum in full and give a receipt for it." They had settled up with Paul.

Their gifts then were a sacrifice to God, not to Paul. God is pleased when his believers sacrifice their material goods, their time, and abilities to do the work of his kingdom (Ro 12:1; Heb 13:16). Any sacrifices we offer will be stained with sin. Yet they are still acceptable to God through our Lord Jesus Christ. What a joy it is to know that what we do in faith pleases our holy God!

> vv. 19,20 — *And my God will meet all your needs according to his glorious riches in Christ Jesus. To our God and Father be glory for ever and ever. Amen.*

They can sacrifice with confidence. Just as God strengthened Paul to do all things in every situation, the same God will meet all their needs—physical and spiritual. He will use the riches Jesus has won for them to fill them with peace, faith, contentment, joy, and trust. And for the sake of the riches Jesus earned on the cross, God will take care of their physical needs as well (cf. Ps 37:25). They and we don't have to worry that we will give ourselves into the poor house as we offer our sacrifices to God.

Paul ends this section and this letter by thanking God for his undeserved love. God does not owe believers contentment and peace, the promise to care for our needs. Yet God in his grace gives these promises and more. What else can Paul, the Philippians, and we do than to give God all glory and praise "for ever and ever"? Let us join in the "Amen" as we see all God has done for us and continues to do!

Homiletical Suggestions

If one tries to treat this entire text in one 20-minute sermon, he won't be able to do justice to all the important thoughts in these verses. Many of the key thoughts—peace, thanks, contentment, and trust—need to be addressed head on because Satan is attacking them ferociously in our time.

It may be best to divide the text in half, preaching either on verses 6-9 or verses 10-20. This would also allow variety from one year to the next, since both Series B and Series C of ILCW have this text for the Thanksgiving Epistle.

All of the key ideas have direct application to our Festival of Thanksgiving. We need peace because our troubles threaten to rob us of our thanks for all God has done. We naturally want to thank God for his indescribable riches. Contentment, not possessions, will fill our hearts and homes with thanks. When we trust our God to meet all our needs we are free to thank him for all he has done without worry about the future.

If you preach on verses 6-9, you may want to use this outline:

Present Your Requests to God

1. Thankfully (v. 6)
2. Confidently (v. 7)
3. Devoutly (vv. 8,9)

If you treat verses 10-20, consider these outlines:

God Will Meet All Our Needs

1. To be grateful (v. 10)
2. To be content (vv. 11-13)
3. To be generous (vv. 14-20)

We Know the Secret of Being Content

1. God gives us strength (vv. 10-13)
2. God meets our needs (vv. 14-20)

Sometimes to cope with prosperity is at least as challenging as to cope with need. Verses 11b-13 can be the basis for a sermon dealing with that truth:

The Secret of Contentment Is Christ Who Strengthens Us

1. Through him we can cope with need
2. Through him we can cope with prosperity